P9-BYU-324

Student Course Guide
for

Shaping America

U.S. History to 1877

Third Edition

KENNETH G. ALFERS, Ph.D.
Dallas County Community College District

DALLAS TeleLearning
Dallas County Community College District
R. Jan LeCroy Center for Educational Telecommunications

BEDFORD / ST. MARTIN'S
Boston • New York

I would like to dedicate this work to Molly, Andrew, and Michael and to all students of history. Special thanks and recognition are due to some special people who greatly enhanced the quality of this course. Janice Christophel, instructional designer, constantly kept the focus of my work on student learning from the time of our first organizational meeting until the last page of this student course guide went to press. She always provided her thoughtful guidance with cordiality and grace. The brilliant mind and talent of Julia Dyer, producer/director, is most obvious in the twenty-six video programs that give this course its exceptional and unique quality. What is not obvious from the videos is what a truly marvelous colleague she is, and I will always treasure my opportunity to have worked with her. Angie Meyer, production coordinator, has been the vital link in shaping this course. She willingly applied her superb organizational skills to every imaginable task, and she kept us relaxed (and groovy) with her delightful sense of humor and infectious good spirit.

Craig Mayes, director of production, gave us all the benefit of his experience and encouragement. His steady hand always steered us toward the best path. Evelyn J. Wong, telecommunications information specialist, is a master of the art and technology needed to pull together Word files from all directions and make them clear and understandable. Russell Blair, videographer, and Marcia Henke, sound recordist, not only enhanced the videos, but also helped make our production trips enjoyable learning experiences. My colleagues on the national and local advisory committees have my gratitude for their constructive comments throughout the entire process.

Finally, I would like to thank all the members of the staff of the R. Jan LeCroy Center for Educational Telecommunications for making my work with the Center so pleasant and rewarding. This was my third stint at doing a project like this, and, with the help and support of everyone, this was the best experience yet!

R. Jan LeCroy Center for Educational Telecommunications

Provost/LeCroy Center: Pamela K. Quinn
Vice President of Instruction: Jim Picquet
History Content Specialist: Kenneth G. Alfers, Ph.D.
Project Director: Craig Mayes
Producer/Director: Julia Dyer
Instructional Designer: Janice Christophel
Director of Product Design: Suzanne Dunn, Ph.D.
Production Coordinator: Angie Meyer
Research Assistant: Andrea Boardman
Telecommunications Information Specialist: Evelyn J. Wong

Student Course Guide ISBN (10): 0-312-47003-7; ISBN (13): 978-0-312-47003-6
Copyright © 2009 by Dallas County Community College District.

All rights reserved. No part of this work may be reproduced, stored in a retrieval system, or transcribed in any form or by any means—electronic, mechanical, photocopying, recording, or otherwise—without the prior written permission of Dallas County Community College District.

Requests for permission to make copies of any part of the work should be mailed to:
DALLAS TeleLearning
9596 Walnut Street
Dallas, Texas 75243

BEDFORD / ST. MARTIN'S
75 Arlington Street
Boston, MA 02116

Printed in the United States of America
10 9 8 7 6 5 4 3 2 1

Contents

To the Student

Dear Student:

How many times have you wondered about how and why America has become what it is today? Too often in our fast-paced information age, we seem to be overwhelmed with the needs of the present. Those of us in the production of this distance learning course, *Shaping America,* have endeavored to create a comprehensive course of study that challenges you to take the time to think about America and what it means. I urge you to use this opportunity to broaden your knowledge and to reflect upon the past, the present, and the connection between the two.

I have been teaching American history at the college level for over thirty years. During the 1999–2000 and 2000–2001 academic years, I concentrated totally on preparing materials for this distance learning course. Friends, colleagues, and former students sometimes smile and question why I devoted so much time to the creation of a new history course. After all, what changes in history? Indeed, that is a great part of my fascination with the discipline, for there is always more to learn. For example, I hope you will be as intrigued as I was by the remarks of the seventy-five nationally recognized historical experts whom we interviewed for *Shaping America.* Their insights make this course truly unique.

Shaping America surveys U.S. history to 1877 in twenty-six lessons. In each lesson, we try to connect you with people who lived in earlier times. In addition, each video program uses location footage and visual images to remind us that we encounter the past in our daily lives and in our contemporary communities.

In summary, I want you to think about the American people, past and present, and to consider our relationship with the rest of the world. Our personal lives, our nation, and our world demand that we analyze, evaluate, and make reasoned judgments about people, leaders, positions, and issues. Our future depends on the prudent application of our knowledge. Through this course of study, it is my hope and expectation that you will gain greater awareness and understanding about the shaping of America. I also hope that you will come to appreciate your opportunity to shape its future.

—Kenneth G. Alfers

About the Author

Dr. Kenneth G. Alfers is a teacher, writer, and historian. He received the Dallas County Community College District's Outstanding Teacher Award in 1983 and was selected as a Piper Professor of 2005 in the state of Texas. He was the content specialist for *America: The Second Century* and *America in Perspective*, distance learning courses used around the country since 1980. He received his B.A. and M.A. degrees from Creighton University and his M.Ph. and Ph.D. degrees from The George Washington University.

A Final Note

With careful and thoughtful application of your time and energy to the material presented in this course, you should have a rewarding experience in the broadest sense of that term. I, along with other members of the production team, have put forth our best efforts to create a quality course. However, my experience teaches me that any course can be improved, so I encourage you to share any ideas about it with me. Please send your comments to Kenneth G. Alfers, R. Jan LeCroy Center for Educational Telecommunications, 9596 Walnut Street, Dallas, TX 75243-2112.

Course Organization

Shaping America is designed as a comprehensive learning package consisting of four elements: student course guide, textbook, video programs, and interactive activities.

STUDENT COURSE GUIDE

The guide for this distance learning course is:

Alfers, Kenneth G. *Student Course Guide for Shaping America*. 4th ed. Boston: Bedford/St. Martin's, 2009. ISBN (10): 0-312-47003-7; ISBN (13): 978-0-312-47003-6

This student course guide acts as your daily instructor. Each lesson gives you an Overview, Lesson Assignments, Lesson Objectives, Lesson Focus Points, a Practice Test with an Answer Key, Enrichment Ideas, Suggested Readings, Resources, and a list of historians interviewed. Some lessons present you with relevant primary sources in a "Documents" section. If you follow the student course guide closely and study each lesson carefully, you should successfully meet all of the requirements for this course.

TEXTBOOK

In addition to the student course guide, the textbook required for this course is:

Roark, James L., Michael P. Johnson, Patricia Cline Cohen, Sarah Stage, Alan Lawson, and Susan M. Hartmann. *The American Promise: A History of the United States, Volume I: To 1877*. 4th ed. Boston: Bedford/St. Martin's, 2009. ISBN (10): 0-312-45292-6; ISBN (13): 978-0-312-45292-6

VIDEO PROGRAMS

The video program series for this distance learning course is:

Shaping America

Each video program is correlated with the student course guide and the reading assignment for that lesson. Be sure to read the Lesson Focus Points in the student course guide before you watch the program. The video programs are presented in a documentary format and are divided into distinct but connected segments. Some videos have "short-takes," brief segments on interesting and relevant topics connected to the lesson. Every video brings analysis and perspective to the issues being discussed. Watch them closely.

If the video programs are broadcast more than once in your area, or if DVDs are available at your college, you might find it helpful to watch the video programs more than once, or listen to an audio tape for review. Since examination questions will be taken from the video programs as well as from the reading, careful attention to both is vital to your success.

COMPUTER-BASED INTERACTIVE ACTIVITIES

Self-graded interactive tutorials, formative self-assessments, and scenario-based application exercises are available to students whose institutions have opted to offer these. Offered in CD-ROM, DVD-ROM, and Internet formats, these activities are useful for reinforcement and review of lesson content and learning objectives. Ask your instructor how to access these activities if they are listed in your syllabus as a course requirement.

Use the publisher's website at www.bedfordstmartins.com/roark for online practice quizzes and other study tools related to material in the textbook.

Course Guidelines

Follow these guidelines as you study the material presented in each lesson:

1. OVERVIEW:
   Read the Overview for an introduction to the lesson material.

2. LESSON ASSIGNMENTS:
   Review the Lesson Assignments in order to schedule your time appropriately. Pay careful attention, as the titles and numbers of the textbook chapters are different from the student course guide lessons and the video programs.

3. LESSON OBJECTIVES:
   To get the most from your reading, review the Lesson Objectives in the student course guide.

4. LESSON FOCUS POINTS:
   The Lesson Focus Points are designed to help you get the most benefit from the resources selected for each lesson. To maximize your learning experience:
   - Scan the focus point questions.
   - Read the material assigned.
   - View the video.
   - Write answers to or make notes on the focus point questions. (References in parentheses following each question can be used to locate information in the text and video that relates to each question.)

5. HISTORICAL EXPERTS INTERVIEWED:
   These individuals are being acknowledged for their valuable contributions to this distance learning course. The titles and locations were accurate when the video programs were recorded, but may have changed since the original taping.

6. PRACTICE TEST:
   Complete the Practice Test to help you evaluate your understanding of the lesson.

7. ANSWER KEY:
   Use the Answer Key at the end of the lesson to check your answers or to locate material related to each question of the Practice Test.

8. ENRICHMENT IDEAS:
   These activities are not required unless your instructor assigns them. They are offered as suggestions to help you learn more about the material presented in this lesson.

9. SUGGESTED READINGS/RESOURCES:
   These reading materials are not required but are offered as suggestions if you wish to examine other books and resources related to the material presented in this lesson.

10. DOCUMENTS:
    The purpose of this part of your student course guide is to give you additional opportunities to "do" history by dealing directly with primary sources. By reviewing this material and relating it to that in the textbook, you should be able to increase your understanding of the lesson.

11. REVIEWING THE CHAPTER:
    At the end of each chapter in the text, you will find helpful review steps. Follow these steps to strengthen your understanding of the material in that chapter.

<u>Unit One</u>

Colonial America
To 1760
"A City on a Hill?"

1. A World Apart
2. Worlds Transformed
3. Settling the Southern Colonies
4. Settling in New England
5. Diversifying British America
6. A Distinctive Society

THEME

As John Winthrop and his fellow Puritan emigrants approached America in 1630, he expressed a vision for the community they were about to establish in Massachusetts: "We must consider that we shall be as a city upon a hill. The eyes of all people are upon us." In many ways, people are still watching the United States of America to see if it can live up to its promise. Today, like in the past, most people hope and perhaps expect that life can and will get better. Making that happen, however, often leads to a reality check. Limits, whether environmental, economic, cultural, political, and/or personal, constrain what individuals and communities can accomplish. This process of development has shaped America from its beginnings.

The cultures of the indigenous peoples who lived in North America prior to European contact were as diverse as the ecosystems in which they lived. While many groups had experienced decline prior to European contact, the effects of the Columbian Exchange were devastating to most Indian peoples who encountered the Europeans.

In colonial America, a variety of Europeans with a variety of visions for a better life came to places already inhabited by native people who had their own established lifestyles. Spain proceeded to establish an extensive American empire, part of which extended up the Rio Grande River to present-day New Mexico. Meanwhile, British settlers founded colonies at Jamestown and Plymouth. The Dutch presence in New Amsterdam illustrated the diversity of Europeans who would expand throughout the middle colonies in the late seventeenth and early eighteenth centuries. Africans were brought to America against their wishes and without much hope for a better life, but their cultures contributed to the development of a distinctive American society by 1760. In the converging experiences of these people of colonial America, we can see the roots of much of what makes America what it is today.

Lesson 1

A World Apart

OVERVIEW

When we asked Professor Gerald Danzer about studying the past, he replied that it is like being invited to a party. You want to know when it is, where it is, and who's coming. Time, place, and people — keep those things in mind as you proceed to enhance your understanding of how America took shape. Make connections between your time and place and what happened in the past. And try to have fun along the way!

This first video provides you with some perspectives on why history matters, and it introduces you to the themes that recur throughout this course. Think about American identity, that is, what America is and what being an American means. Part of American identity is based on place, so geography is stressed throughout this course. American identity also comprises ideas that developed and eventually became associated with the nation. Foremost among these ideas are freedom and equality, concepts that are contested from beginning to end. As a third part of American identity, we want you to consider an old and persistent question: Who is an American? How do race and ethnicity fit into being an American? How and why has this changed over time?

This lesson begins to address those themes by examining America before 1492. A diverse array of indigenous peoples occupied the area that would eventually become the United States of America long before they had any sustained contact with Europeans. Over time, these Native Americans adapted to the various ecosystems in which they lived and developed distinct cultures. Not all of these cultures survived until the late fifteenth century, but there is a lot to learn about and from them. Their experiences, like ours, play a vital part in the shaping of America.

LESSON ASSIGNMENTS

Text: Roark, et al., *The American Promise,* Chapter 1, "Ancient America," pp. 3–33

Video: "A World Apart" from the series *Shaping America*

Documents:
     "Iroquois and Penobscot Myths of Creation" found at the end of this lesson

LESSON OBJECTIVES

This lesson introduces the main themes of the course and describes America before 1492. Upon completing this lesson, you should be able to:

1. Describe how and why historians study the past.

2. Describe the geographical and human origins of North American history.

3. Explain the development and characteristics of major indigenous cultures found in six distinct regions of the area that would become the United States of America.

4. Describe the Mexica culture of Meso-America prior to contact with Europeans.

5. Assess the legacy of Native American cultures and their status as of 1492.

LESSON FOCUS POINTS

The following questions are designed to help you get the most benefit from the sources selected for this lesson. For reference purposes, the titles for the video segments are: (1) Introduction, (2) "Defining America," (3) "The Pacific Northwest," (4) "The California Coast," (5) "The Pueblo People," (6) "The Mississippi Valley," (7) "The Southeast," (8) "The Northeast," (9) Summary Analysis: "We Have a Great Deal to Learn…"

1. According to historians quoted in the video, why does history matter? What themes will recur throughout this course? (video segment 1)

2. How do historians differ from archaeologists in their study of the past? What is meant by the term *prehistory*? How do we learn about ancient Americans? What limits our learning? (textbook, pp. 3–5)

3. Why were human beings relatively late in arriving in the Western Hemisphere? What made it possible for them to get there? (textbook, pp. 6–7)

4. Why did Paleo-Indians spread relatively rapidly across the Americas? What characterized this culture? (textbook, p. 10)

5. Why did Paleo-Indians face a crisis about 11,000 years ago? How did they adapt? What resulted from these adaptations? (textbook, pp. 10–11)

6. What does the term "archaic" connote about cultures indigenous to America? (textbook, p. 11)

7. Examine the maps on pages 6, 12 and 24. How did environmental factors help define the cultural boundaries and characteristics of the first Americans? (textbook, pp. 6, 12, 24)

8. What roles did the salmon, totems, and kin groups play in the pre-Columbian Indian cultures of the Pacific Northwest? (textbook, pp. 13, 16; video segment 3)

9. What were the characteristics of the Chumash culture along the California coast? (textbook, p. 16; video segment 4)

10. How did the ancestral pueblo peoples of the Southwest adapt to their environment? What characterized their social organization and village life? (textbook, pp. 17–20; video segment 5)

11. What characterized the culture that developed at Cahokia? How is this culture similar to that found at Adena and Hopewell? What purposes did mounds serve? (textbook, pp. 20–22; video segment 6)

12. How did the environment affect pre-Columbian Indian cultures in the Southeast? What characterized these groups? (video segment 7)

13. Why did indigenous peoples of the Northeast often inhabit villages that were seasonal sites? What else characterized these people? (textbook, pp. 22–23, 26; video segment 8)

14. What characterized the Mexica culture of Meso-America before European contact? (textbook, pp. 28–30)

15. Generally, what was the status of Native American cultures in 1490s? (textbook, pp. 22–25, 28; video segment 9)

16. In summary, what is the legacy of the indigenous peoples of ancient America? (textbook, p. 30; video segment 9)

17. Many cultures have stories concerning the origin of the universe. Compare the stories from Iroquois and Penobscot traditions with each other and to the tradition with which you are familiar. (Documents)

HISTORICAL EXPERTS INTERVIEWED

Michael Adler, Associate Professor, Southern Methodist University, Dallas, TX
Alex Barker, Curator of Archaelogy, Dallas Museum of Natural History, Dallas, TX
Colin Calloway, Professor, Dartmouth College, Hanover, NH
Gerald Danzer, Professor of History, University of Illinois at Chicago, Chicago, IL
R. David Edmunds, Watson Professor of American History, University of Texas at Dallas, Richardson, TX
Brian Fagan, Professor of Anthropology, University of California at Santa Barbara, Santa Barbara, CA
Eric Foner, Professor of History, Columbia University, New York, NY
James Oliver Horton, Benjamin Banneker Professor of American Civilization and History, The George Washington University, Washington, DC
William Iseminger, Public Relations Director, Cahokia Mounds State Historic Site, Collinsville, IL
Linda Kerber, May Brodbeck Professor in Liberal Arts, University of Iowa, Iowa City, IA
Frank Lemos, Director, Chumush Interpretive Center, Thousand Oaks, CA
Chad Smith, Principal Chief, Cherokee Nation, Tahlequah, OK

PRACTICE TEST

The following items will help you evaluate your understanding of this lesson. Use the Answer Key at the end of the lesson to check your answers or to locate material related to each question.

Multiple choice: Choose the BEST answer.

1. According to historians cited in the video, the study of history should do all of the following EXCEPT _____.
   A. provide a sense of who we are
   B. include multiple stories
   C. spark our curiosity
   D. emphasize dates and battles

2. The basic reason for the early, prolonged absence of humans in the Western Hemisphere is that _____.
   A. the warm climate of Africa attracted most of the earth's population
   B. large herds of mammoths made migration to the Americas too dangerous
   C. North and South America had become detached from the gigantic continent of Pangaea
   D. food was too plentiful for northern European tribes to seek a different home

3. About 11,000 years ago the Paleo-Indians faced a major crisis: _____.
   A. the people had difficulty living in a cooling climate
   B. the large animals they hunted had difficulty adapting to a warming climate
   C. an over-concentration on hunting small animals eliminated much of the food sources of the large mammals
   D. water became scarce as the climate cooled

4. The Northwest archaic peoples _____.
   A. erected small tents of buffalo skins adorned with highly intricate quillwork
   B. carved out pueblo dwellings in the side of mountains, adorned with sandpaintings
   C. constructed large, multifamily cedar houses adorned with totems
   D. created small, single-family structures from glacial ice adorned with ironwork

5. At Cahokia, Monk's Mound likely served as a site for _____.
   A. burying women
   B. the ruling chief
   C. dispatching hunters
   D. observing nearby tribes

6. The human sacrifices practiced by the Mexica are said to have been on a scale unequaled in human history; to the Mexica, human sacrifice was _____.
   A. an intuitive remedy to a protein deficiency
   B. a ritual modeled by their one god, Quetzalcoatl, who methodically sacrificed all the other gods as he created the universe
   C. a normal and reasonable activity to demonstrate their religious devotion
   D. a ritual necessary to make crops grow fruitfully

7. The greatest similarity among the diverse cultures that inhabited North America at the dawn of European colonization was that each _____.
   A. employed some form of written language
   B. no longer depended upon hunting and gathering for a major portion of their food
   C. used domesticated animals for hunting and agricultural production
   D. developed a distinct culture because of specific adaptations made to their own local natural environment

Short Answer: Your answers should be one or two paragraphs long and specifically address the points indicated.

8. Explain the following statement in reference to archaic Americans: The absence of written sources means that ancient human beings remain anonymous.

9. What were the similarities of the cultures of indigenous peoples in America in 1492, and how did they differ from the culture of Europe at the time?

10. What were the main features of the Mexica culture prior to European contact?

Essay Question: Your answer should be several paragraphs long and express a clear understanding of the points indicated.

11. Describe and explain the characteristics of the pre-Columbian indigenous cultures that existed in the Pacific Northwest, the California coastal region, the Southwest, the Mississippi Valley, the Southeast, and the Northeast. What is the legacy of these cultures?

ANSWER KEY

Answer	Learning Objectives	Focus Points	References
1. D	LO 1	FP 1	video segment 1
2. C	LO 2	FP 3	pp. 6–7
3. B	LO 2	FP 5	pp. 10–11
4. C	LO 3	FP 8	pp. 13–16; video segment 3
5. B	LO 3	FP 11	pp. 20–22; video segment 6
6. C	LO 4	FP 14	pp. 28–30
7. D	LO 5	FP 15	pp. 22–25, 28; video segment 9

8. ....LO 1..................FP 2 ....pp. 3–5
   - How do we learn about cultures that did not use written languages?
   - What can we learn about those cultures?
   - What elements do written sources bring to our knowledge about people?

9. ....LO 5..................FP 5 ....pp. 10–11
   - Consider the adaptations to the environment in order to survive.
   - Are social and political organizations similar? How did various cultures communicate?
   - Contrast indigenous cultures with European technology and domesticated animals, etc.

10. ....LO 4................FP 14 .... pp. 28–30
    - What was the extent of their empire in the Americas?
    - How was their society structured?
    - What role did tribute play in their empire?

11. ....LO 3, 5.......FP 8–13, 15–16 .... pp. 13–30; video segments 3–9
    - Consider how the environment affected the economy of each culture.
    - How did they organize their communities?
    - Identify at least one feature of each culture.
    - What can we learn from them?

ENRICHMENT IDEAS

These activities are not required unless your instructor assigns them. They are offered as suggestions to help you learn more about the material presented in this lesson.

1. In the video for this lesson, you heard many brief responses to the question, "Why does history matter?" In a well-developed essay, explain which responses were most interesting to you. Why does history matter to you?

2. Using the "Beyond America's Borders- Nature's Immigrants" segment of the text, pp. 8–9, consider immigration patterns as you research your local geography and the history of indigenous animals in your area. Then submit a report on your findings. How did the indigenous animals adapt to the environmental conditions?

3. Choose a place in North America before 1492. Now organize a food-gathering trip using the available resources and technology. Submit a report describing your plan.

SUGGESTED READINGS/RESOURCES

See the "Bibliography" on pages 30–31 of the text if you wish to examine other books and resources related to the material presented in this lesson.

DOCUMENTS

Many cultures have stories concerning the origin of the universe. Compare these stories from Iroquois and Penobscot traditions with each other and to tradition with which you are familiar.

Iroquois and Penobscot Myths of Creation

Iroquois Account of the Origins of Human Life

In a house in the Sky World, a man and a woman lived on opposite sides of a fireplace. The two had great spiritual power because each had been isolated from other people until the age of puberty. Every day after the housemates went out to work, the woman crossed to the other side of the fire to comb the man's hair. Through mysterious means, she became pregnant and bore a daughter. Shortly thereafter, the man fell ill and announced that he would soon die. Because no one in the Sky World knew what death was, he had to explain to the woman what would happen to him and instruct her how to preserve his body. After he died, the woman's growing daughter endured fits of weeping that, despite the best efforts of village neighbors to comfort her, could be relieved only by visits to the preserved corpse of the deceased, whose spirit told her that he was her father and taught her many things.

When the daughter, whom the Iroquois called Sky Woman, reached adulthood, her father's spirit instructed her to take a dangerous journey to the village of a man destined to become her spouse. She brought her prospective husband loaves of bread baked with berries and then, enduring great travail, cooked him a potent soup that cured him of a long-troublesome ailment. In exchange, he sent her home with a burden of venison that nearly filled her family's house. After Sky Woman returned to her husband, the pair always slept on opposite sides of the fire and refrained from sexual intercourse. Nevertheless, she, like her mother before her, inexplicably became pregnant. Stricken by jealousy, the husband again became ill and dreamed that a great tree near his house must be uprooted so that he and his spouse could look down through the resulting hole to the world below. To cure his sickness, all the people of the village worked together to pull it up. When Sky Woman looked over the edge of the abyss, her husband pushed her down.

As Sky Woman fell toward the endless waters below, the spirit birds and animals of the sea held a council to decide how to rescue her, Ducks flew up to catch her on their wings and bring her safely down, and the Turtle agreed to provide a place for her to rest on his back. Meantime, various animals tried to dive to the bottom of the lake and bring up earth on which the woman could walk; only the Muskrat succeeded. The material he placed on the Turtle's back grew, with Sky Woman's help, into the living dry land of North America. Soon the celestial visitor gave birth to a daughter, who in time became supernaturally pregnant by the spirit of the Turtle. In the younger woman's womb grew male twins, who began arguing over the best way to emerge from her body. The Good Twin (Upholder of the Heavens, or Sky Grasper) was born normally. The second, the Evil Twin, burst forth from his mother's side and thus killed her. When Sky Woman asked which of her grandsons had slain her daughter, they blamed each other, but the Evil Twin was the more persistent and persuasive. The Grandmother cherished him, and she turned the body and head of the boys' deceased mother into the sun and moon, respectively; and she threw the Good Twin out of her house, assuming he would die.

But he did not. Instead, with the aid of his father the Turtle, the Good Twin improved Iroquoia, making various animals, learning the secrets of cultivating maize and other crops, and bringing into existence mortal human beings. All of these things he did not create from nothingness; they grew through a process of transformation and infusion of supernatural power from the living earth and from a kind of spirit beings who dwelled in the Sky World and under the waters. With each new creation, however, Sky Woman and the Evil Twin partially undid the Good Twin's efforts in ways that forever after would make life difficult for humans. When the Good Twin constructed straight rivers for canoeing, with the water flowing in both ways at once, the Evil Twin threw in rocks and hills to twist the streams and make their waters fall in only one direction. When the Good Twin grew succulent ears of corn, Sky Woman threw ashes into his cooking pot and decreed that maize must be parched and ground before it could be eaten. When the Good Twin made animals readily give themselves to humans as food, the Evil Twin sealed them all in a cave, from which Sky Grasper could rescue only a portion; the rest the Evil Twin turned into enemies of humans.

Finally, the two brothers also fought, and the Good Twin won. He could not, however, undo all the evil that his brother and Grandmother had left in the world. So he taught humans how to grow corn, and how to keep harm at bay with ceremonies of thanksgiving and peacekeeping with the spirits. Sky Grasper made these ceremonies easier by designating clans named after certain animals such as Wolf, Bear, Turtle. But he knew that mortals could never keep the ritual well enough. But Sky Grasper also predicted the time would come when all peoples would fall into great dispute and destroy one another. Good Twin went home, where he never died, but instead continually passed through stages of aging and then rejuvenating himself.

Corn Mother: A Penobscot Myth

When Kloskurbeh, the All-maker, lived on earth, there were no people yet. But one day when the sun was high, a youth appeared and called him "Uncle, brother of my mother." This young man was born from the foam of the waves, foam quickened by the wind and warmed by the sun. It was the motion of the wind, the moistness of water, and the sun's warmth, which gave him life. And the young man lived with Kloskurbeh and became his chief helper.

Now, after these two powerful beings had created all manner of things, there came to them, as the sun was shining at high noon, a beautiful girl. She was born of the wonderful earth plant, and of the dew, and of warmth. Because a drop of dew fell on a leaf and was warmed by the sun, and the warming sun is life, this girl came into being from the green living plant, from moisture, and from warmth.

"I am love," said the maiden. "I am a strength giver, I am the nourisher, I am the provider of men and animals. They all love me."

Then Kloskurbeh thanked the Great Master Above for having sent them the maiden. The youth, the Great Nephew, married her, and the girl conceived and thus became First Mother. And Kloskurbeh, the Great Uncle, who teaches humans all they need to know, taught their children how to live. Then he went away to dwell in the north, from which he will return sometime when he is needed.

Now, the people increased and became numerous. They lived by hunting, and the more people there were, the less game they found. They were hunting it out, and as the animals decreased, starvation came upon the people. And First Mother pitied them.

The little children came to First Mother and said: "We are hungry. Feed us." But she had nothing to give them, and she wept. She told them: "Be patient. I will make some food. Then your little bellies will be full." But she kept weeping.

Her husband asked: "How can I make you smile? How can I make you happy?"

"There is only one thing that will stop my tears."

"What is it?" asked her husband.

"It is this: you must kill me."

"I could never do that."

"You must, or I will go on weeping and grieving forever."

The husband traveled far, to the end of the earth, to the north he went, to ask the Great Instructor, his uncle Kloskurbeh, what he should do.

"You must do what she wants. You must kill her," said Kloskurbeh. Then the young man went back to his home, and it was his turn to weep. But First Mother said: "Tomorrow at high noon you must do it. After you have killed me, let two of our sons take hold of my hair and drag my body over that empty patch of earth. Let them drag me back and forth, back and forth, over every part of the patch, until all my flesh has been torn from my body. Afterwards, take my bones, gather them up, and bury them in the middle of this clearing. Then leave that place."

She smiled and said, "Wait seven moons and then come back, and you will find my flesh there, flesh given out of love, and it will nourish and strengthen you forever and ever."

So it was done. The husband slew his wife and her sons, praying, dragged her body to and fro as she had commanded, until her flesh covered all the earth. Then they took up her bones and buried them in the middle of it. Weeping loudly, they went away.

When the husband and his children and his children's children came back to that place after seven moons had passed, they found the earth covered with tall, green, tasseled plants. The plants' fruit — corn — was First Mother's flesh, given so that people might live and flourish. And they partook of First Mother's flesh and found it sweet beyond words. Following her instructions, they did not eat all, but put many kernels back into the earth. In this way her flesh and spirit renewed themselves every seven months, generation after generation.

And at the spot where they had burned [sic] First Mother's bones, there grew another plant, broad-leafed and fragrant. It was First Mother's breath, and they heard her spirit talking: "Burn this up and smoke it. It is sacred. It will clear your minds, help your prayers, and gladden your hearts."

And First Mother's husband called the first plant Skarmunal, corn, and the second plant utarmur-yayeh, tobacco.

"Remember," he told the people, "and take good care of First Mother's flesh, because it is her goodness become substance. Take good care of her breath, because it is her love turned into smoke. Remember her and think of her whenever you eat, whenever you smoke this sacred plant, because she has given her life that you might live. Yet she is not dead, she lives: in undying love she renews herself again and again."

"Iroquois and Penobscot Myths of Creation" taken from *The Ordeal of the Longhouse: The People of the Iroquois League in the Era of European Colonization* by Daniel Richter. Published for the Institute of Early American History and Culture, copyright 1992 by the University of North Carolina Press.

Lesson 2

Worlds Transformed

OVERVIEW

When Christopher Columbus encountered the Taino people on the island they called Guanahani in 1492, he touched off an exchange of plants, animals, diseases, and cultures that transformed worlds. Natives inhabiting the "New World," as the Europeans called it, would pay a heavy price for living in an area now coveted by aggressive outsiders. At the same time, people living in the "Old World" would have their lives altered by the repercussions of this contact. Indeed, after 1492 the world would never be the same again, either geographically or culturally.

Spain, whose monarchs financed Columbus' voyage, proceeded to take the lead among European nations seeking to capitalize on their "discoveries." Spanish explorers traversed much of the Americas, including areas that eventually became part of the south and southwestern United States. Spanish conquistadors subdued many of the native populations, setting the stage for a Spanish empire in the New World. Part of this empire reached into the area we now know as New Mexico. The blending of cultures there reflected the dynamics of continuing contact in frontier regions, a process that played a vital role in the shaping of America.

LESSON ASSIGNMENTS

Text: Roark, et al., *The American Promise*, Chapter 2, "Europeans Encounter the New World," pp. 35–67

Video: "Worlds Transformed" from the series *Shaping America*

Documents:
           "Justifying Conquest," pp. 54–55 in the textbook

LEARNING OBJECTIVES

This lesson describes the effects of European contact with the Americas. After completing this lesson, you should be able to:

1. Explain the changes taking place in Western Europe that stimulated interest in overseas expansion and colonization.

2. Analyze the ways in which the peoples of the New and Old Worlds affected each other when their cultures met, with specific emphasis on the "Columbian exchange."

3. Describe the geographic revolution that took place in the late fifteenth and early sixteenth centuries.

4. Analyze the development of Spain's New World empire and how it affected both Europe and the Americas.

LESSON FOCUS POINTS

The following questions are designed to help you get the most benefit from the resources selected for this lesson. For reference purposes, the titles for the video segments are: (1) Introduction, (2) "Columbian Exchange," (3) "The Conquest of the Americas," (4) "New Spain," and (5) Summary Analysis: "A Blending of Cultures."

1. What was happening in Europe in the late fifteenth and early sixteenth centuries that explains the urge to look outward? (textbook, pp. 35–38)

2. Examine Map 2.1 on page 38 of the textbook. What trade goods were being exchanged between Europe and Asia? What was the incentive to secure a water route from Europe to Asia? (textbook, pp. 37–38)

3. How and why was Portugal exploring ways to get access to Asia? What were the effects of the Portuguese explorations? (textbook, pp. 39–40)

4. What was Columbus's vision? In what ways did Columbus reflect the spirit of his times? (textbook, pp. 41–42; video segment 2)

5. Define the term *Columbian exchange*. What were the short- and long-term consequences of this exchange? (textbook, pp. 42–46; video segment 2)

6. How did Columbus's voyages and those of other European explorers bring about a geographic revolution? (textbook, pp. 42–46)

7. Examine Map 2.2 on page 43 of the textbook. Who were the early European explorers? What countries did they represent? Where did they go? (textbook, p. 43)

8. What were the motivations behind Spanish conquests in the Americas? How did the Spaniards justify conquering the Indians? (textbook, pp. 46–51; video segment 3)

9. Why was Cortés' entry into Tenochtitlán a unique moment in history? (video segment 3)

10. How and why was Cortés able to conquer Mexico? (textbook, pp. 46–48, 50–51; video segment 3)

11. What areas of America did de Soto, Coronado, and Cabrillo explore? What were the effects of their explorations? (textbook, p. 49; video segment 3)

12. How was Cabeza de Vaca's experience in America different from most other Spanish conquistadors? (video segment 3)

13. Examine Map 2.3 on page 52 of the textbook. What major areas of North and South America composed the Spanish empire in America? (textbook, p. 52)

14. What were the economic, political, and social characteristics of Spain's empire in the New World in the sixteenth century? (textbook, pp. 52–60; video segments 4, 5)

15. What is the significance of the *encomienda* system in Spanish America? In what ways was this system changed by the *repartimiento?* What were the effects of both systems? (textbook, pp. 52–56)

16. What role did the religious missionaries play in New Spain? (textbook, pp. 53–59; video segment 4)

17. What was the toll of Spanish conquest and colonization on the Indians? (textbook, p. 60)

18. Why did the Spanish found a settlement at St. Augustine? (textbook, pp. 60–61; video segment 4)

19. Why did the Spanish settle in the area that became New Mexico? What led to the Acoma rebellion? How did Juan de Oñate suppress that rebellion? Why was Santa Fe founded in 1608? (textbook, pp. 60–61; video segment 4)

20. What were the effects of the mixing of Spanish, Indian, and African peoples and cultures in the New World? Why does cultural blending tend to happen in frontier zones? How is this blending reflected in American society today? (textbook, pp. 57, 60; video segment 5)

21. How did the Spanish empire in America affect Spain and other European countries? (textbook, pp. 62–65)

HISTORICAL EXPERTS INTERVIEWED

Alfred Crosby, Professor Emeritus, University of Texas at Austin, Austin, TX
Deena J. Gonzalez, Professor of History, Pomona College, Claremont, CA
Frances Levine, Division Head, Arts and Sciences, Santa Fe Community College, Santa Fe, NM
Stuart B. Schwartz, George Burton Adams Professor of History, Yale University, New Haven, CT
David Weber, Professor of History, Southern Methodist University, Dallas, TX

PRACTICE TEST

The following items will help you evaluate your understanding of this lesson. Use the Answer Key at the end of the lesson to check your answers or to locate material related to each question.

Multiple choice: Choose the BEST answer.

1. While it was unfortunate that the bubonic plague killed about a third of Europe's population, it was beneficial in that it _____.
   A. eased food shortages and weakened the feudal system
   B. eased pressure on food resources and created greater opportunities for advancement
   C. created a food surplus which stimulated exploration for new marketplaces
   D. created a more even distribution of food and weakened the authority of the Catholic Church

2. Portugal's early interest in exploration and expansion stemmed from a desire to _____.
   A. expel Muslims from Europe and control the African trade for wheat and gold
   B. control the gold and slave trade of Africa
   C. shift the balance of power in Europe from France to itself
   D. shift the balance of power in Europe from England to itself

3. Columbus' first impression of the Tainos was that they _____.
   A. would be good slaves
   B. possessed strong religious values
   C. would be good and intelligent servants
   D. could pass as ordinary European peasants

4. Some historians believe that because of the effects of the Columbian exchange, the so-called discovery of America was _____.
   A. beneficial to the indigenous peoples
   B. the most important event in the history of the world
   C. of little benefit to Europe and Asia
   D. all of the above

5. If you were Martin Waldseemüller in 1500, you were among the very first to understand that _____.
   A. the earth was a sphere and not flat
   B. a round globe, rather than a flat map, depicted the earth with greater accuracy
   C. the Treaty of Tordesillas line shifted power from Italy to Spain and Portugal
   D. the discoveries of Columbus, Balboa, and Vespucci proved there was a continent which existed west of Europe and east of Asia

6. Hernán Cortés was eventually able to defeat the Mexicans in 1521 by enlisting the help of _____.
   A. a Mayan chief and his followers
   B. tribes of the Yucatan, and Catholic priests
   C. the Aztec peoples
   D. tens of thousands of Indian allies who favored the destruction of the Aztecs

7. The Spanish introduced the *encomienda* as a way to _____.
   A. reward conquistadors who claimed territory in the New World
   B. provide housing for the Indians who labored in the silver mines
   C. divide the wealth of the New World between the monarchy and the Catholic Church
   D. punish wrong-doers

8. In the video, Professor David Weber reminds us that in frontier regions _____.
   A. people tend to develop a new culture
   B. democracy always emerges among settlers
   C. indigenous culture is totally destroyed
   D. expansion moves almost invariably from east to west

Short Answer: Your answers should be one or two paragraphs long and specifically address the points indicated.

9. How and why was Cortés able to conquer Mexico?

10. Explain the role Portugal played in the age of European exploration.

11. How and why did a geographic revolution take place in the sixteenth century?

12. Why did Spain become the dominant European power in the New World in the sixteenth century?

13. Why did Spain establish settlements in areas that became Florida and New Mexico?

Essay Questions: Your answers should be several paragraphs long and express a clear understanding of the points indicated.

14. Describe and explain the meaning of the Columbian exchange. How did both the Old and New Worlds experience gains and losses because of the exchange? Which world benefited the most? Why? In what ways does the exchange continue today?

15. During the sixteenth century, Spain became the most powerful country in both Europe and the Americas. How and why did this happen? How did Spain transform America? How is the Spanish influence still visible in the United States today?

ANSWER KEY

	Answer	Learning Objectives	Focus Points	References
1.	B	LO 1	FP 1	pp. 35–38
2.	A	LO 1	FP 3	pp. 39–40
3.	C	LO 2	FP 4	pp. 41–42; video segment 2
4.	B	LO 2	FP 5	pp. 42–46; video segment 2
5.	D	LO 3	FP 6	pp. 42–46
6.	D	LO 4	FP 10	pp. 46–48, 50–51; video segment 3
7.	A	LO 4	FP 15	pp. 52-56
8.	A	LO 2, 4	FP 20	pp. 57, 60; video segment 5
9.		LO 2, 4	FP 9, 10	pp. 46–48, 50–51; video segment 3

- What technological advantages did Cortés have?
- How and why was he able to get help from some of the indigenous peoples?

10. ....LO 1.................FP 3 ....pp. 39–40

- Where was Portugal located?
- Why did Portugal encourage voyages around Africa?
- What technological advances are associated with Portugal's efforts?

11. ....LO 3.................FP 6 ....pp. 42–46

- How did mapmakers depict the world prior to this time?
- How did Martin Waldseemüller map the world? What information did he have?
- What effect did the European "discovery" of the Pacific Ocean have?

12. ....LO 4.................FP 21 ....pp. 62–65

- What areas did Spain colonize? By what authority?
- What resources in the Americas did Spain use to its advantage?
- How were they able to control and use the native peoples?

13. ....LO 4.............FP 18, 19 ....pp. 60–61; video segment 4

- How would a colony in Florida solidify its claim and protect its ships?
- What were the Spanish seeking in New Mexico? What did they end up doing there?

14. ....LO 2, 4.........FP 5, 20, 21 .... pp. 42–46, 57–65; video segments 2, 5

- What is the Columbian exchange?
- How did New World food products, crops, and mineral resources affect Europe and Asia?
- How did diseases affect both areas?
- Did the New World gain anything from Europe? What?
- How does the exchange of organisms continue?

15. ....LO 4...........FP 1, 5, 7–21 .... pp. 35–38, 42–65; video segments 2–5
    - What geographic advantages did Spain have?
    - How did Spain use the resources it gained in the Americas?
    - Why was Spain able to establish its empire? What parts of their culture did they impose?
    - How is the influence reflected in people, language, religion, architecture, etc.?

ENRICHMENT IDEAS

1. In a well-developed position paper, take a stand on the issue of whether or not Columbus Day should be a national holiday in the United States.

2. If you live in a region that was colonized by Spain, examine how the effects of that colonization are still in evidence today. Summarize your findings in a well-documented essay.

3. Research the life of Amerigo Vespucci. In a well-developed essay, explain his contribution to geography and why America was named after him.

4. You are an Indian or a Spanish observer to Cortés' entrance into Tenochtitlán. Write a commentary on what you observe.

5. Read the book *Longitude* by Dava Sobel, and then write a report on the main points discussed in that book.

SUGGESTED READINGS/RESOURCES

See the "Bibliography" on pages 66–67 of the textbook if you wish to examine other books and resources related to the material presented in this lesson.

Lesson 3

Settling the Southern Colonies

OVERVIEW

The Spanish experience in the New World caused other European nations, particularly England, to envision expanded world power and fabulous riches. British investors hoped to make money and set out to sponsor permanent settlement in the Chesapeake region of eastern North America.

The settlers had their own hopes and dreams, but they were the ones who had to face the realities of establishing new communities in an area already inhabited by American Indians. An initial attempt by the British to establish a settlement at Roanoke in the late 1580s ended with the mysterious disappearance of the colonists. Nearly thirty years later, another British settlement, this time at Jamestown, survived—but just barely. The struggles the colonists experienced there brought about some adjustments in land and labor policies. Further south in Carolina, close ties with British colonies in the Caribbean affected the development of Charleston, another distinctive colony. Characterized by the production of staple crops, a servant labor system, and an emerging racial hierarchy, the southern colonies established by the British in the seventeenth century would ultimately affect all Americans for generations to come.

LESSON ASSIGNMENTS

Text: Roark, et al., The American Promise, Chapter 2, "Europe and the Spanish Example," pp. 63–64, and Chapter 3, "The Southern Colonies in the Seventeenth Century," pp. 69–101

Video: "Settling the Southern Colonies" from the series *Shaping America*

Documents:
     "Virginia Laws Governing Servants and Slaves," pp. 84–85 in the textbook
     "Manifesto Concerning the Troubles in Virginia" found at the end of this lesson

LEARNING OBJECTIVES

This lesson describes the enduring effects of the British colonies established along the southeastern coast of North America in the seventeenth century. Upon completing this lesson, you should be able to:

1. Describe the experience of the British colony at Roanoke.

2. Describe the relations between English colonists and the American Indians in the Chesapeake region.

3. Explain the development of the Chesapeake colonies in the seventeenth century.

4. Explain the causes and significance of Bacon's Rebellion.

5. Describe the development of the West Indian sugar economy of Barbados, the subsequent establishment of the Carolina colony, and the connections between the two.

6. Explain the ways in which slavery and racism affected the social and political order of the Chesapeake and Carolina colonies.

LESSON FOCUS POINTS

The following questions are designed to help you get the most benefit from the resources selected for this lesson. For reference purposes, the titles for the video segments are:
(1) Introduction, (2) "Jamestown," (3) Short-take: "The Stinking Weed," (4) "The Changing Chesapeake," (5) Short-take: "Sugar, Sugar," (6) "The Caribbean Connection," and (7) Summary Analysis: "A Dividing Line."

1. Why did the British attempt to found a colony at Roanoke? What likely happened to this colony? (textbook, p. 64; video segment 1)

2. Why was a colony established at Jamestown? (textbook, p. 71; video segment 2)

3. Why was the Jamestown settlement so fragile? (textbook, pp. 71–73; video segment 2)

4. How did the settlers at Jamestown cope with the hardships they encountered? (textbook, pp. 73–75; video segment 2)

5. What factors explain the relationship of the settlers with the Indians in the surrounding area? Why was there no major Indian attack between 1607 and 1622? Why did the relationship change in 1622? (textbook, pp. 69–75; video segment 2)

6. How important was John Smith to the survival of the Jamestown colony? Why did Pocahontas save Smith's life in 1607? What was ironic about that by the end of the seventeenth century? (textbook, pp. 69–75; video segment 2)

7. Why were the Jamestown settlers unable to feed themselves for more than a decade? How important was the corn crop to their survival? (textbook, pp. 73–75)

8. What significant political changes took place in the Jamestown colony in 1619 and 1624? Why were these changes important? (textbook, pp. 75–76)

9. How and why did the Virginia Company decide to parcel out land to individual property owners? (textbook, pp. 77–78; video segment 2)

10. What was the short- and long-term significance of tobacco? (textbook, pp. 77–87; video segments 2, 3, 4)

11. Examine Map 3.1 on page 78 of the textbook. Why was access to navigable water so important? What is the "fall line"? (textbook, p. 78)

12. What were the characteristics of the indentured servant labor system that developed in the Chesapeake area? What was life like for the servant laborers? (textbook, pp. 78–79, 82–86; video segment 4)

13. Why were Africans brought into Virginia? What does the life of Anthony Johnson illustrate about the life of Africans in early Virginia? (video segment 4)

14. Why did the English colonists consider themselves superior to Indians and Africans? (textbook, pp. 88–89)

15. As British settlement expanded in the Chesapeake region, what social, economic, and political conflicts emerged? Why did this happen? (textbook, pp. 87, 90; video segment 4)

16. Why did Bacon's Rebellion occur? (See Bacon's "Manifesto.") What is important about Bacon's Rebellion? (textbook, pp. 90–92; video segment 4; document)

17. Why was a British colony established at Charleston, in the Carolina region of North America? How was this colony linked to Barbados in the West Indies? (textbook, pp. 94–96; video segment 6)

18. Examine Map 3.2 in the text. Answer the questions related to it. (textbook, p. 95)

19. Why were the British colonies in the Chesapeake region and the Carolinas moving toward a slave labor system in the last thirty years of the seventeenth century? What were the effects of this change? (textbook, pp. 96–98; video segment 7)

20. In summary, what can we learn from the experiences of British settlers, Indians, and Africans in the Chesapeake and Carolina areas in the seventeenth century? (textbook, pp. 69–101; all video segments)

HISTORICAL EXPERTS INTERVIEWED

Michael Johnson, Professor of History, Johns Hopkins University, Baltimore, MD
Karen Kupperman, Professor of History, New York University, New York, NY
Daniel Littlefield, Professor of History, University of South Carolina, Columbia, SC
Jonathan Poston, Director of Museums and Preservation Initiatives, Historic Charleston
    Foundation, Charleston, SC

PRACTICE TEST

The following items will help you evaluate your understanding of this lesson. Use the Answer Key at the end of the lesson to check your answers or to locate material related to each question.

Multiple choice: Choose the BEST answer.

1. In the video, Professor Karen Kupperman speculates that the "lost" colonists of Roanoke likely _____.
    A. were killed by Indians
    B. melded in with the Indian population in the area
    C. abandoned the island to go to the West Indies
    D. starved due to laziness

2. The story of Pocahontas saving Captain John Smith from her father's death sentence was told to inform the reader _____.
    A. of Pocahontas' great love of John Smith
    B. about the origins of the "noble savage"
    C. about how inadequately Englishmen understood Indian rituals
    D. that Powhatan never truly understood the English

3. Relations between Jamestown colonists and Indians changed by 1622 because _____.
    A. Powhatan was losing power
    B. Virginia became a royal colony
    C. John Smith took over as governor
    D. expansion of the settlement now encroached on Indian land

4. Richard Hakluyt, a strong proponent of colonization, argued that English colonies would _____.
    A. enhance England's ability to maintain a balance of power in Europe and throughout the Mediterranean world
    B. provide a market for English goods and a place for the unemployed
    C. provide raw materials for England and a strategic political outpost
    D. provide a dumping ground for England's surplus goods and disenfranchised younger sons of the nobility

5. If you wanted to be a highly profitable tobacco farmer in the 1600s in Virginia, the biggest obstacle you were likely to face was _____.
    A. lack of affordable land
    B. lack of workers
    C. getting the crop to grow
    D. being able to afford the technology needed to grow tobacco

---

6. Bacon's Rebellion erupted in 1676 as a dispute over Indian policy, and it ended as a conflict between the _____.
   A. planter elite and the small farmers
   B. indentured servants and their masters
   C. Indians and Virginia militia
   D. small farmers and newly freed servants

7. It is important to study the economy and slave labor system of the Caribbean sugar islands because it helps us better understand _____.
   A. the first major settlement of slaves and slave owners in Carolina
   B. the resistance to slavery by abolitionists
   C. why the Chesapeake did not pursue sugar agriculture
   D. the relationship between West Indians and Africans

8. In the video, Professor Dan Littlefield observes that the shift in seventeenth century Virginia away from indentured servant labor was accompanied by _____.
   A. increasing tobacco production
   B. slowing rates of population growth
   C. accelerating movement toward democracy
   D. using race as a dividing line among the poor

Short Answer: Your answers should be one or two paragraphs long and specifically address the points indicated.

9. Why was John Smith a critical person in the survival of Jamestown?

10. How did Nathaniel Bacon justify his rebellion in 1676?

11. In what ways was seventeenth century South Carolina a frontier outpost for Barbados?

Essay Question: Your answer should be several paragraphs long and express a clear understanding of the points indicated.

12. Why did the British establish colonies in the Chesapeake and Carolina? How and why did life and labor in these colonies change during the seventeenth century? What developments occurred then that continued to shape America for generations?

ANSWER KEY

Answer	Learning Objectives	Focus Points	References
1. B	LO 1	FP 1	p. 64; video segment 1
2. C	LO 2	FP 5	pp. 69–75; video segment 2
3. D	LO 2	FP 5	pp. 69–75; video segment 2
4. B	LO 3	FP 2	p. 71; video segment 2
5. B	LO 3	FP 10	pp. 77–87; video segments 2, 3, 4
6. A	LO 4	FP 15, 16	pp. 87, 90–92; video segments 2, 4; document
7. A	LO 5	FP 17	pp. 94–96; video segment 5
8. D	LO 6	FP 19	pp. 96–98; video segment 7

9. .... LO 2, 3 .... FP 6 .... pp. 69–75; video segment 2
   - Why was the initial settlement suffering from a leadership void?
   - What did he force the settlers to do?
   - How did he get along with the Indians in the area?

10. .... LO 4 .... FP 16 .... pp. 90–92; video segment 4; document
    - What is Bacon complaining about?
    - Who does he blame for the troubles?
    - Was he guilty of treason?

11. .... LO 5 .... FP 17 .... pp. 94–96; video segment 5
    - Who settled the Carolina region?
    - What socioeconomic system was put in place in Carolina?
    - What products were traded between Barbados and Carolina?

12. .... LO 2, 4, 5 ... FP 2, 8–14, 16–18 .... pp. 71, 75–92, 94–96; document; video segments 2–4, 6
    - Consider the economic motives for each region. What adaptations were made economically?
    - What social system developed? How was land parceled out?
    - Why did a servant labor system change to a slave labor system?
    - How would you characterize these colonies by the late seventeenth century? What were the long-term economic, social, and political patterns established?

ENRICHMENT IDEAS

These activities are not required unless your instructor assigns them. They are offered as suggestions to help you learn more about the material presented in this lesson.

1. Research the status of the tobacco industry today. How important is tobacco to the economy? What is the current product liability and consumer protection situation in the tobacco industry? Write a thoughtful essay in which you discuss your findings and take a stand on the consumer protection issue.

2. Research the background of your political representative at the state or national level of government. What socioeconomic class does he/she come from? Where does her/his funding come from? Who does he/she really represent? Address these questions in a well-organized essay, and be sure to support your opinion when addressing the last question.

3. Maps and narratives related to this lesson mention the Fall Line. After researching the Fall Line, write a thoughtful essay in which you describe what the Fall Line is and what it meant for patterns of settlement and economic and political development in colonial America.

SUGGESTED READINGS/RESOURCES

See the "Bibliography" on pages 98–99 of the textbook if you wish to examine other books and resources related to the material presented in this lesson.

DOCUMENTS

Nathaniel Bacon, recently arrived from England, led western Virginia settlers in a bitter fight against the governor of Virginia, William Berkeley. The fight began over Indian policy, but continued with demands for colonial reforms. The resulting conflict brought significant changes to the colony.

As you read this document, focus on answering the following questions:

1. What "troubles" does Bacon identify? Who does he blame for them?
2. How did Bacon defend himself against charges of treason?

"Manifesto Concerning the Troubles in Virginia" (1676) by Nathaniel Bacon

If virtue be a sin, if piety be guilt, all the principles of morality, goodness and justice be perverted, we must confess that those who are now called rebels may be in danger of those high imputations. Those loud and several bulls would affright innocents and render the defence of our brethren and the inquiry into our sad and heavy oppressions, treason. But if there be, as sure there is, a just God to appeal to; if religion and justice be a sanctuary here; if to plead the cause of the oppressed; if sincerely to aim at his Majesty's honour and the public good without any reservation or by interest; if to stand in the gap after so much blood of our dear brethren bought and sold; if after the loss of a great part of his Majesty's colony deserted and dispeopled, freely with our lives and estates to endeavour to save the remainders be treason; God Almighty judge and let guilty die. But since we cannot in our hearts find one single spot of rebellion or treason, or that we have in any manner aimed at the subverting of the settled government or attempting of the person of any either magistrate or private man, notwithstanding the several reproaches and threats of some who for sinister ends were disaffected to us and censured our innocent and honest designs, and since all people in all places where we have yet been can attest our civil, quiet, peaceable behaviour far different from that of rebellion and tumultuous persons, let truth be told and all the world know the real foundations of pretended guilt. We appeal to the country itself what and of what nature their oppressions have been, or by what cabal and mystery the designs of many of those whom we call great men have been transacted and carried on; but let us trace these men in authority and favour to whose hands the dispensation of the country's wealth has been committed. Let us observe the sudden rise of their estates composed with the quality in which they first entered this country, or the reputation they have held here amongst wise and discerning men. And let us see whether their extractions and education have not been vile, and by what pretence of learning and virtue they could so soon [come] into employments of so great trust and consequence. Let us consider their sudden advancement and let us also consider whether any public work for our safety and defence or for the advancement and propagation of trade, liberal arts, or sciences is here extant in any way adequate to our vast charge. Now let us compare these things together and see what sponges have sucked up the public treasure, and whether it has not been privately contrived away by unworthy favourites and juggling parasites whose tottering fortunes have been repaired and supported at the public charge. Now if it be so, judge what greater guilt can be than to offer to pry into these and to unriddle the mysterious wiles of a powerful cabal; let all people judge what can be of more dangerous import than to suspect the so long safe proceedings of some of our grandees, and whether people may with safety open their eyes in so nice a concern.

Another main article of our guilt is our open and manifest aversion of all, not only the foreign but the protected and darling Indians. This, we are informed, is rebellion of a deep dye for that both the governor and council are by Colonel Cole's assertion bound to defend the queen and the Appamatocks with their blood. Now, whereas we do declare and can prove that they have been for these many years enemies to the king and country, robbers and thieves and invaders of his Majesty's right and our interest and estates, but yet have by persons in authority been defended and protected even against his Majesty's loyal subjects, and that in so high a nature that even the complaints and oaths of his Majesty's most loyal subjects in a lawful manner proffered by them against those barbarous outlaws, have been by the right honourable governor rejected and the delinquents from his presence dismissed, not only with pardon and indemnity, but with all encouragement and favour; their firearms so destructful to us and by our laws prohibited, commanded to be restored them, and open declaration before witness made that they must have ammunition, although directly contrary to our law. Now what greater guilt can be than to oppose and endeavour the destruction of these honest, quiet neighbors of ours?

The Declaration of the People

For having upon specious pretences of public works, raised unjust taxes upon the commonalty for the advancement of private favourites and other sinister ends, but no visible effects in any measure adequate.

For not having during the long time of his government in any measure advanced his hopeful colony, either by fortification, towns or trade.

For having abused and rendered contemptible the majesty of justice, of advancing to places of judicature scandalous and ignorant favourites.

For having wronged his Majesty's prerogative and interest by assuming the monopoly of the beaver trade.

By having in that unjust gain bartered and sold his Majesty's country and the lives of his loyal subjects to the barbarous heathen.

For having protected, favoured and emboldened the Indians against his Majesty's most loyal subjects, never contriving, requiring, or appointing any due or proper means of satisfaction for their many invasions, murders, and robberies committed upon us.

For having, when the army of the English was just upon the track of the Indians, which now in all places burn, spoil, and murder, and when we might with ease have destroyed them who then were in open hostility, for having expressly countermanded and sent back our army by passing his word for the peaceable demeanour of the said Indians, who immediately prosecuted their evil intentions, committing horrid murders and robberies in all places, being protected by the said engagement and word passed of him, the said Sir William Berkeley, having ruined and made desolate a great part of his Majesty's country, have now drawn themselves into such obscure and remote places and are by their successes so emboldened and confirmed, and by their confederacy so strengthened that the cries of blood are in all places, and the terror and consternation of the people so great, that they are now become not only a difficult, but a very formidable enemy who might with ease have been destroyed, etc. When upon the loud outcries of blood, the Assembly had with all care raised and framed an army for the prevention of future mischiefs and safeguard of his Majesty's colony.

For having with only the privacy of some few favourites, without acquainting the people, only by the alteration of a figure, forged a commission by we know not what hand, not only without but against the consent of the people, for raising and effecting of civil wars and distractions, which being happily and without bloodshed prevented.

For having the second time attempted the same thereby calling down our forces from the defence of the frontiers, and most weak exposed places, for the prevention of civil mischief and ruin amongst ourselves, whilst the barbarous enemy in all places did invade, murder, and spoil us, his Majesty's most faithful subjects.

Of these, the aforesaid articles, we accuse Sir William Berkeley, as guilty of each and every one of the same, and as one who has traitorously attempted, violated and injured his Majesty's interest here, by the loss of a great part of his colony, and many of his faithful and loyal subjects by him betrayed, and in a barbarous and shameful manner exposed to the incursions and murders of the heathen.

And we further declare these, the ensuing persons in this list, to have been his wicked, and pernicious counsellors, aiders and assisters against the commonalty in these our cruel commotions:

Sir Henry Chicherly, Knt.
Col. Charles Wormley
Phil. Dalowell
Robert Beverly
Robert Lee
Thos. Ballard
William Cole
Richard Whitacre
Nicholas Spencer
Mathew Kemp

Jos. Bridger
Wm. Clabourne
Thos. Hawkins, Jr.
William Sherwood
Jos. Page, Clerk
Jo. Cliffe, Clerk
Hubberd Farrell
John West
Thos. Reade

And we do further demand, that the said Sir William Berkeley, with all the persons in this list, be forthwith delivered up, or surrender themselves, within four days after the notice hereof, or otherwise we declare as followeth: that in whatsoever house, place, or ship any of the said persons shall reside, be hid, or protected, we do declare that the owners, masters, or inhabitants of the said places, to be confederates and traitors to the people, and the estates of them, as also of all the aforesaid persons, to be confiscated. This we, the commons of Virginia, do declare desiring a prime union amongst ourselves, that we may jointly, and with one accord defend ourselves against the common enemy. And let not the faults of the guilty be the reproach of the innocent, or the faults or crimes of the oppressors divide and separate us, who have suffered by their oppressions.

These are therefore in his Majesty's name, to command you forthwith to seize the persons above mentioned as traitors to the king and country, and them to bring to Middle Plantation, and there to secure them, till further order, and in case of opposition, if you want any other assistance, you are forthwith to demand it in the name of the people of all the counties of Virginia.

[signed]   NATH BACON, Gen'l.
                By the Consent of the People.

Warren Billings, ed., *The Old Dominion in the Seventeenth Century: A Documentary History of Virginia, 1601–1689* (Chapel Hill: University of North Carolina Press, 1975) pp. 277–279.

Lesson 4

Settling in New England

OVERVIEW

Settlement along the Chesapeake and further south set in motion a process of development which ultimately affected all Americans. Likewise, British settlements to the north, although quite different, had profound and lasting effects on the shaping of America.

In New England, religious zealots took the initiative in trying to establish what they envisioned would be "a city upon a hill." From Plymouth to Boston and beyond, Pilgrims and Puritans sought to create communities that conformed to their religious views. As with others, their visions had to be tempered by the realities of life. Dissenters appeared almost immediately, and, although the early malcontents might be banished to the hinterlands, rigid religious authority seemed to erode after the first generation of settlement. Indians in the region, who were initially cooperative, undertook a devastating war against the expanding Puritan communities in the mid-1670s. Finally, the excessive actions taken in Salem, Massachusetts, in 1692 to the perceived threat of witchcraft ultimately weakened Puritan control even more. Still, the Puritans' vision of America as a special place of opportunity and their emphasis on community would eventually reach far beyond their New England roots.

LESSON ASSIGNMENTS

Text: Roark, et al., *The American Promise*, Chapter 3, "Religion and Revolt in the Spanish Borderland," pp. 92–93; Chapter 4, "The Northern Colonies in the Seventeenth Century," pp. 103–135

Video: "Settling in New England" from the series *Shaping America*

Documents:
            "King Philip Considers Christianity," pp. 110–111 in the textbook

LEARNING OBJECTIVES

This lesson explains the significance of British settlement in the New England area in the seventeenth century. Upon completing this lesson, you should be able to:

1. Explain the background, founding, and early development of the Plymouth and Massachusetts Bay colonies.

2. Explain the conditions in Puritan Massachusetts that spawned dissenters such as Roger Williams and Anne Hutchinson and how the Puritan communities dealt with dissent.

3. Analyze the relations between the Puritan communities and American Indians and how that relationship compares to the relationships between Indians and other European colonizers at that time.

4. Explain what happened during the Salem witchcraft episode in 1692.

5. Assess the lasting effects of Puritanism on American society.

6. Analyze the economic, social, political, and religious development of the New England colonies in the seventeenth century and how that helped shape America.

LESSON FOCUS POINTS

The following questions are designed to help you get the most benefit from the resources selected for this lesson. For reference purposes, the titles of the video segments are:
(1) Introduction, (2) "Pilgrims," (3) "The Puritan Dilemma," (4) "Encountering the Wilderness," (5) Short-take: "The Pueblo Revolt," (6) "Witch Hunt," and (7) Summary Analysis: "The Puritan Influence."

1. Who were the Pilgrims and the Puritans? Where did they come from? Why did they end up in the area that became Massachusetts? (textbook, pp. 103–107; video segment 2)

2. How and why did the Indians in the region initially cooperate with the Pilgrims? (textbook, p. 107; video segments 1, 2)

3. Why did the Pilgrim story at Plymouth become so mythological in America? (video segment 2)

4. What was unique about the charter authorizing the founding of Massachusetts Bay Colony? How did that charter affect the operations of that colony? (textbook, pp. 108–109, 112)

5. What was John Winthrop's vision for Massachusetts Bay Colony? How did that vision and Puritan beliefs regarding family, church, and community shape seventeenth century New England? (textbook, pp. 108–109, 112; video segment 3)

6. Examine Map 4.1 on page 109 of the text. Identify the New England colonies founded in the seventeenth century. What major towns were established? Why were towns so important in New England? (textbook, pp. 109, 115–116)

7. Generally, how were the New England colonies governed? How was land distributed? (textbook, pp. 114–116)

8. How did the Puritans deal with dissent? Why were Roger Williams and Anne Hutchinson considered threats to the community? (textbook, pp. 103–104, 116–120; video segment 3)

9. How did Puritans react to the American wilderness? What fundamental question was brought forward when Puritan settlers were taken captive by Indians? (video segment 4)

10. Read the excerpt from *Indian Dialogues* in the text. How does this passage reveal cultural differences between the people living in New England in the seventeenth century? (textbook, pp. 110–111)

11. Why did King Philip's war take place in the 1670s? What were the consequences of this war? (textbook, pp. 127–129; video segment 4)

12. How is the Pueblo Revolt near Santa Fe similar to King Philip's war? (textbook, pp. 92–93; video segment 5)

13. What explains the witch-hunt in Salem and the surrounding communities in 1692? What were the consequences? (textbook, pp. 122–123; video segment 6)

14. Generally, what changes came about in the economy, politics, and society of the New England communities from the 1640s to 1700? (textbook, pp. 117–120, 126–132)

15. To what extent is the Puritan influence still found in the United States? (video segment 7)

16. What characterized the colony of "New France" in North America? How did this colony affect American Indians and British colonists in the northern borderlands? (textbook, pp. 130–131)

HISTORICAL EXPERTS INTERVIEWED

James Baker, Web Master and Senior Historian, Plimoth Plantation, Plymouth, MA
Jon Butler, Coe Professor of History, Yale University, New Haven, CT
Colin Calloway, Professor of History, Dartmouth College, Hanover, NH
John Demos, Samuel Knight Professor of History, Yale University, New Haven, CT
Curtis Thomas, Professor of History, Richland College, Dallas, TX

PRACTICE TEST

The following items will help you evaluate your understanding of this lesson. Use the Answer Key at the end of the lesson to check your answers or to locate material related to each question.

Multiple choice: Choose the BEST answer.

1. Sixteenth-century English Puritanism _____.
   A. was a well-organized, centrally administered religious reform movement
   B. took few ideas from Martin Luther and John Calvin
   C. was a set of broadly interpreted ideas and religious principles held by those seeking to purify the Church of England
   D. interpreted Protestantism as a call for increased influence of the clergy in the lives of average parishioners

2. In the video, historian Jim Baker observes that American Indians in the area of Plymouth colony signed a treaty of friendship with the Pilgrims because they _____.
   A. realized the military superiority of the Pilgrims
   B. sought allies against neighboring Indian tribes
   C. wanted to acquire agricultural products from the Pilgrims
   D. all of the above

3. Anne Hutchinson's emphasis on the "covenant of grace" stirred religious controversy in early Massachusetts because _____.
   A. she said only her followers would achieve salvation
   B. it was feared she was disrupting the good order in the colony
   C. she encouraged other women to take an active part in religious governance
   D. she said the Puritan leaders should be excommunicated

4. Metacomet (King Philip) led a war against New England settlers in the 1670s because _____.
   A. trade was declining between the settlers and Indians
   B. Puritan missionaries had become too aggressive
   C. settlers continued to encroach upon Indian lands
   D. he needed to divert attention away from internal problems

5. By the 1680s New England's population had grown large and somewhat religiously splintered to the point that _____.
   A. most people who had formerly considered themselves Puritans were now called Calvinists
   B. some towns did not have enough churches to accommodate all congregants
   C. heated debates between factions were common
   D. Puritan leaders repealed all statutes making church attendance compulsory

6. In seventeenth-century New England, accusing someone of witchcraft often became a useful way to _____.
   A. perform the valuable public service of ridding the community of pesky witches
   B. cast oneself as a victim and blame one's misfortune on evil forces beyond the control of mere mortals
   C. demonstrate important leadership and administrative abilities
   D. prosper economically, as convicted witches forfeited all their worldly possessions to those identifying them as devilish menaces to New England

7. In the video, Professor Curtis Thomas observes that the Puritan influence on Americans can still be seen in their tendency to assume _____.
   A. religion controls their lives
   B. people are basically evil
   C. economic forces determine how communities organize
   D. government will provide for them

8. The seventeenth-century New England economy mainly consisted of _____.
    A. diversified agriculture producing staples for the world market
    B. subsistence farming mixed with fishing and timber harvesting for markets in Europe and the West Indies
    C. reexporting commodities shipped from England
    D. little more than subsistence farming with some produce for the local market

Short Answer: Your answers should be one or two paragraphs long and specifically address the points indicated.

9. How and why were the northern colonies different from the southern colonies in the seventeenth century?

Essay Question: Your answer should be several paragraphs long and express a clear understanding of the points indicated.

10. Describe the Puritan "city on a hill" envisioned by John Winthrop. Analyze the ways in which the Puritans attempted to realize this vision in the New England colonies. What tensions and conflicts did this bring about? To what extent did Puritan influences shape America? How is this reflected today?

ANSWER KEY

	Answer	Learning Objectives	Focus Points	References
1.	C	LO 1	FP 1	pp. 103–107; video segment 2
2.	B	LO 1	FP 2	pp. 107; video segment 2
3.	B	LO 2	FP 8	pp. 103–104, 116–120; video segment 3
4.	C	LO 3	FP 11	pp. 127–129; video segment 4
5.	C	LO 4	FP 13	pp. 122–123; video segment 6
6.	B	LO 4	FP 13	pp. 122–123; video segment 6
7.	B	LO 5	FP 15	video segment 7
8.	B	LO 6	FP 14	pp. 117–120, 126–132
9.		LO 6	FP 4, 6, 7, 14	pp. 107–109, 112–116

- Consider the geography of each region and its effects on people and the economy.
- What role did religion and community play in each area?

10.　　..........LO 1, 5, 6.....FP 4–11, 13–15 ....pp. 108–120, 117–129; video segments 3, 4, 6, 7
- What ideals were expressed by Winthrop?
- What role did community play in upholding the vision?
- How were settlements organized and governed?
- Why did dissent occur and how did they deal with it?
- What explains the Salem witchcraft episode?
- How do we see Puritan influences in our society?

ENRICHMENT IDEAS

These activities are not required unless your instructor assigns them. They are offered as suggestions to help you learn more about the material presented in this lesson.

1. The "Protestant work ethic" is often associated with the New England colonies. In a thoughtful essay, examine what this work ethic means, how it is passed on in America, and to what extent it exists in America today. Also, consider how and why different work ethics may have developed in different cultures and generations.

2. Examine maps illustrating the planned communities of New England. In an essay with specific examples, describe how and why the towns were laid out like they were. To what extent do the current communities reflect the original plan?

3. Assume the role of an Anglo captive, a Wampanoag Indian, or a praying Indian during King Philip's war. Describe your situation, what choices you have, and what course of action you plan to take. What is your objective and how will you accomplish it?

4. Should Anne Hutchinson have been banned from Massachusetts? In a well-reasoned essay, defend your position.

5. In a thoughtful essay, compare and contrast the Salem witch-hunt to the McCarthy hearings in the 1950s. What are the lessons of each episode? Are there similar attempts to impose conformity on our communities today? Why or why not?

6. Read *The Crucible* or *The Scarlet Letter* and then write and submit a critical analysis of the work to your instructor.

SUGGESTED READINGS/RESOURCES

See the "Bibliography" on pages 132–133 of the textbook if you wish to examine other books and resources related to the material presented in this lesson.

Lesson 5

Diversifying British America

OVERVIEW

As you have learned, British settlers in the British mainland colonies in the Chesapeake and Carolina areas tried to transplant much of what was British society into a new environment. In New England, most colonists were British in their cultural backgrounds, even though many of them were religious dissenters.

The ethnic diversity in British America, however, was more obvious in the middle colonies: New York, New Jersey, Pennsylvania, and Delaware. When the British took over the Dutch outpost of New Amsterdam in 1664, they inherited a cosmopolitan settlement whose attachment to commerce was already evident. During the next century, New York's growth accentuated the city's commercial and ethnic diversity. In the process, New Yorkers faced the challenge of maintaining an ethnic identity while assimilating into a developing "American" culture.

New Jersey's location between New York and Pennsylvania made it a place that shared in the rich cultural mix becoming evident in the region. The presence of ethnic diversity points to the increasing diversity of religion in colonial America. As people of different traditions lived and worked together in relatively close proximity, their toleration of religious differences emerged.

In keeping with the desire of founder William Penn, toleration was a hallmark of Pennsylvania's colonial development. As Philadelphia grew, so did opportunities for a variety of residents, including the well-known Benjamin Franklin as well as thousands of merchants and artisans. Meanwhile, the Pennsylvania frontier, like those in other colonies, experienced the contact of rapidly expanding non-Indian farmers with the indigenous peoples. It is on the Pennsylvania frontier that the remarkable work of go-betweens like the German immigrant Conrad Weiser and his Indian friend Shikellamy is particularly notable. By the time of their deaths in the mid-eighteenth century, an American identity was emerging from the diversity common in colonial America.

LESSON ASSIGNMENTS

Text: Roark, et al., *The American Promise,* Chapter 4, "The Northern Colonies in the Seventeenth Century," pp. 120–132 and Chapter 5, "Colonial America in the Eighteenth Century," pp. 137–151, pp. 160–161

Video: "Diversifying British America" from the series *Shaping America*

Documents:
          "Father Abraham's Speech" found at the end of this lesson

LEARNING OBJECTIVES

This lesson explains how and why diversity became a characteristic of the middle colonies and how that diversity helped shaped America. Upon completing this lesson, you should be able to:

1. Describe the characteristics of the middle colonies and how they differed from the southern and New England colonies.

2. Explain how and why the middle colonies became so ethnically, religiously, and economically diverse.

3. Evaluate the economic and political relationships between the colonies and England at the end of the seventeenth century.

4. Explain how the British colonies in America differed from the Spanish colonies in New Spain at the end of the seventeenth century.

5. Analyze the changes taking place in the middle colonies and New England colonies in the first half of the eighteenth century.

6. Explain why the middle colonies became "the best poor [white] man's country."

7. Analyze both the short- and long-term effects of the ethnic and religious diversity found in colonial American society.

LESSON FOCUS POINTS

The following questions are designed to help you get the most benefit from the sources selected for this lesson. For reference purposes, the titles for the video segments are: (1) Introduction, (2) "New Amsterdam," (3) "New York," (4) "New Jersey," (5) "Pennsylvania," and (6) Summary Analysis: "I Am Not as You Are…"

1. Examine Map 4.2 on page 120 of the textbook. Which colonies are identified as "middle"? How would the geographical features of these colonies affect their development? (textbook, p. 120)

2. Why did the Dutch found a colony at New Amsterdam? (textbook, pp. 120–121; video segment 2)

3. How did Peter Stuyvesant affect the development of New Amsterdam? Why did the Dutch surrender to the British in 1664? (textbook, pp. 121, 124; video segment 2)

4. Why did New Amsterdam/New York attract a diverse group of people? (textbook, pp. 121, 124; video segments 2 and 3)

5. What was the importance of the trial of John Peter Zenger? (textbook, p. 161; video segment 3)

6. How did New Yorkers maintain a sense of ethnic identity? How and why were they assimilating with people of other groups? (video segment 3)

7. How and why did religion in the middle colonies become markedly different from religion in Europe and the other colonies? (textbook, pp. 124–125; video segment 4)

8. How did William Penn and the Quakers contribute to the diversity and toleration in Pennsylvania in the late seventeenth century? (textbook, pp. 124–125)

9. Examine Map 4.3 in the textbook. Answer the questions below the map. (textbook, p. 126)

10. How and why did the British government tighten its regulation of colonial trade and control over colonial governments in the late seventeenth century? What effects did this have in the colonies? (textbook, pp. 126–129, 132)

11. By 1700, how and why were the British colonies in North America different from those established by Spain? (textbook, p. 132)

12. How do the lives of Benjamin Franklin and Mary Smith illustrate the opportunities available in Philadelphia in the mid-eighteenth century? (textbook, pp. 150–151; video segment 5)

13. Why did the population grow so rapidly in the eighteenth century colonies? Why did the majority of free colonists, especially those in the middle colonies, have a better standard of living than the majority of people elsewhere in the Atlantic world? (textbook, pp. 138–140)

14. Examine Map 5.1 on page 140 of the textbook. What does that map tell you about the ethnic diversity in colonial America in the eighteenth century? (textbook, p. 140)

15. Why did Yankee traders replace Puritan settlers as the dominant group in the New England colonies by the mid-eighteenth century? (textbook, pp. 140–142)

16. Examine Map 5.2 in the textbook. Answer the questions below the map. (textbook, p. 143)

17. Who were the "Pennsylvania Dutch"? Who were the Scots-Irish? How did they shape the social and economic development of the middle colonies? (textbook, pp. 142–143, 146–147)

18. Why did Pennsylvania become the "best poor [white] man's country"? (textbook, pp. 147–151)

19. What advice did "Father Abraham" give in *Poor Richard's Almanac*? (document)

20. Who was Conrad Weiser? Who was Shikellamy? Why were their roles on the frontier important in early and mid-eighteenth century? (video segment 5)

21. Why was there a growing sense of identity among Indians and among European colonists by the end of the colonial period? (video segment 6)

22. What are the long-term consequences of the diversity found in colonial America? (video segment 6)

HISTORICAL EXPERTS INTERVIEWED

Jon Butler, Coe Professor of History, Yale University, New Haven, CT
Michael P. Johnson, Professor of History, Johns Hopkins University, Baltimore, MD
James Merrell, Professor of History, Vassar College, Poughkeepsie, NY
Mike Wallace, Co-author of *Gotham*, John Jay College, New York City, NY

PRACTICE TEST

The following items will help you evaluate your understanding of this lesson. Use the Answer Key at the end of the lesson to check your answers or to locate material related to each question.

Multiple choice: Choose the BEST answer.

1. The colony of New Netherland was marked by a _____.
   A. small, remarkably diverse population
   B. small, remarkably homogeneous population
   C. large population consisting almost exclusively of people from France and Spain
   D. large, remarkably diverse population

2. The trial of journalist John Peter Zenger was significant because the verdict _____.
   A. found the defendant guilty
   B. became a foundation stone for freedom of the press
   C. established freedom of religion for Jews in America
   D. set a precedent for requiring a jury of peers

3. The Quaker maxim, "In souls there is no sex," helps explain _____.
   A. the degree to which Quakers allowed women to assume positions of religious leadership in the seventeenth century
   B. the Quaker belief that men and women would be saved in equal numbers
   C. the fact that Quakers generally frowned upon the customary gender structure of their own day and time
   D. why Quaker women held many important political offices in seventeenth-century Pennsylvania

4. By the end of the seventeenth century, colonial commerce was characterized by _____.
   A. increasing independence from its former ties with the British Empire
   B. stagnation because the colonies were forbidden by England from importing anything but English-made goods
   C. strong ties to England due to royal supervision of merchants, shippers, imports, and exports, and the protection of the British navy
   D. a status of equality with England as the colonies and the mother country cooperated and made joint decisions on trade matters

5. The most important change in eighteenth century colonial America was _____.
   A. a phenomenal population growth
   B. an increase in the British population due to famine in England
   C. more land development
   D. a decrease in the Indian population

6. An early Pennsylvania policy that encouraged settlement was _____.
   A. giving away land to adult white males
   B. paying settlers to farm Indian lands
   C. a very low property tax
   D. negotiating with Indian tribes to purchase land, which reduced frontier clashes

7. One result of the multiplicity of religions in colonial America was the _____.
   A. persecution of the Jews
   B. tightening of the affiliation with colonial governments
   C. marked improvement in relations with American Indians
   D. growing sense of toleration for different faiths

Short Answer: Your answers should be one or two paragraphs long and specifically address the points indicated.

8. Explain how and why New York became a diverse community in the colonial period. How was this diversity reflected? How was ethnic identity maintained?

9. Why did Pennsylvania become "the best poor [white] man's country" in colonial America?

10. Describe the role of go-betweens on the frontier. How did they help maintain some degree of stability?

11. By 1700, how and why were the British colonies in North America different from those established by Spain?

Essay Question: Your answer should be several paragraphs long and express a clear understanding of the points indicated.

12. How and why did the middle colonies become more diverse than the southern and New England colonies? What are the short- and long-term economic, social, and political consequences of this diversity?

ANSWER KEY

	Answer	Learning Objectives	Focus Points	References
1.	A	LO 2	FP 4	p. 121, 124; video segments 2, 3
2.	B	LO 5	FP 5	video segment 3
3.	A	LO 2	FP 8	pp. 124–125
4.	C	LO 3	FP 10	pp. 126–129; 132
5.	A	LO 5	FP 13	pp. 138–140
6.	D	LO 6	FP 18	pp. 147–151
7.	D	LO 7	FP 8, 22	pp. 124–125; video segment 6

8. ....LO 2, 5, 7.........FP 4, 6, 7.........pp. 121, 124–125; video segments 2, 3, 4
   - What effect did the Dutch origins of the colony have?
   - Why did commerce attract diverse peoples? What ethnic groups and religions were reflected?
   - What roles did religion and neighborhood settlement play in identity?

9. ....LO 1, 2, 6.........FP 18.........pp. 147–151
   - What geographic advantages did Pennsylvania have?
   - How did the attitude of its founders encourage opportunity? What types of people settled there?
   - How did it blend agriculture with commerce?

10. ....LO 5, 7.........FP 20.........video segment 5
   - What types of problems did these people deal with?
   - What skills did they have that helped resolve conflicts?
   - How were they able to establish respect and understanding?

11. ....LO 4.........FP 11.........p. 132

12. What role did geography play?
   - How were the people different? How were their relations with Indian peoples different?
   - How was the economy different? Religion? Politics?

13. ....LO 1, 2, 6, 7..FP 4, 6–8, 12–14, 17–18, 20.........pp. 121, 124–125, 138–140, pp. 142–143, 146–151; video segments 2, 3, 4, 5
   - What role did geography play?
   - Who founded these colonies? How tolerant were the founders and early settlers?
   - What types of people settled there? What religions and talents did they bring?
   - How did these colonies blend agriculture and commerce?
   - How did diversity contribute toward further toleration and freedom?
   - How did diversity help shape an American identity?

ENRICHMENT IDEAS

These activities are not required unless your instructor assigns them. They are offered as suggestions to help you learn more about the material presented in this lesson.

1. Imagine yourself to be an immigrant from Europe to the British mainland colonies in 1730. Where would you want to live? Explain your choice in a well-developed essay.

2. Immigration is a consistent theme in American history. Based on what you have learned in this lesson, compose an essay in which you examine the issues of ethnic identity and assimilation. Do we see a melting pot beginning in colonial America? Do we see a "salad bowl," in which the cultural identities are distinct? To what extent did the immigrant groups have to conform to Anglo dominance?

3. If the ethnic group and/or religious community with which you identify was present in colonial America, find out where they were located and how they were faring at that time. Submit your findings in a well-developed essay.

4. The middle colonies were referred to as "the best poor [white] man's country." Research how different societies dealt with their poor populations during the colonial period. Then write an essay in which you describe your findings.

5. Diversity initiated in the colonial period can still be found in New York and in the Pennsylvania Dutch country. After doing research on this topic, submit an essay describing how these areas still reflect their colonial roots.

6. *Poor Richard's Almanac* became a popular guide to many Americans. Why did that happen? After reviewing a copy of it and considering the function of almanacs in general, write an essay in which you explain the popularity and purpose of almanacs. Which ones are currently popular? Why?

SUGGESTED READINGS/RESOURCES

See the "Bibliography" on pages 132–133, and 170–171 of the textbook if you wish to examine other books and resources related to the material presented in this lesson.

DOCUMENTS

Benjamin Franklin, the son of a candle maker in Boston, moved to Philadelphia and became a successful printer and colonial leader. In his *Poor Richard's Almanac*, he not only informed Americans but also tried to school them in basic virtues. One such attempt was "Father Abraham's Speech."

As you read this document, focus on answering the following questions:

1. What temptations, most likely, lead one astray according to Father Abraham?
2. How did the people respond to Father Abraham's admonitions?

"Father Abraham's Speech from *Poor Richard's Almanac*, 1757" by Benjamin Franklin

Courteous Reader,

I have heard that nothing gives an Author so great Pleasure, as to find his Works respectfully quoted by other learned Authors. This Pleasure I have seldom enjoyed. . . . I concluded at length, that the People were the best judges of my Merit; for they buy my Works; and besides, in my Rambles, where I am not personally known, I have frequently heard one or other of my Adages repeated, with, as Poor Richard says, at the End on't; this gave me some Satisfaction, as it showed not only that my Instructions were regarded, but discovered likewise some Respect for my Authority; and I own, that to encourage the Practice of remembering and repeating those wise Sentences, I have sometimes quoted myself with great Gravity.

Judge then how much I must have been gratified by an Incident I am going to relate to you. I stopt my Horse lately where a great Number of People were collected at a Vendue of Merchant Goods. The Hour of Sale not being come, they were conversing on the Badness of the Times, and one of the Company call'd to a plain clean old Man, with white Locks, Pray, Father Abraham, what think you of the Times? Won't these heavy Taxes quite ruin the Country? How shall we be ever able to pay them? What would you advise us to? — Father Abraham stood up, and reply'd, If you'd have my Advice, I'll give it you in short, for a Word to the Wise is enough, and many Words won't fill a Bushel, as Poor Richard says. They join'd in desiring him to speak his Mind, and gathering round him, he proceeded as follows;

"Friends," says he, "and Neighbours, the Taxes are indeed very heavy, and if those laid on by the Government were the only Ones we had to pay, we might more easily discharge them; but we have many others, and much more grievous to some of us. We are taxed twice as much by our Idleness, three times as much by our Pride, and four times as much by our Folly, and from these Taxes the Commissioners cannot ease or deliver us by allowing an Abatement. However let us hearken to good Advice, and something may be done for us; God helps them that help themselves, as Poor Richard says.

It would be thought a hard Government that should tax its People one tenth Part of their Time, to be employed in its Service. But Idleness taxes many of us much more, if we reckon all that is spent in absolute Sloth, or doing of nothing, with that which is spent in idle Employments or Amusements, that amount to nothing. Sloth, by bringing on Diseases, absolutely shortens Life. Sloth, like Rust, consumes faster than Labour wears, while the used Key is always bright, as Poor Richard says. — How much more than is necessary do we spend in Sleep! forgetting that The sleeping Fox catches no Poultry, and that there will be sleeping enough in the Grave, as Poor Richard says. If Time be of all Things the most precious, wasting Time must be, as Poor Richard says, the greatest Prodigality, since, as he elsewhere tells us, Lost Time is never found again. Let us then up and be doing, and doing to the Purpose; so by Diligence shall we do more with less Perplexity. Sloth makes all Things difficult, but Industry all easy, as Poor Richard says; and He that riseth late, must trot all Day, and shall scarce overtake his Business at Night. While Laziness travels so slowly, that Poverty soon overtakes him, as we read in Poor Richard, who adds, Drive thy Business, let not that drive thee; and Early to Bed, and early to rise, makes a Man healthy, wealthy and wise.

So what signifies wishing and hoping for better Times. We may make these Times better if we bestir ourselves. Industry need not wish, as Poor Richard says, and He that lives upon Hope will die fasting. There are no Gains, without Pains. . . . And, as Poor Richard likewise observes, He that hath a Trade hath an Estate, and He that hath a Calling hath an Office of Profit and Honour; but then the Trade must be worked at, and the Calling well followed, or neither the Estate, nor the Office, will enable us to pay our Taxes. —If we are industrious we shall never starve; for, as Poor Richard says, At the working Man's House Hunger looks in, but dares not enter. Nor will the Bailiff or the Constable enter, for Industry pays Debts, while Despair encreaseth them, says Poor Richard. —What though you have found no Treasure, nor has any rich Relation left you a Legacy, Diligence is the Mother of Good-luck, as Poor Richard says, and God gives all Things to Industry. Then plough deep, while Sluggards sleep, and you shall have Corn to sell and to keep, says Poor Dick. Work while it is called To-day, for you know not how much you may be hindered To-morrow which makes Poor Richard say, One Today is worth two Tomorrows; and farther, Have you somewhat to do To-morrow, do it To-day. If you were a Servant, would you not be ashamed that a good Master should catch you idle? Are you then your own Master, be ashamed to catch yourself idle, as Poor Dick says.

Methinks I hear some of you say, Must a Man afford himself no Leisure? I will tell thee, my Friend, what Poor Richard says, Employ thy Time well if thou meanest to gain Leisure; and, since thou art not sure of a Minute, throw not away an Hour. Leisure is Time for doing something useful; this Leisure the diligent Man will obtain, but the lazy Man never. . . . Do you imagine that Sloth will afford you more Comfort than Labour? No, for as Poor Richard says, Trouble springs from Idleness, and grievous Toil from needless Ease. . . . Whereas Industry gives Comfort, and Plenty, and Respect: . . . The diligent Spinner has a large Shift and now [that] I have a Sheep and a Cow, every Body bids me Good morrow.

But with our Industry, we must likewise be steady, settled and careful, and oversee our own Affairs with our own Eyes, and not trust too much to others; for, as Poor Richard says,

I never saw an oft removed Tree,
Nor yet an oft removed Family,
That throve so well as those that settled be.

And again, Three Removes is as bad as a Fire; and again, Keep thy Shop, and thy Shop will keep thee; and again, If you would have your Business done, go; If not, send. . . . And again, The Eye of a Master will do more Work than both his Hands; and again, Want of Care does us more Damage than Want of Knowledge; and again, Not to oversee Workmen, is to leave them your Purse open. Trusting too much to others Care is the Ruin of many; for, as the Almanack says, In the Affairs of this World, men are saved, not by Faith, but by the Want of it. . . . And farther, If you would have a faithful Servant, and one that you like, serve yourself.

So much for Industry, my Friends, and Attention to one's own Business; but to these we must add Frugality, if we would make our Industry more certainly successful. A Man may, if he knows not how to save as he gets, keep his Nose all his Life to the Grindstone, and die not worth a Groat at last. A fat Kitchen makes a lean Will, as Poor Richard says; and,

Many Estates are spent in the Getting,
Since Women for Tea forsook Spinning and Knitting,
And Men for Punch forsook Hewing and Splitting.

If you would be wealthy, says he, in another Almanack, think of Saving as well as of Getting: The Indies have not made Spain rich, because her Outgoes are greater than her Incomes. Away then with your expensive Follies, and you will not have so much Cause to complain of hard Times, heavy Taxes, and chargeable Families. . . . And farther, What maintains one Vice, would bring up two Children. You may think perhaps, That a little Tea, or a little Punch now and then, Diet a little more costly, Clothes a little finer, and a little Entertainment now and then, can be no great Matter; but remember what Poor Richard says, Many a Little makes a Nickle; and farther, Beware of little Expences; a small Leak will sink a great Ship; and again, Fools make Feasts, and wise Men eat them.

Here you are all got together at this Vendue of Fineries and Knicknacks. You call them Goods, but if you do not take Care, they will prove Evils to some of you. You expect they will be sold cheap, and perhaps they may for less than they cost; but if you have no Occasion for them, they must be dear to you. Remember what Poor Richard says, Buy what thou hast no Need of, and ere long thou shalt sell thy Necessaries. . . . He means, that perhaps the Cheapness is apparent only, and not real; or the Bargain by straitning thee in thy Business, may do thee more Harm than Good. . . . Many a one, for the Sake of Finery on the Back, have gone with a hungry Belly, and half starved their Families; Silks and Sattins, Scarlet and Velvets, as Poor Richard says, put out the Kitchen Fire. These are not the Necessaries of Life; they can scarcely be called the Conveniencies, and yet only because they look pretty, how many want to have them. The artificial Wants of Mankind thus become more numerous than the natural. By these, and other Extravagancies, the Genteel are reduced to Poverty, and forced to borrow of those whom they formerly despised, but who through Industry and Frugality have maintained their Standing; in which Case it appears plainly, that a Ploughman on his Legs is higher than a Gentleman on his Knees, as Poor Richard says, If you would know the Value of money, go and try to borrow some; for, he that goes a borrowing goes a sorrowing; and indeed so does he that lends to such People, when he goes to get it in again. Poor Dick farther advises, and says, Fond Pride of Dress, is sure a very Curse. When you have bought one fine Thing you must buy ten more, that your Appearance may be all of a Piece; but Poor Dick says, 'Tis easier to suppress the first Desire, than to satisfy all that follow it. And 'tis as truly Folly for the Poor to ape the Rich, as for the Frog to swell, in order to equal the Ox.

Great Estates may venture more,
But little Boats should keep near Shore.

'Tis however a Folly soon punished; for . . . Pride breakfasted with Plenty, dined with Poverty and supped with Infamy. And after all, of what Use is this Pride of Appearance, for which so much is risked, so much is suffered? It cannot promote Health, or ease Pain; it makes no Increase of Merit in the Person, it creates Envy, it hastens Misfortune. . . . But what Madness must it be to run in Debt for these Superfluities! We are offered, by the Terms of this Vendue, Six Months Credit; and that perhaps has induced some of us to attend it, because we cannot spare the ready Money, and hope now to be fine without it. But, ah, think what you do when you run in Debt; You give to another Power over your Liberty. If you cannot pay at the Time, you will be ashamed to see your Creditor; you will be in Fear when you speak to him; you will make poor pitiful sneaking Excuses, and by Degrees come to lose your Veracity, and sink into base downright lying; for, as Poor Richard says. . . Lying rides upon Debt's Back. Whereas a freeborn Englishman ought not to be ashamed or afraid to see or speak to any Man living. But Poverty often deprives a Man of all Spirit and Virtue: 'Tis hard for an empty Bag to stand upright, as Poor Richard truly says. What would you think of that Prince, or that Government, who should issue an Edict forbidding you to dress like a Gentleman or a Gentlewoman, on Pain of Imprisonment or Servitude? Would you not say, that you are free, have a Right to dress as you please, and that such an Edict would be a Breach of your Privileges, and such a Government tyrannical? And yet you are about to put yourself under that Tyranny when you run in Debt for such Dress! Your Creditor has Authority at his Pleasure to deprive you of your Liberty, by confining you in Goal [sic] for Life, or to sell you for a Servant, if you should not be able to pay him! When you have got your Bargain, you may, perhaps, think little of Payment; but Creditors, Poor Richard tells us, have better Memories than Debtors. . . . The Borrower is a Slave to the Lender, and the Debtor to the Creditor, disdain the Chain, preserve your Freedom; and maintain your Independency: Be industrious and free; be frugal and free. At present, perhaps, you may think yourself in thriving Circumstances, and that you can bear a little Extravagance without Injury; but,

> For Age and Want, save while you may;
> No Morning Sun lasts a whole Day. . . .

This Doctrine, my Friends, is Reason and Wisdom; but after all, do not depend too much upon your own Industry, and Frugality, and Prudence, though excellent Things, for they may all be blasted without the Blessing of Heaven; and therefore ask that Blessing humbly, and be not uncharitable to those that at present seem to want it, but comfort and help them. Remember Job suffered, and was afterwards prosperous.

And now to conclude, remember this, They that won't be counselled, can't be helped, as Poor Richard says: And farther, That if you will not hear Reason, she'll surely rap your Knuckles.

Thus the old Gentleman ended his Harangue. The People heard it, and approved the Doctrine, and immediately practised the contrary, just as if it had been a common Sermon; for the Vendue opened, and they began to buy extravagantly, notwithstanding all his Cautions, and their own Fear of Taxes.

I am, as ever,
Thine to serve thee,
July 7, 1757   Richard Saunders.

Poor Richard's Almanac, in Benjamin Franklin's *Writings*, ed. J. A. Leo Lemay (New York: Library of America, 1987) pp. 1294–1303.

Lesson 6

A Distinctive Society

OVERVIEW

While many people living in the northern colonies in the first half of the eighteenth century experienced more diverse economic and social opportunities, those living in the southern colonies were increasingly affected by the institution of slavery. As you have learned, the foundation for this society had been laid in the seventeenth century, when the emergence of staple crops, a slave labor system, and a racial hierarchy became apparent in the Chesapeake and Carolina regions (See Lesson 3).

The continued development of the plantation system and improvement in the mortality rates of southern colonists heightened the demand for a permanent slave labor force. Coupled with the ready supply of Africans subject to possible enslavement, the Atlantic slave trade exploded in the early eighteenth century. Perhaps the most horrific aspect of this trade was the infamous Middle Passage from Africa to the Americas. Those Africans who survived were forced to cope with the cruelties of the slave labor system in America. Out of these conditions, an African American culture as well as a region characterized by a distinctive economic, political, and social structure emerged.

Even though southern and northern colonies had developed along different paths, America itself was becoming more distinctive. As you will notice in the textbook and assigned video for this lesson, you are encouraged to think about the unifying experiences of colonial America before moving on to examine the revolutionary era. Colonists still recognized themselves as British subjects, but they were also becoming "American" in many other ways. In your deliberations, consider how American identity and the themes of freedom and equality so often associated with America were taking shape by the 1750s.

LESSON ASSIGNMENTS

Text: Roark, et al., *The American Promise,* Chapter 5, "Colonial America in the Eighteenth Century," pp. 137–138; 151–173

Video: "A Distinctive Society" from the series *Shaping America*

Documents:
            "Missionaries Report on California Missions," pp. 168–169 in the textbook

LEARNING OBJECTIVES

This lesson explains how and why slavery began, distinguishes the southern colonies, and reveals how America itself was becoming a distinctive society by the 1750s. Upon completing this lesson, you should be able to:

1. Describe the African slave trade.

2. Explain the conditions of slave labor and the emergence of an African American culture.

3. Analyze the effects of the slave labor system on the economic, social, and political structure of the southern colonies.

4. Analyze the unifying experiences shared by the colonists throughout British North America.

5. Assess how the experiences and developments of the colonial period shaped American identity.

LESSON FOCUS POINTS

The following questions are designed to help you get the most benefit from the sources selected for this lesson. For reference purposes, the titles for the video segments are: (1) Introduction, (2) "Middle Passage," (3) "African American Culture," (4) Short-take: "Gullah," (5) "A Distinctive Society," and (6) Unit Close: "City on a Hill?"

1. What developments in the southern colonies in the late seventeenth century provided an economic rationale that contributed to a booming Atlantic slave trade in the early eighteenth century? (video segment 1)

2. Who were the Africans being sold into slavery? Why were they being sold? (textbook, pp. 137–138, 151–153; video segment 2)

3. Examine Map 5.3 on p. 152 of the textbook. Why were the number of slave imports so much greater in the eighteenth century than before or after? Where in the Americas were most of the Africans being shipped? Why was this the case? (textbook, pp. 152–153)

4. Who is Olaudah Equiano? Why is he important? (textbook, p. 153; video segment 2)

5. Why were conditions on the Middle Passage so horrible? How did the slaves cope with these conditions? What choices did they have? (textbook, pp. 153–155; video segment 2)

6. What characterized the slave labor system? How did the slaves cope? What choices did they have? (textbook, pp. 155–156 video segment 3)

7. To what extent was an African American culture emerging in colonial America? What characterized this culture? (textbook, pp. 155–156; video segment 3)

8. How did African cultures affect South Carolina? What is the Gullah culture? How is it reflected in America? (video segments 3, 4)

9. What happened during the Stono rebellion? How did white southerners react to it? (textbook, pp. 155–156; video segment 3)

10. How did the slave labor system affect the southern economy, politics, and social system? (textbook, pp. 156–157; video segment 5)

11. How did commerce and consumption unify the colonists? (textbook, pp. 158, 161)

12. What was the Enlightenment and how did it affect colonial America? (textbook, p. 162)

13. What factors explain the emergence of the "Great Awakening"? How did that awakening affect the colonial people? (textbook, pp. 162–163)

14. How did the colonies fit into the British Empire by 1760? What were the benefits to England and the colonists? How were developments on the borderlands affecting the British colonies and the people living in North America? To what extent did the colonists have a distinctive political system in place by 1760? (textbook, pp. 163–170)

15. How had an American identity emerged by 1760? How were minorities, including women and American Indians fitting into this identity? To what extent was freedom present in colonial America? (textbook, p. 170; video segment 6)

HISTORICAL EXPERTS INTERVIEWED

Ira Berlin, Professor of History, University of Maryland, College Park, MD
Nemata Blyden, Assistant Professor, University of Texas at Dallas, Richardson, TX
R. David Edmunds, Watson Professor of American History, University of Texas at Dallas, Richardson, TX
Eric Foner, Professor of History, Columbia University, New York, NY
James Oliver Horton, Benjamin Banneker Professor of American Civilization and History, The George Washington University, Washington, DC
Michael Johnson, Professor of History, Johns Hopkins University, Baltimore, MD
Linda K. Kerber, May Brodbeck Professor of Liberal Arts, University of Iowa, Iowa City, IA
Daniel Littlefield, Carolina Professor of History, University of South Carolina, Columbia, SC

PRACTICE TEST

The following items will help you evaluate your understanding of this lesson. Use the Answer Key at the end of the lesson to check your answers or to locate material related to each question.

Multiple choice: Choose the BEST answer.

1. In the video, Professor Dan Littlefield makes the point that Africans being sold in Africa were _____.
   A. shipped out according to a specific order of preference
   B. not always exactly what slave traders and buyers preferred
   C. most often people with royal heritage
   D. willing to leave Africa since conditions were so bad there

2. The main reason why southern masters preferred black slaves over white indentured servants was that _____.
   A. masters had to pay indentured servants a small sum each year
   B. indentured servants would not work as many hours as slaves
   C. indentured servants were surly and talked back
   D. slaves served for life and could be beaten into submission

3. The Stono rebellion proved that slaves _____.
   A. were dangerous in large organized numbers
   B. could not overturn slavery nor win in the fight for freedom
   C. would continue to rebel until they received their freedom
   D. could not organize themselves against the smart, armed masters

4. While the eighteenth-century southern gentry privately looked down upon poor whites, they publicly acknowledged them as _____.
   A. necessary to the growth of Southern economy
   B. their equals, belonging to the superior white race
   C. a contemptible group of lost souls
   D. having the opportunity to become gentry someday

5. The South was a distinctive society by 1750 due to its commitment to slavery and because _____.
   A. religious diversity was more widespread there
   B. most of the people lived in booming port cities
   C. an emerging middle class dominated political life
   D. the British considered it to be the most valuable part of North America

6. A communication medium that brought the colonies closer together as it evolved was _____.
   A. published newspapers
   B. printed pamphlets
   C. lending libraries
   D. philosophical societies

7. During the eighteenth century, the colonists in America _____.
   A. thought of themselves as both British subjects and colonists
   B. were ready to break with England
   C. became remarkably homogeneous given the number of immigrants
   D. worked incessantly to make their society thoroughly colonial, rejecting as much of British culture and fashion as possible

Short Answer: Your answers should be one or two paragraphs long and specifically address the points indicated.

8. Describe the process known as "seasoning" in the African slave trade. Why did this process help make slaves more valuable to planters?

9. To what extent was an African American culture emerging in colonial America? How was this culture expressed?

Essay Questions: Your answers should be several paragraphs long and express a clear understanding of the points indicated.

10. How and why had the southern colonies become a distinctive society by 1760? What were the short- and long-term consequences of this distinctiveness?

11. Compare and contrast the northern, middle, and southern colonies by 1760. What experiences were unifying the colonies? How were the British colonies in North America different from Spain's colonies?

12. How and why were the British colonists becoming "American" by 1760? What characterized this society?

ANSWER KEY

Answer	Learning Objectives	Focus Points	References
1. B	LO 1	FP 2	video segment 2
2. D	LO 2	FP 6	pp. 155–156; video segment 3
3. B	LO 2	FP 9	pp. 155–156; video segment 3
4. B	LO 3	FP 11	pp. 158–161; video segment 5
5. D	LO 3	FP 11	pp. 158–161; video segment 5
6. A	LO 4	FP 12	p. 162
7. A	LO 5	FP 15	p. 170

8.   ....LO 1.................FP 5 ....pp. 153–155; video segment 2
- How was the physical condition of the slaves arriving from Africa restored?
- What sort of cultural changes had to take place?
- How would a healthier and more communicative slave population benefit planters?

9.   ....LO 2.................FP 7–9 .... pp. 155–156; video segments 3, 4
- How important were kin networks to the slaves? How were they expressed?
- How did names and language reflect a new culture?
- How did food crops and music fit into this scheme?

10.   ....LO 2, 3..........FP 6–11, 15 .... pp. 155–161, 170; video segments 3–5
- What role did geography play?
- What crops were developed?
- Why did a slave labor system develop?
- How did the slave labor system affect race relations? How did slavery influence the class system and politics?
- How would slavery ultimately affect relations with other colonies and eventually states (after the Revolution)?

11.   ....LO 3, 4............FP 12–15 ....pp. 162–170
- What role did geography play?
- How were the economy and diversity issues different?
- How did commerce and consumption unify them?
- What role did religion play?
- What did it mean that they were all British subjects?
- How did they differ from Spain regarding geography, religion, agriculture, and types of people present?

12.   ....LO 5.................FP 15 ....p. 170; video segment 6
- How had the encounters with Indian peoples forged an identity?
- To what extent was freedom becoming associated with America?
- How and why was diversity shaping a different identity?
- To what extent had an "American" economic and political identity emerged?

ENRICHMENT IDEAS

These activities are not required unless your instructor assigns them. They are offered as suggestions to help you learn more about the material presented in this lesson.

1. If you are an African American, can you trace your family history back to the colonial period? If so, what do you know about the African roots of your family? How is African culture still represented? Submit your story and cite the sources of your information.

2. Imagine yourself to be a slave in the South who is organizing a rebellion in 1740. In a well-developed essay, describe your plan. What will you do to ensure your success?

3. Consider the geographic and demographic maps of the British colonies in 1760. Which groups of people tended to settle where? Why did these patterns of settlement develop? How did this process affect the shaping of America? Compose a well-developed essay in which you report on your conclusions.

SUGGESTED READINGS/RESOURCES

See the "Bibliography" on pages 170–171 of the textbook if you wish to examine other books and resources related to the material presented in this lesson.

Unit Two

Revolutionary America
1754–1801
"All Men Are Created Equal?"

THEME

When the delegates to the Second Continental Congress approved the Declaration of Independence in July 1776, they endorsed one of the most remarkable political documents in world history. More than two hundred twenty-five years later, Americans take an annual holiday to commemorate what happened then. In the midst of the social gatherings and fireworks which mark the day, some may even reflect on what happened in 1776 and what the statements in the Declaration actually mean to us today. Most notably, that elusive goal of equality is still there.

How and why did the revolutionaries in thirteen colonies take such a bold step in 1776? What in the world were they thinking? Declaring independence was one thing, winning it was another! How could they propose to engage and actually defeat the British in a revolutionary war? What kind of nation could be created in such an environment? Would that nation have enough stability to survive? Could power be transferred without a violent revolution? Exploring the answers to these questions can provide us with new perspectives not only on the revolutionary generation but also on the enduring effects of that generation's choices.

Lesson 7

Making a Revolution

OVERVIEW

Revolutions still occur in world history, but they are never simple affairs. Many ingredients need to coalesce to form a revolutionary movement. Enough committed people have to be dedicated to bringing about fundamental changes. These changes are political, to be sure, but the revolutionary process can lead to unforeseen social and economic consequences as well.

On the surface, mid-eighteenth-century British colonists in America appeared to be unlikely revolutionaries. While they were forming a society distinct from England, they were still predominantly British in their thinking and loyalty. However, in the 1760s and 1770s, these colonial people turned into a revolutionary people. How and why did this happen?

A key turning point in this revolutionary process was the British victory in the French and Indian War. The British had removed the French from the North American chessboard, but they still had to deal with hostile Indians and an imposing war debt. British decisions regarding these and other issues led to a series of actions in America that made a revolution possible.

Americans from thirteen different colonies could not agree on a Plan of Union in 1754, but during the next twenty years, a revolutionary mindset began to take shape. James Otis' appeal to natural rights in 1761 gave an American expression to the idea that governments are limited. Then a series of British moves prompted colonial Americans to challenge the authority of the British government. Americans began to talk more forcefully about their liberties. Revolutionary leaders emerged, and propagandists portrayed victims of British gunfire as martyrs. Finally, British patience with American provocations expired after the Boston Tea Party, and they took steps in 1774 to force the colonials to comply with British policy. By this time, however, the Americans were willing and able to make a unified response. Indeed, they were on the brink of declaring independence.

LESSON ASSIGNMENTS

Text: Roark, et al., *The American Promise*, Chapter 6, "The British Empire and the Colonial Crisis," pp. 175–211

Video: "Making a Revolution" from the series *Shaping America*

Documents:
          "How News of the Powder Alarm Traveled," pp. 202–203 in the textbook

LEARNING OBJECTIVES

This lesson focuses on how and why the American revolutionary movement took shape in the 1760s and 1770s. Upon completing this lesson, you should be able to:

1. Explain why the French and Indian War took place and how it affected relations between England and the people in the British colonies in North America.

2. Explain the shifting British policies toward colonial America in the 1760s and 1770s and why these actions aroused so much colonial opposition.

3. Describe the evolution of American political thought and tactics in opposing British policies between 1754 and 1774.

4. Analyze the complexity of revolutions in general and the American revolutionary movement in particular.

LESSON FOCUS POINTS

The following questions are designed to help you get the most benefit from the sources selected for this lesson. For reference purposes, the titles for the video segments are: (1) Introduction, (2) "Opening Moves," (3) "The Gambit," (4) "The Middle Game," (5) "The Blunder," (6) "Queen's Corner," and (7) "Endgame."

1. What does the term *revolution* mean? Why do people get involved? Why were the Americans ripe for a revolution by the 1770s? (video segment 1)

2. Who was fighting whom in the French and Indian War? Why were they fighting? Where were they fighting? (textbook, pp. 176–179; Map 6.1, p. 178; video segment 2)

3. What was the purpose of the Albany Congress? What was the Albany Plan of Union? What did the Congress and the fate of the Plan of Union indicate about the colonies? (textbook, p. 179; video segment 2)

4. What were the consequences of the French and Indian War in terms of geography? What were the consequences in terms of British policy? (textbook, pp. 180–182; Map 6.2, p. 181; video segment 2)

5. What were "writs of assistance"? Why did James Otis argue against them? How did his arguments form a philosophical basis for revolution? What were the short- and long-term effects of this issue? (video segment 3)

6. Why did Pontiac initiate an uprising in 1763? Where did this take place? How is the uprising connected to the Proclamation Act of 1763? What is the significance of this proclamation? (textbook, pp. 182–185)

7. What steps did the British take in 1764–1765 to raise revenue from the colonists? Why was the Stamp Act so controversial? How did arguments about the stamp tax illustrate differing views about representation and the right to tax? (textbook, pp. 186–187; video segment 4)

8. How did the Americans resist the Stamp Act? What forms of resistance were particularly effective? Who were the Sons of Liberty, and what did they do? What role did "crowd politics" begin to play in the revolutionary movement? (textbook, pp. 187–191; video segment 4)

9. Why did the Americans link "liberty and property" in their arguments against British taxes? Why did they think England was trying to enslave them? To what extent were the arguments about liberty and slavery applicable to black Americans at this time? (textbook, pp. 192–193; video segment 4)

10. Why did the British impose the Townshend duties? How were they resisted in America? Why and how did women play an active role in this resistance? (textbook, pp. 193–196)

11. Why did the Boston Massacre take place? What really happened? What was the significance of this event? (textbook, pp. 196–197; video segment 5)

12. How and why did the British reaction to the burning of the *Gaspee* and their proposals to pay justices provoke colonial opposition? How were the revolutionaries able to form a communications network? What was important about that? (textbook, pp. 197–198)

13. Why did tea get invested with a lot of political meaning during the 1760s and 1770s? What were the causes and consequences of the Boston Tea Party? (textbook, pp. 197–200; video segment 6)

14. Read the document segment on the "Powder Alarm." Answer the questions posed in the text. (textbook, pp. 202–203)

15. What were the Coercive Acts? What effects did these acts have on the colonials? (textbook, pp. 199–203; video segment 6)

16. What was the purpose of the First Continental Congress? What actions were taken at this meeting? (textbook, pp. 201, 204; video segment 6)

17. How and why had a "national consciousness" emerged among the colonies between the Albany Congress (1754) and the First Continental Congress (1774)? Do you think the American Revolution was inevitable by the end of 1774? (video segment 7)

HISTORICAL EXPERTS INTERVIEWED

Jon Butler, Coe Professor of History, Yale University, New Haven, CT
Patricia Cline Cohen, Professor, University of California at Santa Barbara, Santa Barbara, CA
Edward Countryman, University Distinguished Professor, Southern Methodist University, Dallas, TX
Sheila Skemp, Professor, University of Mississippi, Oxford, MS
Gordon Wood, Alva O. Way University Professor and Professor of History, Brown University, Providence, RI

PRACTICE TEST

The following items will help you evaluate your understanding of this lesson. Use the Answer Key at the end of the lesson to check your answers or to locate material related to each question.

Multiple choice: Choose the BEST answer.

1. In the video, Professors Sheila Skemp and Jon Butler indicate that the American colonies were ripe for revolution prior to 1776 for all of the following reasons EXCEPT that they _____.
    A. had developed a new political order
    B. had a clear blueprint for a new national government
    C. were steeped in the English tradition of rights
    D. lived in diverse social and economic communities

2. The Albany Plan of Union as proposed by Benjamin Franklin and Thomas Hutchinson was _____.
    A. accepted by all of the colonies
    B. accepted by the colonies and turned down by England
    C. helpful in gaining the pledge of the Iroquois to fight the French
    D. approved by neither the colonies nor England

3. After the French and Indian War, the Earl of Bute decided to keep ten thousand British troops in America to _____.
    A. keep the peace between the colonists and the Indians
    B. punish the colonists for their smuggling activities during the war
    C. prevent the French from trying to regain lost territory
    D. protect settlers who moved west of the Appalachian Mountains

4. The Stamp Act of 1765 _____.
    A. affected only New England
    B. was consistent with past parliamentary efforts to regulate trade
    C. seemed to set an ominous precedent in the eyes of the colonists
    D. required the consent of the colonial assemblies before going into effect

5. According to the British, the major purpose of the Tea Act of 1773 was to _____.
    A. break the American boycott of tea imported from England
    B. raise more revenue from the sale of tea to cover military costs in North America
    C. boost sales for the financially strapped British East India Company
    D. punish the Americans for importing tea from Holland

6. The First Continental Congress created the Continental Association, whose purpose was to _____.
    A. abolish individual colonial governments
    B. enforce a staggered and limited boycott of trade
    C. provide a forum to share plans for resisting British oppression
    D. devise a method of collecting taxes until the former Massachusetts charter was restored

Short Answer: Your answers should be one or two paragraphs long and specifically address the points indicated.

7. After listening to and reflecting upon James Otis' arguments against the writs of assistance, John Adams observed that "then and there, the child of independence was born." Explain why Adams made this statement. Do you agree with him? Why or why not?

Essay Question: Your answers should be several paragraphs long and express a clear understanding of the points indicated.

8. Describe and explain the evolution of American political thought and tactics in opposing British policies between 1754 and 1774. Why and how had the revolutionary movement brought the colonies to the brink of declaring independence? Do you think that the American Revolution was inevitable by 1774? Why or why not?

ANSWER KEY

Answer	Learning Objectives	Focus Points	References
1. B	LO 4	FP 1	video segment 1
2. D	LO 1	FP 3	p. 179; video segment 2
3. A	LO 1	FP 4	pp. 180–182; video segment 2
4. C	LO 3	FP 7	pp. 186–187; video segment 4
5. C	LO 2	FP 13	pp. 197–200; video segment 6
6. B	LO 3	FP 16	pp. 201, 204; video segment 6

7. ....LO 3.................FP 5 ....video segment 3
   - What was Otis' central argument?
   - How could Otis' argument be applied to other issues in the 1760s and 1770s?
   - How does Otis' argument connect to a right of revolution? . . . to the Declaration of Independence?

8. ....LO 1– 4 ....FP 1–17 .... pp. 176–204; video segments 1–7
   - Consider the ingredients necessary to make a revolution.
   - What was the status of colonial political union in 1754?
   - How did the Americans begin to apply natural rights to their situation?
   - Why and how did the Americans connect ideas of liberty and property? Why would this connection lead them toward more revolutionary positions?
   - Describe the various tactics the Americans used to express their disagreement with the British. How and why did their tactics and actions coalesce into a revolutionary movement?
   - What was the status of colonial political union in 1774?
   - Take a position on the inevitability question and defend it.

ENRICHMENT IDEAS

These activities are not required unless your instructor assigns them. They are offered as suggestions to help you learn more about the material presented in this lesson.

1. Are there issues and/or policies in the communities in which you live and work that you do not agree with? Select one and then proceed to write a well-developed essay in which you describe the issue and explain how you propose to change it.

2. Research the killings that took place at Kent State University in 1970. Then submit an essay in which you compare and contrast that event with the Boston Massacre of 1770.

3. Imagine yourself to be the lawyer defending Captain Thomas Preston, the British officer charged with murder in the Boston Massacre. In a carefully worded essay, describe how you plan to convince the jury that he is innocent of the charge.

4. There are many ingredients necessary to make a revolution: natural rights arguments, violence, propaganda, charismatic leadership, martyrdom, et cetera. Research one of these factors in a revolution *other than* the American fight for independence. Then submit a report in which you discuss the importance of that ingredient in the revolution you have examined.

SUGGESTED READINGS/RESOURCES

See the "Bibliography" on pages 208–209 of the text if you wish to examine other books and resources related to the material presented in this lesson.

Lesson 8

Declaring Independence

OVERVIEW

By 1775, relations between England and its mainland colonies were obviously severely strained, but they were not yet at the breaking point. However, the revolutionary movement, which had been inching toward independence, picked up momentum when armed insurrection erupted at Lexington and Concord, Massachusetts, in April of that year.

The Second Continental Congress assembled a month later and began assuming political and military authority for the colonies. However, the delegates, like the American people, were not yet united on their ultimate objective, and many continued to express loyalty to the King of England. The sense of that loyalty was severely challenged by Thomas Paine in January 1776. Six months later, the Congress adopted one of the most revolutionary documents in world history, the Declaration of Independence.

In the short term, that document justified both independence from England and a war against that nation. Beyond that, the revolutionary philosophy enunciated there would help spark democratic revolutions throughout the world for over two hundred years. At home, the Declaration of Independence became part of an American creed. Most especially, the phrase that "all men are created equal" turned into a goal that would challenge the United States throughout its history.

LESSON ASSIGNMENTS

Text: Roark, et al., *The American Promise,* Chapter 6, "The British Empire and the Colonial Crisis," pp. 204–208; Chapter 7, "The War for America," pp. 213–222; and Appendix, pp. A1–A3 (The Declaration of Independence)

Video: "Declaring Independence" from the series *Shaping America*

LEARNING OBJECTIVES

This lesson examines the background, purpose, and meaning of the Declaration of Independence. Upon completing this lesson, you should be able to:

1. Analyze the historical significance of the "domestic insurrections" at Lexington and Concord and those directed against slavery.

2. Analyze the steps taken by the Second Continental Congress to assume political and military authority in the colonies.

3. Explain the significance of Thomas Paine's *Common Sense*.

4. Explain the purpose and meaning of the Declaration of Independence.

5. Analyze the short- and long-term effects of the Declaration of Independence.

LESSON FOCUS POINTS

The following questions are designed to help you get the most benefit from the sources selected for this lesson. For reference purposes, the titles for the video segments are: (1) Introduction, (2) "Justifying Revolution," (3) "Declaring Equality," (4) "The Unanimous Declaration," (5) Short-take: "The Men Who Signed," and (6) Summary Analysis: "From This Time Forward."

1. Why were the British troops advancing on Lexington and Concord on April 18–19, 1775? (textbook, pp. 204–206; video segment 2)

2. How and why did the colonial militia resist the British advance and attack their retreat? What was the significance of these military engagements? (textbook, pp. 205–206; video segment 2)

3. How did slaves pursue their version of liberty at the same time that militant colonials were resisting British attempts to reduce them to "slavery." How does this display an irony of history? (textbook, pp. 206–208)

4. How did the story of Deborah Sampson illustrate the personal experiences of the American Revolution? (textbook, pp. 213–214)

5. How and why was royal control breaking down in the colonies and local communities in 1774–1775? What initial steps did the Second Continental Congress take to assume political and military authority in the colonies? Why was George Washington chosen to command the Continental army? (textbook, pp. 215, 218–219)

6. What happened at the Battle of Bunker Hill? What was its significance? (textbook, p. 218)

7. How and why did the Second Continental Congress continue to pursue reconciliation with England in the summer and fall of 1775? (textbook, p. 220)

8. Who was Thomas Paine? Why did he write *Common Sense*? What was the significance of that pamphlet? (textbook, pp. 220–221; video segment 2)

9. Why was Thomas Jefferson chosen to be the primary author of the Declaration of Independence? Where did his ideas come from? (video segment 3)

10. What was the purpose of the Declaration in 1776? What is the basic political philosophy expressed in the Declaration? Why are charges brought against the King in the document? Are the charges accurate? Do the charges justify the revolution? (textbook, pp. 221–222, A1–A3; video segments 2, 3)

11. What did the statement that "all men are created equal" mean in 1776? (video segment 3)

12. Why did Congress excise Jefferson's proposed passage in the Declaration that blamed the King for slavery? How does Jefferson's life reflect the American perspective on the issue of slavery? (video segment 3)

13. What effect did the editing by Congress have on the Declaration? (video segment 4)

14. Why was the signing of the Declaration difficult and meaningful? (textbook, p. 222; video segments 4, 5)

15. Why and how has the Declaration been used since its adoption in 1776? Why did the Declaration become part of the American creed? How has it shaped our identity? (video segments 5, 6)

HISTORICAL EXPERTS INTERVIEWED

Patricia Cline Cohen, Professor, University of California at Santa Barbara, Santa Barbara, CA

Edward Countryman, University Distinguished Professor, Southern Methodist University, Dallas, TX

Joseph J. Ellis, Professor of History (Ford Foundation), Mount Holyoke College, South Hadley, MA

James Oliver Horton, Benjamin Banneker Professor of American Civilization and History, The George Washington University, Washington, DC

Gordon Wood, Alva O. Way University Professor and Professor of History, Brown University, Providence, RI

PRACTICE TEST

The following items will help you evaluate your understanding of this lesson. Use the Answer Key at the end of the lesson to check your answers or to locate material related to each question.

Multiple choice: Choose the BEST answer.

1. General Gage planned a surprise attack on an ammunition storage site in Concord _____.
   A. to put down the small group of rabble-rousers he believed was causing all the colonial dissent
   B. because the site contained all the firepower in the area
   C. because he knew it would be unguarded
   D. because he was ordered to quell the dissenters before they became more organized

2. Northern slave Phillis Wheatley used bitter sarcasm in a 1774 newspaper essay exposing the hypocrisy of local slave owners; her other accomplishments included _____.
   A. leading Bostonian women in promoting spinning bees
   B. writing poetry about freedom for slaves
   C. inciting slaves to rebel against the British in Boston
   D. starting the Underground Railroad

3. The Continental Congress delegates chose George Washington as commander in chief because _____.
   A. he was an excellent general
   B. he had done such a good job in the French and Indian War
   C. picking a southerner would show England that there was widespread commitment to war outside New England
   D. he was a wealthy plantation owner and had the time to commit to an all-out war

4. The author of the radical pamphlet *Common Sense* _____.
   A. called for independence and republicanism
   B. was actually Benjamin Franklin writing under a pseudonym
   C. asked the colonists to reconsider their cry for independence to restore harmony in the colonies
   D. urged the common people to revolt against the wealthy merchants and planters

5. Professor Edward Countryman states in the video that he thinks Thomas Jefferson's vision of equality at the time of the writing of the Declaration of Independence meant _____.
   A. the American people were equal to other people
   B. the west was equal to the east
   C. women were equal to men
   D. free blacks were equal to slaves

6. Congress excised the passage in the Declaration of Independence condemning George III for slavery because _____.
   A. they wanted stronger language used
   B. they were still awaiting a response to the olive branch petition
   C. the issue itself was too divisive and controversial
   D. slaves had already joined the British army

7. In the video, Professor James Oliver Horton says that for African Americans the Declaration of Independence _____.
   A. is a living document
   B. should be amended
   C. is meaningless
   D. applies only to the nineteenth century

Short Answer: Your answers should be one or two paragraphs long and specifically address the points indicated.

8. What were the contradictory tasks of the Second Continental Congress in 1775? How did they pursue each one?

9. Why was Thomas Jefferson chosen to be the primary author of the Declaration of Independence? What was important about that?

10. Explain the key points of political philosophy contained in the Declaration of Independence.

Essay Question: Your answer should be several paragraphs long and express a clear understanding of the points indicated.

11. Describe and explain the background, purpose, and meaning of the Declaration of Independence. Why did this document become part of the American creed?

ANSWER KEY

	Answer	Learning Objectives	Focus Points	References
1.	D	LO 1	FP 1	pp. 204–206; video segment 2
2.	B	LO 1	FP 3	pp. 206–208
3.	C	LO 2	FP 5	pp. 215, 218–219,
4.	A	LO 3	FP 8	pp. 220–221; video segment 2
5.	A	LO 4	FP 11	video segment 3
6.	C	LO 4	FP 12	video segment 3
7.	A	LO 5	FP 15	video segments 5, 6

8. .... LO 2 .... FP 5, 7 .... pp. 215, 218–220
   - Consider the situation when the Congress convened.
   - What steps did they take to prepare for war?
   - How did they continue to pursue peace with King George?

9. .... LO 2 .... FP 9 .... video segment 3
   - Who were the likely authors?
   - What role did Jefferson play in the Congress?
   - Why did others turn down the job?
   - What talents did Jefferson have? How did he see the world?
   - Why was it important that he was from Virginia?

10. .... LO 4, 5 .... FP 10 .... pp. 221–222, A1–A3; video segments 2, 3
   - How are natural rights expressed in the document?
   - What is the purpose of government?
   - What do the people have a right to do in case the government falls short?

11. .... LO 4, 5 .... FP 1–15 .... pp. 204–208, 213–222, A1–A3;
   .... video segments 1–6
   - Consider the significant events and actions that brought the delegates to consider a formal declaration of independence.
   - What are some of the key grievances in the document?
   - How does the document justify revolution?
   - What did the document mean in 1776?
   - Why did the statement about equality change over time?
   - What key individuals and groups have applied the Declaration to pursue principles stated in the document?
   - Why does the document have meaning today?

ENRICHMENT IDEAS

These activities are not required unless your instructor assigns them. They are offered as suggestions to help you learn more about the material presented in this lesson.

1. Imagine yourself to be a slave in Virginia, and you have just heard about Lord Dunmore's Proclamation. Relate your reaction to the proclamation and what you plan to do about it.

2. Imagine yourself to be a delegate at the Second Continental Congress. You are charged with editing Thomas Jefferson's draft passage on the slavery issue. In a well-developed essay, describe how you propose to edit the passage and why you are proposing these changes.

3. Imagine yourself to be a free black in New York City or in Charleston, South Carolina, in July/August 1776, and you have just read a copy of the Declaration of Independence. Write a letter to the publisher of one of the local newspapers in which you describe your reaction to the document.

4. Research the work of Phillis Wheatley. Then submit an essay in which you describe her writing and her place in American literature.

5. Research how the Declaration of Independence was used during the 1960s, both in reference to the civil rights movement and the Vietnam War. Then submit an essay in which you describe your findings and what that says about the document.

SUGGESTED READINGS/RESOURCES

See the "Bibliography" on pages 208–209 and 247 of the text if you wish to examine other books and resources related to the material presented in this lesson.

Lesson 9

Winning Independence

OVERVIEW

Declaring independence was one thing; actually winning it was another. At the beginning of the Revolutionary War, the odds of the newly created United States of America actually defeating one of the most powerful nations in the world were slim.

This war was both a colonial war for liberation and a civil war at home. An army had to be raised, organized, armed, maintained, and led. Support, both at home and abroad, had to be pursued and nurtured. Hardship was shared by soldiers, their patriotic backers, and loyalists. Women took on new roles at home and sometimes on the military front. Free blacks hoped that the cause of liberty would spread, while slaves had to choose what side might better bring them freedom. American Indians were caught in the middle.

Although it was not clear to people engaged in the events at that time, in the end, we know the United States won. The revolutionary generation had now secured independence and unleashed ideals that would shape the generations to come.

LESSON ASSIGNMENTS

Text: Roark, et al., *The American Promise,* Chapter 7, "The War for America,"
            pp. 213–214, 222–249

Video: "Winning Independence" from the series *Shaping America*

Documents:
            "Families Divide over the Revolution," pp. 234–235 in the textbook
            "The Unreliable Militia" and "Memoir, 1830" found at the end of this lesson

LEARNING OBJECTIVES

This lesson examines how and why the United States won the Revolutionary War and what that meant to the American people. Upon completing this lesson, you should be able to:

1. Explain the relative strengths and weaknesses of the Americans and the British at the start of the Revolutionary War.

2. Describe how struggles on the home front affected the war.

3. Explain the key turning points on the military front.

4. Assess why the British lost and the Americans won.

5. Explain how the war and its outcome affected the American people, including women, African Americans, American Indians, and loyalists.

LESSON FOCUS POINTS

The following questions are designed to help you get the most benefit from the sources selected for this lesson. For reference purposes, the titles for the video segments are: (1) Introduction, (2) "The War Takes a Turn," (3) "Wartime Allies," (4) "The Long Winter," (5) "Monmouth and the Molly Pitchers," (6) "Tories," and (7) Summary Analysis: "A World Turned Upside Down."

1. Why were the odds stacked against American victory in the war? Did they have any advantages? How could they win? (video segment 1)

2. How did the Americans raise an effective military force? Where did the troops come from? Who joined the military? Why was George Washington concerned about the militia? (textbook, pp. 222–225; document; video segment 2)

3. What was the British strategy for winning the war? (textbook, p. 225)

4. Examine Map 7.1 on page 226. Why was so much of the war fought in New York and New Jersey between 1776 and 1778? Where were Washington's winter quarters in 1776–1777 and 1777–1778? (textbook, pp. 225–227)

5. What was important about General George Washington's escape from New York in late 1776? Why did Washington attack German mercenaries at Trenton? Why was the victory at Trenton important for the Americans? (textbook, pp. 227–228; video segments 1, 2)

6. Why and how were African Americans participating in the war? Why were many slaves attracted to the British side? (textbook, pp. 224–225; video segment 2)

7. How was patriotism assured at the local level? What roles did white women play on the home front? (textbook, pp. 228–229; video segment 5)

8. How many British loyalists were there in America? Who were they? Why were they loyal? Where were they most numerous? (textbook, pp. 229, 231–232; video segment 6)

9. How was a traitor defined? What happened to them? (textbook, pp. 230–231, 233, 236; video segment 7)

10. Why was there so much financial instability and corruption during the war? (textbook, p. 236)

11. What happened at the Battle of Oriskany in August 1777? What did this battle and other engagements indicate about the role of American Indians in the war? How did the outcome

of this battle affect what would happen later at Saratoga? (textbook, pp. 236–240; video segment 3)

12. What happened at the Battle of Saratoga in October 1777? Why was this a critical American victory? (textbook, pp. 237–238, 236; video segment 3)

13. Why did France form an alliance with the United States? What was important about that? (textbook, pp. 240–241; video segment 3)

14. What were conditions like at Valley Forge in the winter of 1777–1778? Why did the soldiers there stick it out? What did George Washington and Baron von Steuben do at Valley Forge? How did Joseph Plumb Martin describe his wartime experiences? (textbook, p. 238; document; video segment 4)

15. What happened at the Battle of Monmouth? Who were "Molly Pitchers," and how did Molly Ludwig Hayes represent their roles in the war? What else was important about the Battle of Monmouth? (video segment 5)

16. Examine Map 7.4 on page 242. Why did the British take the war south? Why and how did General Cornwallis move from Charleston to Yorktown? (textbook, pp. 241–243; video segment 6)

17. Why did Benedict Arnold commit treason? What effect did it have on the patriots? (textbook, p. 242)

18. Why did guerilla war break out in the backcountry in the south? What characterized this type of war? (textbook, pp. 242–243; video segment 6)

19. What happened at Yorktown? Why was Cornwallis forced to surrender? (textbook, pp. 243–244; video segment 6)

20. What were the key provisions of the Treaty of Paris, 1783? (textbook, pp. 245–246)

21. In summary, why had the British lost and the Americans won? (textbook, pp. 246–247; video segment 6)

22. In summary, how did the war affect loyalists, America Indians, women, and African Americans? How and why did the results of the war unleash a dynamic that would continue to change America and the world? (textbook, pp. 244–247; video segment 7)

HISTORICAL EXPERTS INTERVIEWED

Carol Berkin, Professor of History, City University of New York, New York City, NY
Richard Brookhiser, Senior Editor, *National Review*, New York, NY
Calvin L. Christman, Professor of History, Cedar Valley College, Lancaster, TX
Lincoln Rolling, Professor of History, Cedar Valley College, Lancaster, TX
Sheila Skemp, Professor of History, University of Mississippi, Oxford, MS
Richard White, Margaret Byrne Professor of American History, Stanford University, Stanford, CA
Anthony Wonderly, Nation Historian, Oneida Indian Nation, Oneida, NY
Gordon Wood, Alva O. Way University Professor and Professor of History, Brown University, Providence, RI

PRACTICE TEST

The following items will help you evaluate your understanding of this lesson. Use the Answer Key at the end of the lesson to check your answers or to locate material related to each question.

Multiple choice: Choose the BEST answer.

1. All of the following were advantages of the British at the beginning of the Revolutionary War EXCEPT _____.
    A. Americans were poorly armed
    B. a majority of the American people were loyal to Britain
    C. Americans lacked adequate financing
    D. the British army and navy were considered among the best in the world

2. During the Revolution, both the Continental Congress and the states issued paper money, which resulted in _____.
    A. deflation and low prices
    B. making it easy to sell bonds
    C. inflation and escalating prices
    D. low interest foreign credit becoming available

3. In the Battle of Long Island, _____.
    A. British troops, led by General Howe, forced the Americans to retreat to Manhattan Island
    B. Washington and the Continental army scored their first major victory over British forces
    C. General Howe demanded the unconditional surrender of Washington and his troops
    D. British troops and a Loyalist regiment accidentally fired on each other

4. Burgoyne's defeat at the Second Battle of Saratoga, October 17, 1777, was a decisive moment in the Revolutionary War because _____.
   A. it caused Benedict Arnold to defect to the British
   B. it brought France into the war on the side of the patriots
   C. it discredited Horatio Gates, resulting in his being replaced by Nathaniel Greene
   D. it vindicated Burgoyne's strategy for mounting an attack from Canada

5. After the Battle of Monmouth, _____.
   A. British forces never faced Washington's army again in the North
   B. American forces retreated in disgrace
   C. women were accepted as regular combat troops
   D. the French agreed to become allies

6. In the course of the southern campaign late in the Revolutionary War, _____.
   A. small bands of American guerrillas fought a series of fierce battles in the southern backcountry
   B. British forces were buoyed by increasing loyalist strength in the South
   C. Cherokee units in the Carolina backcountry switched to the patriot side
   D. the French convinced the Indians to fight the British along with their forces

7. In the video, Professor Sheila Skemp observes that loyalists in the South were _____.
   A. firmly opposed to slavery
   B. quickly joining the regular British army
   C. mostly recent immigrants from Barbados
   D. less numerous than the British thought

8. The British lost the Revolutionary War primarily because _____.
   A. their food supply was cut off by heavy rains every few months
   B. there were very few loyalists to help them win the war
   C. the French alliance doomed them to defeat
   D. royal governors were imprisoned early in the war

Short Answer: Your answers should be one or two paragraphs long and specifically address the points indicated.

9. Who were the loyalists in the Revolutionary War? Why were they the "true losers" in the war?

10. How and why did the Battle of Oriskany affect the outcome of the Battle of Saratoga?

11. Who were the "Molly Pitchers" of the war? How did women support the war effort?

12. What effect did the French alliance have on the outcome of the Revolutionary War?

Essay Questions: Your answers should be several paragraphs long and express a clear understanding of the points indicated.

13. Describe and explain the roles played by loyalists, African Americans, women, and American Indians during the Revolutionary War. How did the outcome of the war affect them?

14. Describe and explain why the British lost and the Americans won the Revolutionary War. In your answer, cite key military battles as well as other factors.

ANSWER KEY

	Answer	Learning Objectives	Focus Points	References
1.	B	LO 1	FP 1, 2, 3	pp. 222–225; video segments 1, 2
2.	C	LO 2	FP 10	p. 236
3.	A	LO 3	FP 5	pp. 227–228; video segments 1, 2
4.	B	LO 3	FP 12	pp. 237–238; video segment 3
5.	A	LO 3	FP 15	video segment 5
6.	A	LO 3	FP 18	pp. 242–243; video segment 6
7.	D	LO 4, 5	FP 16	pp. 241–243; video segment 6
8.	C	LO 4	FP 21	pp. 246–247; video segment 6

9. ....LO 1, 2, 5.........FP 8, 9, 22 .... pp. 229–233, 236, 244–247; video segments 6, 7
- Consider the economic status, political positions, and location of the loyalists.
- What did they have at stake in the Revolution? What happened to them at the end of the war?

10. ....LO 3.................FP 11 ....pp. 236–240; video segment 3
- What happened at Oriskany, particularly in reference to the American Indians' role?
- What did the British army do after Oriskany?
- How did lack of reinforcement affect Burgoyne at Saratoga?

11. ....LO 2, 5.............FP 7, 15 ....p. 213–214, 228–229; video segment 5
- What does the term *pitcher* indicate about what these women were doing?
- How were some of these women drawn into combat?
- What roles did women play on the home front? How did they help the military?

12. ....LO 4.............FP 13, 21 ....pp. 240–241, 246–247 ; video segment 3
- What types of support did the French provide?
- Why would the French alliance give concern to Britain?
- How did Yorktown illustrate the French effect?

13.   LO 5   FP 22   pp. 244–247; video segment 7

- Who were the loyalists? How did they help the British? What happened to them?
- How were African Americans pursuing freedom? What happened to them?
- What did women do during the war? How did this affect post-war conditions?
- How and why were American Indians caught in the middle of the war? Why was the outcome of the war likely to cause them more problems?

14.   LO 1–4   FP 21   pp. 246–247; all video segments

- Consider the British task and mistakes: Could they conquer the countryside? Did they take the Americans seriously? Did they overestimate the loyalist support? Did they have a cause which would sustain the fight?
- Consider American strengths: How important was George Washington? How critical was French help? How committed were American troops and political leaders? How compelling was the American cause?
- Consider the battles of Long Island, Trenton, Oriskany, Saratoga, Monmouth, and Yorktown.

ENRICHMENT IDEAS

These activities are not required unless your instructor assigns them. They are offered as suggestions to help you learn more about the material presented in this lesson.

1. Imagine yourself to be a young man or woman in August 1776. In a thoughtful essay, write an explanation of why you are choosing to be a patriot or a loyalist. How are you going to act upon your convictions?

2. In the video, Professor Calvin L. Christman observes that during the Revolutionary War the British army was like an iron hammer thrown into a silo of shucked corn. In a well-developed essay, explain what he meant, citing key military engagements to illustrate your points.

3. If you live in an area where significant military action took place during the Revolutionary War, research what happened. Then submit a report in which you describe what happened and how it affected the course of the war.

4. Recruitment of troops is usually a challenge for any nation. Research how the United States recruited military personnel during the Revolutionary War and how it recruits them at the present time. Then submit a report on your findings. What are the similarities and differences? Why do recruits join the military? What are the rewards and risks?

5. The Revolutionary War is often referred to as "England's Vietnam." After researching the Vietnam conflict, write an essay in which you compare and contrast the position of England with that of the United States in Vietnam.

SUGGESTED READINGS/RESOURCES

See the "Bibliography" on page 247 of the text if you wish to examine other books and resources related to the material presented in this lesson.

DOCUMENTS

As George Washington took command of colonial forces in 1775, he suffered from concern over the fitness of his command, and the usefulness of the state militia forces. In the following letter he vents his frustration with the militia.

As you read this document, focus on answering the following questions:

1. What were his primary concerns?
2. Did his objections seem realistic, or was he just biased about these untraditional forces?

"The Unreliable Militia" (1776) by George Washington

To place any dependence upon militia is assuredly resting upon a broken staff. Men just dragged from the tender scenes of domestic life, unaccustomed to the din of arms, totally unacquainted with every kind of military skill, which (being followed by want of confidence in themselves when opposed to troops regularly trained, disciplined, and appointed, superior in knowledge and superior in arms) makes them timid and ready to fly from their own shadows.

Besides, the sudden change in their manner of living (particularly in the lodging) brings on sickness in many, impatience in all, and such an unconquerable desire of returning to their respective homes that it not only produces shameful and scandalous desertions among themselves, but infuses the like spirit in others.

Again, men accustomed to unbounded freedom and no control cannot brook the restraint which is indispensably necessary to the good order and government of an army, without which licentiousness and every kind of disorder triumphantly reign.

The jealousies [suspicions] of a standing army, and the evils to be apprehended from one, are remote, and, in my judgment, situated and circumstanced as we are, not at all to be dreaded. But the consequence of wanting [lacking] one, according to my ideas formed from the present view of things, is certain and inevitable ruin. For, if I was called upon to declare upon oath whether the militia have been most serviceable or hurtful upon the whole, I should subscribe to the latter.

J. C. Fitzpatrick, ed., *The Writings of George Washington* (1931), vol. 6, pp.110–112 (September 24, 1776).

In 1830, Joseph Plumb Martin recalled his military service as a common soldier during the American Revolutionary War. Enlisting at age sixteen, he was involved in many of the important military events of the war. He left the most extensive account of any "common soldier."

As you read this document, focus on answering the following questions:

1. What were his recollections of his enlistment?
2. How did he describe his life as a soldier? What were his concerns?

"Memoir, 1830" by Joseph Plumb Martin

During the winter of 1775–76, by hearing the conversation and disputes of the good old farmer politicians of the times, I collected pretty correct ideas of the contest between this country and the mother country (as it was then called). I thought I was as warm a patriot as the best of them; the war was waged; we had joined issue, and it would not do to "put the hand to the plough and look back." I felt more anxious than ever, if possible, to be called a defender of my country.

However, the time soon arrived that gratified all my wishes. In the month of June, this year, orders came out for enlisting men for six months from the 25th of this month. The troops were styled new levies; they were to go to New York. And notwithstanding I was told that the British army at that place was reinforced by 15,000 men, it made no alteration in my mind; I did not care if there had been 15 times 15,000, I should have gone just as soon as if there had been but 1,500. I never spent a thought about numbers; the Americans were invincible in my opinion. If anything affected me, it was a stronger desire to see them.

I used frequently to go to the rendezvous, where I saw many of my young associates enlist, had repeated banterings to engage with them, but still when it came "case in hand," I had my misgivings. If I once undertake, thought I, I must stick to it; there will be no receding. Thoughts like these would, at times, almost overset my resolutions.

But . . . I one evening went off with a full determination to enlist at all hazards. When I arrived at the place of rendezvous I found a number of young men of my acquaintance there. The old bantering began — come, if you will enlist I will, says one; you have long been talking about it, says another — come, now is the time. "Thinks I to myself," I will not be laughed into it or out of it, at any rate; I will act my own pleasure after all. But what did I come here for tonight? Why, to enlist; then enlist I will. So seating myself at the table, enlisting orders were immediately presented to me; I took up the pen, loaded it with the fatal charge. . . . Well, thought I, I may as well go through with the business now as not. So I wrote my name fairly upon the indentures. And now I was a soldier, in name at least, if not in practice.

I now bid a final farewell to the service.

When those who engaged to serve during the war enlisted, they were promised a hundred acres of land each, which was to be in their own or the adjoining states. When the country had drained the last drop of service it could screw out of the poor soldiers, they were turned adrift like old worn-out horses, and nothing said about land to pasture them upon. Congress did, indeed, appropriate lands under the denomination of "Soldiers' lands," in Ohio state, or some state, or a future state; but no care was taken that the soldiers should get them. The truth was, none cared for them; the country was served, and faithfully served, and that was all that was deemed necessary. It was, soldiers, look to yourselves, we want no more of you.

They were likewise promised the following articles of clothing per year. One uniform coat, a woolen and a linen waistcoat, four shirts, four pair of shoes, four pair of stockings, a pair of woolen and a pair of linen overalls, a hat or a leather cap, a stock for the neck, a hunting shirt, a pair of shoe buckles, and a blanket. Ample clothing, says the reader; and ample clothing, say I. But what did we ever realize of all this ample store—why, perhaps a coat (we generally did get that) and one or two shirts, the same of shoes and stockings, and, indeed, the same may be said of every other article of clothing—a few dribbled out in a regiment two or three times in a year, never getting a whole suit at a time, and all of the poorest quality; and blankets thin enough to have straws shot through without discommoding the threads. How often have I had to lie whole stormy, cold nights in a wood, on a field, or a bleak hill with such blankets and other clothing like them, with nothing but the canopy of the heavens to cover me. All this too in the heart of winter when a New England farmer, if his cattle had been in my situation, would not have slept a wink from sheer anxiety for them. And if I stepped into a house to warm me when passing, wet to the skin and almost dead with cold, hunger, and fatigue, what scornful looks and hard words have I experienced.

Almost every one has heard of the soldiers of the Revolution being tracked by the blood of their feet on the frozen ground. This is literally true; and the thousandth part of their sufferings has not, nor ever will be told. That the country was young and poor at that time, I am willing to allow; but young people are generally modest, especially females. Now, I think the country (although of the feminine gender, for we say "she" and "her" of it) showed but little modesty at the time alluded to, for she appeared to think her soldiers had no private parts; for on our march from the Valley Forge, through the jerseys, and at the boasted Battle of Monmouth, a fourth part of the troops had not a scrip of anything but their ragged shirt flaps to cover their nakedness, and were obliged to remain so long after. I had picked up a few articles of light clothing during the past winter, while among the Pennsylvania farmers, or I should have been in the same predicament. "Rub and go" was always the Revolutionary soldier's motto.

When we engaged in the service we were promised the following articles for a ration: One pound of good and wholesome fresh or salt beef, or three fourths of a pound of good salt pork, a pound of good flour, soft or hard bread, a quart of salt to every hundred pounds of fresh beef, a quart vinegar to a hundred rations, a gill of rum, brandy, or whiskey per day, some little soap and candies, I have forgot how much, for I had so little of these two articles that I never knew the quantity. And as to the article of vinegar, I do not recollect of ever having any except a spoonful at the famous rice and vinegar thanksgiving in Pennsylvania in the year 1777.

But we never received what was allowed us. Oftentimes have I gone one, two, three, and even four days without a morsel, unless the fields or forests might chance to afford enough to prevent absolute starvation. Often when I have picked the last grain from the bones of my scanty morsel, have I ate the very bones, as much of them as possibly could be eaten, and then have had to perform some hard and fatiguing duty when my stomach has been as craving as it was before I had eaten anything at all. When General Washington told Congress, "The soldiers eat every kind of horse fodder but hay," he might have gone a little farther and told them that they eat considerable hog's fodder and not a trifle of dog's, when they could get it to eat.

We were also promised six dollars and two thirds a month, to be paid us monthly, and how did we fare in this particular? Why, as we did in every other. I received the six dollars and two thirds, till (if I remember rightly) the month of August, 1777, when paying ceased. And what was six dollars and sixty-seven cents of this "Continental currency," as it was called, worth? It was scarcely enough to procure a man a dinner. Government was ashamed to tantalize the soldiers any longer with such trash, and wisely gave it up for its own credit. I received one month's pay in specie while on the march to Virginia, in the year 1781, and except that I never received any pay worth the name while I belonged to the army. Had I been paid as I was promised to be at my engaging in the service, I needed not to have suffered as I did, nor would I have done it; there was enough in the country, and money would have procured it if I had had it. It is provoking to think of it. The country was rigorous in exacting my compliance to my engagements to a punctilio, but equally careless in performing her contracts with me; and why so? One reason was because she had all the power in her own hands, and I had none. Such things ought not to be.

The poor soldiers had hardships enough to endure without having to starve; the least that could be done was to give them something to eat. "The laborer is worthy of his meat" at least, and he ought to have it for his employer's interest, if nothing more. But as I said, there were other hardships to grapple with. How many times have I had to lie down like a dumb animal in the field and bear "the pelting of the pitiless storm," cruel enough in warm weather, but how much more so in the heart of winter. Could I have had the benefit of a little fire, it would have been deemed a luxury. But when snow or rain would fall so heavy that it was impossible to keep a spark of fire alive, to have to weather out a long, wet, cold, tedious night in the depth of winter with scarcely clothes enough to keep one from freezing instantly, how discouraging it must be I leave to my reader to judge.

It is fatiguing, almost beyond belief, to those that never experienced it, to be obliged to march 24 to 48 hours (as very many times I have had to) and often more, night and day without rest or sleep, wishing and hoping that some wood or village I could see ahead might prove a short resting place, when, alas, I came to it almost tired off my legs, it proved no resting place for me. How often have I envied the very swine their happiness, when I have heard them quarreling in their warm dry sties, when I was wet to the skin and wished in vain for that indulgence. And even in dry, warm weather, I have often been so beat out with long and tedious marching that I have fallen asleep while walking the road, and not been sensible of it till I have jostled against someone in the same situation; and when permitted to stop and have the superlative happiness to roll myself in my blanket and drop down on the ground in the bushes, briars, thorns, or thistles, and get an hour or two's sleep, O! how exhilarating.

Fighting the enemy is the great scarecrow to people unacquainted with the duties of an army. To see the fire and smoke, to hear the din of cannon and musketry and the whistling of shot; they cannot bear the sight or hearing of this. They would like the service in an army tolerably well but for the fighting part of it. I never was killed in the army; I never was wounded but once; I never was a prisoner with the enemy; but I have seen many that have undergone all these; and I have many times run the risk of all of them myself. But, reader, believe me, for I tell a solemn truth, that I have felt more anxiety, undergone more fatigue and hardships, suffered more every way, in performing one of those tedious marches than ever I did in fighting the hottest battle I was ever engaged in, with the anticipation of all the other calamities I have mentioned added to it.

It was said at that time that the army was idle, did nothing but lounge about from one station to another, eating the country's bread and wearing her clothing without rendering any essential service. You ought to drive on, said they, you are competent for the business; rid the country at once of her invaders. Poor simple souls! It was very easy for them to build castles in the air, but they had not felt the difficulty of making them stand there. It was easier with them taking whole armies in a warm room and by a good fire than enduring the hardships of one cold winter's night upon a bleak hill without clothing or victuals.

James Kirby Martin, ed., *Ordinary Courage*: *The Revolutionary War Adventures of Joseph Plumb Martin* (Saint James, NY: Brandywine Press, 1993), pp. 11–16.

Lesson 10

Inventing a Nation

OVERVIEW

Having won the Revolutionary War and being recognized as independent, the United States now faced the challenges of nation building. Foremost among these challenges was trying to establish a viable representative government. The Declaration of Independence had laid down a clear statement about the source and purpose of government, but it was NOT a constitution.

During the 1780s, the American people grappled with the persistent issue of distributing political power among individuals, states, and the national government. The first written frame of government agreed upon by the states of the new nation was the Articles of Confederation. This document reflected the desires of most American revolutionaries. The central government was weak, and ultimate political sovereignty rested with the states. Some states did take significant steps toward implementing effective republican government, but the lack of a strong central government proved to be increasingly troubling to influential national leaders as the 1780s proceeded.

When the Constitutional Convention convened in 1787, James Madison was ready to direct the meeting toward the creation of a new national government. The Preamble of the Constitution of the United States of America states the purpose of the document, and subsequent articles clearly shift the locus of political power to the central government. Such a drastic change in structure made many people uneasy, and ratification of the Constitution was not a sure thing. Again, Madison stepped forward to reassure the American people that liberty and justice would be made more secure by the larger majority of the whole United States. Once the Bill of Rights was added to the Constitution, opposition to the document itself largely dissipated.

What people did continue to disagree about was what the Constitution meant. Over two hundred years later, that debate still goes on. As Professor Jack Rakove points out in the video, historical experience with the Constitution allows us to know more about what the Constitution means than the founding generation. The Constitution has and will continue to be vital in the process of shaping America.

LESSON ASSIGNMENTS

Text: Roark, et al., *The American Promise,* Chapter 8, "Building a Republic," pp. 251–283 and Chapter 9, "The New Nation Takes Form," pp. 290–291

Video: "Inventing a Nation" from the series *Shaping America*

Documents:
      "The Articles of Confederation," pp. A3–A6 in the textbook
      "The Constitution of the United States of America," pp. A7–A15 in the textbook

LEARNING OBJECTIVES

This lesson examines how and why the United States adopted the Constitution and what that has meant for the American people. Upon completing this lesson, you should be able to:

1. Analyze the successes and failures of the state governments and the national government under the Articles of Confederation during the 1780s.

2. Explain the background and proceedings of the Constitutional Convention.

3. Describe the main features of the Constitution.

4. Describe the process of ratifying the Constitution and the results of that process.

5. Explain the origins and purpose of the Bill of Rights.

6. Analyze both the short- and long-term significance of the Constitution.

LESSON FOCUS POINTS

The following questions are designed to help you get the most benefit from the sources selected for this lesson. For reference purposes, the titles for the video segments are: (1) Introduction, (2) "A More Perfect Union," (3) "Behind Closed Doors," (4) "The Race to Ratify," (5) "The Bill of Rights," and (6) Summary Analysis: "More Than a Blueprint."

1. What was the Newburgh Conspiracy? What did it indicate about George Washington and the state of the nation in 1783? (video segment 1)

2. What type of national government did the Articles of Confederation establish? Why did the Articles of Confederation leave so much political power with the states? Was this a good idea? What are the dangers inherent in this approach? (textbook, pp. A3–A6, 252–255; video segment 2)

3. Why was the cession of western land claims by the states a crucial issue in the 1780s? Examine Map 8.1 on page 254 of the text, and answer the questions posed there. (textbook, pp. 253–255)

4. How did the state constitutions of the 1770s and 1780s address the goals of republican government? How and why did they restrict political participation? (textbook, pp. 255–258)

5. What actions did the states take regarding slavery in the 1770s and 1780s? What were the consequences of these actions? (textbook, pp. 258–262)

6. What explains the financial problems associated with the Confederation period? (textbook, pp. 262–264; video segment 2)

7. How did the Treaty of Fort Stanwix illustrate relations with American Indians? What is significant about the Land Ordinance of 1785 and the Northwest Ordinance of 1787? (textbook, pp. 264–269; video segment 2)

8. What was Shays's Rebellion all about? Why was it important? (textbook, pp. 269–271; video segment 2)

9. Why was a Constitutional Convention called? Who were the delegates? Why did they conduct their business in secret? (textbook, pp. 271–273; video segment 3)

10. How and why did James Madison prepare for the Constitutional Convention? What role did Madison play at the convention? How did the Virginia and New Jersey plans address the major issues at the convention? (textbook, pp. 252, 274; video segment 3)

11. How did the Great Compromise and the three-fifths compromise resolve questions about representation? What other references about slavery were in the Constitution? (textbook, pp. 274; video segment 3)

12. What does the Preamble to the Constitution say? What does it mean? (textbook, p. A7; video segments 2 and 3)

13. How did the Constitution fundamentally differ from the Articles of Confederation? How did it establish a republican and not a democratic government? How was power limited by the Constitution? (textbook, pp. 275, A7–A11; video segment 3)

14. How did the process for ratifying the Constitution proceed? What areas were for and against ratification? Why were Virginia and New York important for ratification? (textbook, pp. 275–279; video segment 4)

15. Who were the Federalists? How and why did they encourage ratification? Why are the *Federalist* papers important? (textbook, pp. 276–279; video segment 4)

16. Who were the Antifederalists? Why did they hold the position that they did? What is the legacy of their views? (textbook, pp. 277–279; video segment 4)

17. How and why did the Constitution address religion as it did? What was important about that? (textbook, pp. 280–281)

18. What is the primary purpose and effect of the Bill of Rights? (textbook, p. 290–291, appendix pp. A12–A15; video segment 5)

19. In summary, what does the Constitution mean to America? (textbook, p. 282; video segment 6)

HISTORICAL EXPERTS INTERVIEWED

Jack Rakove, Coe Professor of History and American Studies, Stanford University, Stanford, CA
Gordon Wood, Alva O. Way University Professor and Professor of History, Brown University,
    Providence, RI
Mel Yazawa, Professor of History, University of New Mexico, Albuquerque, NM

PRACTICE TEST

The following items will help you evaluate your understanding of this lesson. Use the Answer Key at the end of the lesson to check your answers or to locate material related to each question.

Multiple choice: Choose the BEST answer.

1. At Newburgh, New York, in 1783, disgruntled army officers _____.
    A. discussed threatening Congress if their demands were not met
    B. advocated removing George Washington from his commander-in-chief position
    C. established a military academy later relocated to West Point
    D. refused to support ongoing treaty negotiations with the British

2. The weaknesses of Congress under the Articles of Confederation included its lack of _____.
    A. an executive or judicial branch or the power to levy taxes
    B. ability to get money to finance the war
    C. a way to amend the Articles, if that should be needed
    D. ability to conduct foreign relations

3. The states were reluctant to include "equality language" in their bills of rights and constitutions because _____.
    A. they were afraid that the words could be construed to apply to slaves
    B. slaves might sue in court to gain their freedom
    C. women might think they were equal to men and want the vote
    D. children as young as twelve might think they could vote

4. Shays's Rebellion of 1786 was the result of _____.
    A. debt-strapped merchants in Boston
    B. increased taxes and foreclosures on farms in Massachusetts
    C. commercial and eastern creditors' harsh payment terms
    D. Samuel Adams inciting farmers in Massachusetts

5. In the video, Professor Mel Yazawa offers the view that the proceedings of the Constitutional Convention were kept secret so that members could _____.
    A. speak without fear of retribution
    B. cover up their true feelings
    C. more easily skip the meetings
    D. escape the scrutiny of the media

---

6. When the Constitution was drafted, slavery _____.
   A. was not named, but its existence was recognized and guaranteed
   B. was the most hotly debated issue
   C. was euphemistically outlawed
   D. was explicitly named as being a landowner's liberty

7. Before the Constitution could go into effect it had to be ratified by _____.
   A. state legislatures of twelve states
   B. a simple majority of the states
   C. all thirteen states
   D. ratifying conventions in nine states

8. To persuade the powerful state of Virginia to ratify the Constitution, Federalists promised that _____.
   A. George Washington would become the first president
   B. a Bill of Rights would be added to the Constitution
   C. the national debt would be funded at face value
   D. the national capital would be in Virginia

9. In the video, Professor Rakove observes that James Madison believed that a bill of rights would become effective when _____.
   A. people internalized the principles enunciated
   B. the Supreme Court was able to clarify the meaning
   C. states were bound by the same principles
   D. the president enforced the law

Short Answer: Your answers should be one or two paragraphs long and specifically address the points indicated.

10. Why was the decade of the 1780s a "critical period" for the United States?

11. What features of the Land Ordinance of 1785 and the Northwest Ordinance of 1787 had long-term significance in the shaping of America?

12. Why is James Madison called the "Father of the Constitution"?

13. Why is it difficult to determine the "original meanings" of the Constitution? In what ways do we know more about what the Constitution means than the people who wrote the document?

Essay Question: Your answer should be several paragraphs long and express a clear understanding of the points indicated.

14. During the 1780s, the revolutionary generation made fundamental changes in the framework of the national government. In a well-developed essay, address the following questions: (1) Why was the Articles of Confederation replaced by the Constitution? (2) How did the Constitution alter the structure and operation of the national government? (3) What does the Constitution mean to America?

ANSWER KEY

Answer	Learning Objectives	Focus Points	References
1. A	LO 1	FP 1	video segment 1
2. A	LO 1	FP 2	pp. 252–255; video segment 2
3. A	LO 1	FP 5	pp. 258–262
4. B	LO 2	FP 8	pp. 269–271; video segment 2
5. A	LO 2	FP 9	pp. 271–273; video segment 3
6. A	LO 3	FP 11	p. 274; video segment 3
7. D	LO 4	FP 14	pp. 275–279; video segment 4
8. B	LO 4, 5	FP 14	pp. 275–279; video segment 4
9. A	LO 5	FP 18	video segment 5

10. ....LO 1..............FP 1–9 .... pp. 252–273; video segments 1, 2, 3
    - Consider the financial difficulties at the time.
    - What problems with foreign countries existed?
    - How were the state and central governments dealing with pressing issues?

11. ....LO 1..............FP 7 ....pp. 265–269; video segment 2
    - What pattern of survey and sale of land was established?
    - What precedents were set by the Northwest Ordinance?
    - How did these laws affect the future of the United States?

12. ....LO 2–4.........FP 10, 15, 18 .... pp. 252, 274, 276–279, 290–291, A14–A17; .... video segments 3–5
    - What role did Madison play at the Convention?
    - How did he influence the ratification process?
    - What effect did he have on the Bill of Rights?
    - How did he affect our historical record of the times?

13. ....LO 6..................FP 19 ....video segment 6
   - Whose "original meanings" are at issue?
   - What records do we have?
   - To what degree were the framers experimenting at the time?
   - What has experience taught us about the meaning?

14. ....LO 1–6.............FP 1–19..........pp. 252–283, 290–291, A3–A15; video segments 1–6
   - What were the fundamental problems with the Articles?
   - Who was pushing for change and why?
   - Describe the major changes brought about by the Constitution in the operations of the national government.
   - What effect does the Constitution have on stabilizing government?
   - What effect does it have on national identity? How does the average citizen use the Constitution?

ENRICHMENT IDEAS

These activities are not required unless your instructor assigns them. They are offered as suggestions to help you learn more about the material presented in this lesson.

1. Imagine yourself to be either a Federalist or an Antifederalist during the debate over the ratification of the Constitution. In a thoughtful essay, explain your position for or against ratifying that document.

2. The Constitutional Convention was a "closed door" meeting. Write a position paper in which you either defend this type of secrecy or you attack it. How do you balance secret meetings with the people's "right to know"?

SUGGESTED READINGS/RESOURCES

See the "Bibliography" on pages 282–283 of the text if you wish to examine other books and resources related to the material presented in this lesson.

Lesson 11

Searching for Stability

OVERVIEW

By 1789, the American people were searching for stability. They had experienced a successful revolution and just made a significant change in their frame of government. Anxiety was mixed with excitement, for it was still uncertain if the large new republic could survive and, if it did, what kind of nation it would become.

The second video segment of this lesson presents "the state of the nation" in 1789. Revisiting the six geographical locations featured in this course gives a sense of what was happening, both within the new nation and in regions beyond the national boundaries at that time. Then the video goes on to examines how the actions taken to address the most pressing political and economic issues of the time shaped the destiny of the nation.

Politically, a whole new structure of government had to be implemented. Who better than George Washington to direct this process? Once again he assumed power, bringing his leadership and integrity to the new role of president of the United States. Surrounded by domestic and foreign conflicts, Washington provided a monumental stabilizing foundation to the national political scene. And then, once again, he gave up power. Without question, George Washington and his legacy have shaped America.

Economically, recurring questions swirled around debts, taxes, and financial stability. To address these concerns, President Washington turned to Alexander Hamilton, the first secretary of the treasury. Hamilton proceeded to put forward a plan that would stabilize the economy and move the nation toward his vision of an urban capitalist society. Hamilton and his plan attracted spirited opposition, but he prevailed, shaping the American economy both in the short-term and for generations afterward.

LESSON ASSIGNMENTS

Text: Roark, et al., *The American Promise,* Chapter 9, "The New Nation Takes Form,"
          pp. 286–302

Video: "Searching for Stability" from the series *Shaping America*

Documents:
          "Jefferson Versus Hamilton on the Bank" found at the end of this lesson

---

LEARNING OBJECTIVES

This lesson describes the state of the nation in 1789 and how actions taken by George Washington and Alexander Hamilton helped shape America. Upon completing this lesson, you should be able to:

1. Describe the state of the nation in 1789 and in the years immediately following.

2. Analyze how President George Washington provided political stability to the new nation.

3. Analyze Alexander Hamilton's economic plan and his vision for America.

LESSON FOCUS POINTS

The following questions are designed to help you get the most benefit from the sources selected for this lesson. For reference purposes, the titles for the video segments are: (1) Introduction, (2) "The State of the Nation," (3) "Hamilton's Republic," (4) Short-take: "The Whiskey Rebellion," (5) "Washington's Legacy," and (6) Summary Analysis: "The Vision That Prevailed."

1. How did Alexander Hamilton's and Thomas Jefferson's visions for America differ? (video segment 1)

2. How and why did President George Washington and his appointments to his first cabinet provide some hope for stability at the outset of the Washington administration? (textbook, pp. 286–290; video segment 1)

3. How and why did voting qualifications change in the 1790s? To what extent was the role of women changing at that time? (textbook, pp. 290–294)

4. How and why were commercial agriculture, transportation, and commercial banking changing in the 1790s? How did these changes affect the American people? (textbook, pp. 294–295)

5. How would you characterize life in New York City and Charleston at this time? Describe the key features of St. Louis, Sante Fe, San Francisco, and the Willamette Valley. (video segment 2)

6. Why was Alexander Hamilton uniquely qualified to deal with the national economy in 1789? (textbook, pp. 287–288; video segment 3)

7. What did Hamilton propose to do with the national and state debts? Why did he make these proposals? Why did Jefferson and Madison oppose Hamilton's proposals? (textbook, pp. 295–298; video segment 3)

8. How did Washington, D.C., become the federal capital? (textbook, pp. 300–301; video segment 3)

9. What taxes did Hamilton recommend that Congress impose? Why did he take this approach? (textbook, pp. 298–299, 302; video segment 3)

10. Why did Hamilton propose the creation of a national bank? Why did Madison and Jefferson oppose this measure? How did the discussions surrounding this issue illustrate differing interpretations of the Constitution? What was the political fallout from all of this? (textbook, p. 298; document; video segment 3)

11. Why did the Whiskey Rebellion take place? How did Hamilton and Washington deal with it? What did this rebellion illustrate? (textbook, pp. 299, 302; video segment 4)

12. Why is George Washington considered one of the greatest presidents of the United States? What was his legacy to America? (video segment 5)

13. In summary, what were the effects of Hamilton's economic plan? How did it shape America? How has Hamilton's vision shaped modern America? (textbook, pp. 287–290, 294–302; video segment 6)

HISTORICAL EXPERTS INTERVIEWED

Joyce Appleby, Professor of History, University of California at Los Angeles, Los Angeles, CA

Robert Archibald, President, Missouri Historical Society, St. Louis, MO

Carol Berkin, Professor of History, City University of New York, New York City, NY

Richard Brookhiser, Senior Editor, *National Review*, New York City, NY

Alphonso Brown, Owner/Operator, Gullah Tours, Charleston, SC

Charles Fracchia, President, San Francisco Historical Society, San Francisco, CA

John Steele Gordon, Economic Historian, North Salem, NY

Frances Levine, Ph.D., Division Head of Arts and Sciences, Santa Fe Community College, Santa Fe, NM

Chet Orloff, Director, Oregon Historical Society, Portland, OR

Jonathan Poston, Director of Museums and Preservation Initiatives, Historic Charleston Foundation, Charleston, SC

Mike Wallace, Co-author of *Gotham*, John Jay College, New York City, NY

PRACTICE TEST

The following items will help you evaluate your understanding of this lesson. Use the Answer Key at the end of the lesson to check your answers or to locate material related to each question.

Multiple choice: Choose the BEST answer.

1. Among Washington's first duties as a president was _____.
   A. selecting cabinet members to serve him
   B. asking Congress for a judiciary bill
   C. deciding on the number and the names of cabinet offices
   D. choosing a chief justice of the Supreme Court

2. According to republican ideals of the late eighteenth century, the most important role of women and mothers was _____.
   A. teaching virtuous sons
   B. running an orderly household
   C. volunteering for church activities
   D. obeying their husbands

3. In the 1790s, road building and commercial stagecoach travel failed to progress south of the Potomac River like it did in New England and the Middle Atlantic states because _____.
   A. they envisioned the coming of railroads
   B. passenger demand was low
   C. Southerners didn't have the money to build roads and fund stagecoach companies
   D. elite Southerners were opposed to improvements

4. Even though a wealthy elite dominated Charleston, South Carolina, by 1790 _____.
   A. African Americans were playing key roles in the community
   B. backcountry farmers controlled state politics
   C. Indian peoples in the region posed a threat to the city
   D. the rich were reluctant to display their wealth

5. As president, George Washington _____.
   A. was a brilliant thinker and strong political strategist
   B. was congenial and outgoing
   C. was virtuous, aloof, resolute, and dignified
   D. did not like pomp and ceremony

6. Alexander Hamilton's vision for America differed from Thomas Jefferson's in the respect that _____.
   A. Jefferson wanted to foster manufacturing
   B. Hamilton admired the British model
   C. Jefferson favored a hierarchical system
   D. Hamilton encouraged rural development

7. Which of Hamilton's economic programs was attacked as unconstitutional by Thomas Jefferson?
    A. Creation of a national bank
    B. Federal assumption of state debts
    C. Placement of an excise tax on whiskey
    D. Passage of protective tariffs

Short Answer: Your answers should be one or two paragraphs long and specifically address the points indicated.

8. What problems faced Alexander Hamilton as he took the office of secretary of the treasury?

9. Why was Washington, D.C., an area not controlled by any state, chosen as the location of the permanent federal capital?

10. How can the Whiskey Rebellion be seen as more than just a revolt of unhappy farmers?

Essay Questions: Your answers should be several paragraphs long and express a clear understanding of the points indicated.

11. Why is George Washington considered to be one of the United States' greatest presidents? In your answer, be sure to consider the times, his personal qualities, and his legacy. How and why does Washington live on in the American memory?

12. Describe and explain Alexander Hamilton's three-part economic program for the new nation, and analyze the success of each of the three components. To what extent do you think Hamilton's vision of America has prevailed?

ANSWER KEY

Answer	Learning Objectives	Focus Points	References
1. A	LO 2	FP 2	pp. 286–289; video segment 1
2. A	LO 1	FP 3	pp. 290–294
3. B	LO 1	FP 4	pp. 294–295
4. A	LO 1	FP 5	video segment 2
5. C	LO 2	FP 2, 12	pp. 286–290; video segments 1, 5
6. B	LO 3	FP 1	video segment 1
7. A	LO 3	FP 10	p. 298; document; video segment 3

8. ....LO 3.............FP 7, 9, 10 ....pp. 295–299, 302; document; video segment 3
   - What was the debt situation at the national and state level?
   - How much confidence did people have in the national government's ability to deal effectively with economic issues?
   - What revenue could the government count on?
   - What was the banking situation in the country?

9. ....LO 1, 2, 3.............FP 8...pp. 300–301; video segment 3
   - What does the Constitution say about a capital?
   - How was the location connected to the assumption of the state debts?
   - What role did George Washington play in selecting the site?

10. ....LO 2, 3.............FP 11 ....pp. 299, 302; video segment 4
   - How did Hamilton view the rebellion?
   - Why did Washington connect the rebellion to the meaning of the American Revolution?
   - What would have happened if the rebellion had been successful?

11. ....LO 2............FP 2, 11, 12 ....pp. 286–290, 299–302; video segments 1, 4, 5
   - What made the 1790s a particularly important period in American history?
   - Describe Washington's strengths as a leader.
   - What precedents did Washington establish? What was important about his giving up power?
   - Why is it important that the nation have a history, and that Washington plays an important role in that?
   - Where do we see Washington memorialized today?

12. ....LO 3...FP 1, 6, 7, 9, 10, 11, 13 ..... pp. 287–288, 295–302; video segments 1, 3, 4, 6
   - What was the state of the nation economically when Hamilton came to the treasury?
   - How did he propose to deal with the debt issues? What were the results?
   - Why did Hamilton favor a national bank? What did it do? How effective was it?
   - What taxes did Hamilton favor? Why?
   - What were the overall effects of his program?
   - How does the United States mirror "Hamilton's Republic"?

ENRICHMENT IDEAS

These activities are not required unless your instructor assigns them. They are offered as suggestions to help you learn more about the material presented in this lesson.

1. As a new nation, the United States had to search for a usable past in the late eighteenth and early nineteenth centuries. In a well-developed essay, explain how George Washington became a national icon. What myths were created about him? Why? How? Do you think that he is an authentic American hero?

2. Research the similarities and differences between the functions and operations of the first Bank of the United States and the current Federal Reserve System. In a thoughtful essay, report on your findings.

3. Research how and why savings bonds have been used in America. Submit an essay in which you report on your findings.

4. Imagine yourself to be a successful merchant in 1790 who wants to expand your business and personal horizons. Using the available means of transportation at the time, plan and then describe your itinerary for a trip from New York City to Charleston, South Carolina, and then to St. Louis and back to New York. How long will it take you? What will you find?

5. In a well-developed essay, compare and contrast the Whiskey Rebellion with Shays's Rebellion.

6. Research the census data from 1790 and 2000. Submit a report comparing some of the information contained in the reports. For example, where was the demographic center of the country in each instance? How was ethnicity reported? How is census information used? What strikes you as the most interesting aspects of the reports?

SUGGESTED READINGS/RESOURCES

See the "Bibliography" on pages 316–317 of the text if you wish to examine other books and resources related to the material discussed in this lesson.

DOCUMENTS

The passage of a bill creating the Bank of the United States in 1791 occasioned the first debate concerning the constitutionality of an Act of Congress. In the following two pieces, one from Jefferson, and one from Alexander Hamilton, the issues of implied powers and the appropriate use of the "necessary and proper" clause are debated for the first time in the new government.

As you read this document, focus on answering the following questions:

1. What were Jefferson's reservations on creating the Bank? How does he justify his position?
2. How did Hamilton defend the bank bill? How does he justify the use of the "necessary and proper" clause.

"Jefferson Versus Hamilton on the Bank"

Jefferson
February 15, 1791

Hamilton
February 23, 1791

I consider the foundation of the Constitution as laid on this ground—that all powers not delegated to the United States by the Constitution, nor prohibited by it to the states, are reserved to the states, or to the people (12th [10th] amend.). To take a single step beyond the boundaries thus specifically drawn around the powers of Congress is to take possession of a boundless field of power, no longer susceptible of any definition. The incorporation of a bank, and the powers assumed by this bill, have not, in my opinion, been delegated to the United States by the Constitution.

The second general phrase is "to make all laws necessary and proper for carrying into execution the enumerated powers." But they can all be carried into execution without a bank. A bank therefore is not necessary, and consequently not authorized by this phrase.

It has been much urged that a bank will give great facility or convenience in the collection of taxes. Suppose this were true; yet the Constitution allows only the

If the end be clearly comprehended within any of the specified powers, and if the measure have an obvious relation to that end, and is not forbidden by any particular provision of the Constitution, it may safely be deemed to come within the compass of the national authority.

There is also this further criterion, which may materially assist the decision: Does the proposed measure abridge a pre-existing right of any state or of any individual? If it does not, there is a strong presumption in favor of its constitutionality.

"Necessary" often means no more than needful, requisite, incidental, useful, or conducive to. . . . [A] restrictive interpretation of the word "necessary" is also contrary to this sound maxim of construction: namely, that the powers contained in a constitution ought to be construed liberally in advancement of the public good.

A hope is entertained that it has, by this time, been made to appear to the means which are "necessary," not those which are merely "convenient," for effecting the enumerated powers. If such a latitude of construction be allowed to this phrase as to give any non-enumerated power, it [the latitude] will go to every one; for there is not one [power] which ingenuity may not torture into a convenience, in some instance or other, to some one of so long a list of enumerated powers. It would swallow up all the delegated powers [of the states,] and reduce the whole to one power.

satisfaction of the President, that a bank has a natural relation to the power of collecting taxes—to that of regulating trade—to that of providing for the common defense—and that, as the bill under consideration contemplates the government in the light of a joint proprietor of the stock of the bank, it brings the case within the provision of the clause of the Constitution which immediately respects [relates to] the property of the United States. (Evidently Art. N, Sec. III, para. 2: "The Congress shall have power to make all needful rules and regulations respecting the territory or other property belonging to the United States.")

H. C. Lodge, ed., *The Works of Alexander Hamilton* (1904), vol. 3, pp. 458, 452, 455, 485–486; and P. L. Ford, ed., *The Writings of Thomas Jefferson* (New York: G. P. Putnam's Sons, 1895), vol. 5, pp. 285, 287.

Lesson 12

A Peaceful Transfer of Power

OVERVIEW

As you have learned, George Washington's presence and Alexander Hamilton's economic plan provided some stability to the new nation in the early 1790s. Hamilton's critics may have questioned his approach, and the whiskey rebels may have disagreed with federal policy, but the rule of law prevailed. Resolution of other conflicts during the remainder of the 1790s continued to shape the United States by establishing precedents and moving the country toward a peaceful transfer of power.

Conflicts between settlers and American Indians were not new in the 1790s. What did happen was that the area of conflict moved west and precedent-setting treaties were now part of the supreme law of the land. That constitutional provision did not help Indians much in the short term, but ultimately treaties did give them a way to protect their rights or to seek compensation in more recent times.

Conflicts over foreign policy decisions relating to England and France presented another set of challenges to the new nation. While most national leaders agreed that neutrality was the wisest course to follow, sharp disagreements arose when that neutrality was violated. Attempts by those in power to censor their critics during an undeclared war with France brought about strong rebukes from Thomas Jefferson and James Madison.

Out of all the differences of opinion in the 1790s emerged the formation of the nation's first two distinct political parties. While sometimes unsettling, the functioning of political parties sharpened the debates on political issues and established political practices that affected the nation for generations. One of those practices, a peaceful transfer of power, remains a key to the stability of the nation.

As the last segment of the video illustrates, this lesson prompts some reflection on the revolutionary era. America looked quite different in 1801 than it had in 1760. Thirteen separate colonies had become a nation with generous boundaries and an emerging identity. Idealistic principles espousing freedom and equality were becoming part of a national creed. While American Indians were being separated from the rest of the nation, women and African Americans had some hope that they might be included on a more equal basis. Indeed, America did gain a future during the revolutionary era, and America's destiny would continue to be shaped by those who inherited the revolution.

LESSON ASSIGNMENTS

Text: Roark, et al., *The American Promise,* Chapter 9, "The New Nation Takes Form," pp. 302–319 and Chapter 10, "Republicans in Power," p. 323

Video: "A Peaceful Transfer of Power" from the series *Shaping America*

Documents:
     "The Crisis of 1798: Sedition," found on pp. 314–315 in the textbook

LEARNING OBJECTIVES

This lesson examines how and why the precedents established in the 1790s helped shape America. Upon completing this lesson, you should be able to:

1. Explain the origins and results of the conflicts with American Indians in the 1790s.

2. Analyze the foreign policy of the United States in the 1790s.

3. Explain the emergence of the Federalist and Republican political parties of the 1790s, their differing political philosophies, and their effect upon the political traditions of the nation.

4. Analyze the presidential election of 1800 and the importance of its outcome.

5. Analyze the significance of the revolutionary era in the shaping of America.

LESSON FOCUS POINTS

The following questions are designed to help you get the most benefit from the sources selected for this lesson. For reference purposes, the titles for the video segments are: (1) Introduction, (2) "The Treaty of Greenville," (3) Short-take: "The Supreme Law of the Land," (4) "The Quasi War," (5) "The Election of 1800," (6) Short-take: "The Election of 2000," and (7) Unit Summary: "All Men are Created Equal?"

1. Examine Map 9.2 on page 304 of the text. Answer the questions posed in the text. (textbook, p. 304)

2. What happened to General Arthur St. Clair and his military forces in the Ohio Valley region in the fall of 1791? What were the effects of this episode? (textbook, pp. 302–304; video segment 2)

3. What happened at the Battle of Fallen Timbers? (textbook, pp. 304–305; video segment 2)

4. What is the significance of the Treaty of Greenville? (textbook, pp. 304–306; video segment 2)

---

5. Why did treaties between the United States and Indian peoples have long-term significance? (video segments 2 and 3)

6. Why did the United States declare neutrality regarding conflicts between Britain and France in the 1790s? (textbook, pp. 306–308; video segment 4)

7. What was the Jay Treaty? Why was it so controversial? (textbook, pp. 308–309; video segment 4)

8. What was the Haitian Revolution? What effects did it have in the United States? (textbook, pp. 309–310)

9. Why did the results of the 1796 presidential election create a politically awkward situation? (textbook, pp. 310–311)

10. What was the XYZ affair? What effects did it have in the United States? Why did the United States have a "Quasi War" with France? What were the effects of this undeclared war? (textbook, pp. 311–312; video segment 4)

11. What were the Alien and Sedition Acts? What were they intended to accomplish? What effects did they have? (textbook, pp. 312–315; video segment 4)

12. Read the documents concerning "The Crisis of 1798: Sedition" found on pages 314–315 of the text. Answer the questions posed in the text. (textbook, pp. 314–315)

13. Why did Madison and Jefferson write the Virginia and Kentucky Resolutions? What key idea was put forward in these documents? What were the short- and long-term effects of the Resolutions? (textbook, pp. 312–313; video segment 4)

14. Why did President John Adams ultimately pursue peace with France? How did this affect his reelection chances? What does this say about Adams? (textbook, pp. 313, 316; video segment 4)

15. What were the long-term effects of President Washington's approach to neutrality and President Adams' pursuit of peace in the 1790s? (video segment 4)

16. How and why were political parties operating in the presidential election of 1800? What were the major differences between the Federalists and Republicans? (textbook, pp. 316, 323; video segment 5)

17. Why did Thomas Jefferson and Aaron Burr end up with the same number of votes in the electoral college in 1800? What change did this bring about in the electoral voting? (textbook, p. 323; video segment 5)

18. What is the short-term and long-term significance of the election of 1800 and the peaceful transfer of power which followed? (video segment 5)

19. What parallels exist between the elections of 1800 and 2000? (video segment 6)

20. In general, how did the revolutionary era (1760–1801) shape America? (video segment 7)

HISTORICAL EXPERTS INTERVIEWED

Joyce Appleby, Professor of History, University of California at Los Angeles, Los Angeles, CA

Colin Calloway, Professor, Dartmouth College, Hanover, NH

Gerald Danzer, Professor of History, University of Illinois at Chicago, Chicago, IL

R. David Edmunds, Watson Professor of American History, University of Texas at Dallas, Richardson, TX

Joseph J. Ellis, Professor of History, Mount Holyoke College, South Hadley, MA

Eric Foner, Professor of History, Columbia University, New York City, NY

James Oliver Horton, Benjamin Banneker Professor of American Civilization and History, The George Washington University, Washington, DC

Marilyn John, Bear Clan Mother, Oneida Indian Nation, Vernon, NY

Linda Kerber, May Brodbeck Professor in the Liberal Arts and Professor of History, University of Iowa, Iowa City, IA

Richard White, Margaret Byrne Professor of American History, Stanford University, Stanford, CA

Tony Wonderly, Nation Historian, Oneida Indian Nation, Oneida, NY

PRACTICE TEST

The following items will help you evaluate your understanding of this lesson. Use the Answer Key at the end of the lesson to check your answers or to locate material related to each question.

Multiple choice: Choose the BEST answer.

1. When the U.S. government's early policy toward the Indians in the Northwest Territory did not reap the anticipated results, _____.
   A. the troops that had been stationed there were withdrawn
   B. an expansion of military forces led to the total defeat of General St. Clair's army
   C. expanded military efforts by General St. Clair's army pushed the Indians back and made way for new settlement
   D. President Washington told all settlers to refrain from crossing the Ohio River to settle

2. As a result of the Treaty of Greenville (1795), _____.
   A. the British evacuated their forts in the Old Northwest
   B. U.S. military forces withdrew from Ohio
   C. American Indians lost their struggle to preserve the Ohio River as a boundary to white settlement
   D. The United States agreed to respect Indian tribal customs

3. One long-term benefit for Indians of treaties between the United States and Indian peoples is that _____.
   A. Indian lifestyles showed marked improvement in the nineteenth century
   B. liquor was specifically banned as a part of the goods shipped to Indians
   C. states could assert legal authority on reservations
   D. treaties became the basis of Indian rights within the United States

4. What was President Washington's reaction to the war between England and France when it began in 1793?
   A. He supported the French.
   B. He supported the English.
   C. He tried to negotiate peace between the two countries.
   D. He issued a Neutrality Proclamation.

5. "X, Y, and Z" was the code name for _____.
   A. three American diplomats sent to France to avert war
   B. unnamed French agents sent by Tallyrand to meet with American representatives
   C. secret agents sent to France to avert war
   D. English spies located in France to gather intelligence

6. In the video, Professor Joseph Ellis observes that the Alien and Sedition Acts were counterproductive for the Federalists because _____.
   A. they helped Jefferson win the election of 1800
   B. most new immigrants actually tended to support the Federalists
   C. pro-Federalist newspapers were shut down
   D. they could not reveal details of the XYZ affair

7. Issues under the Federalists that divided the country in the late 1790s included _____.
   A. Indian policy
   B. the election of Adams in 1796
   C. the Jay Treaty and the Quasi War
   D. Adams' dismissal of Hamilton as secretary of the treasury

8. When the electoral vote in the 1800 presidential election ended in a tie and the House of Representatives had to choose a winner, _____.
   A. Alexander Hamilton helped Thomas Jefferson prevail
   B. John Adams took his case to the Supreme Court
   C. Aaron Burr challenged Alexander Hamilton to a duel
   D. Thomas Jefferson persuaded Aaron Burr to withdraw before a vote had to be taken

9. In the video, Professor Eric Foner observes that during the revolutionary era, the idea of freedom _____.
   A. narrowed in definition after 1776
   B. was contradicted by Indian removal
   C. applied only to particular groups of people
   D. became universalized and democratized

Short Answer: Your answers should be one or two paragraphs long and specifically address the points indicated.

10. In your opinion, was the Sedition Act of 1798 constitutional? Why or why not?

11. What were the differences between Federalists and Republicans in 1800?

12. Cite three precedents established in the 1790s. What were the long-term effects?

Essay Questions: Your answers should be several paragraphs long and express a clear understanding of the points indicated.

13. Analyze the presidential election of 1800 in respect to the candidates, issues, campaign, and results. Why was a peaceful transfer of power significant in American history?

14. Describe and explain how the revolutionary era (1760–1801) shaped America. In your answer, consider the major changes that took place, particularly relating to American identity and the concepts of freedom and equality. How does that era continue to affect us today?

ANSWER KEY

	Answer	Learning Objectives	Focus Points	References
1.	B	LO 1	FP 2	pp. 302–304; video segment 2
2.	C	LO 1	FP 4	pp. 304–306; video segment 2
3.	D	LO 1	FP 5	video segments 2, 3
4.	D	LO 2	FP 6	pp. 306–308; video segment 4
5.	B	LO 2	FP 10	pp. 311–312; video segment 4
6.	A	LO 2, 4	FP 11	pp. 312–315; video segment 4
7.	C	LO 3	FP 16	pp. 316, 323; video segment 5
8.	A	LO 4	FP 17	p. 323; video segment 5
9.	D	LO 5	FP 20	video segment 7

10. LO 2, 3 .... FP 11, 12, 13 .... pp. 312–315; video segment 4
    - What did the Sedition Act say?
    - What part of the Constitution did it seem to contradict?
    - To what extent can the government restrict expression during times of crisis?

11. LO 3 .... FP 16 .... pp. 316, 323; video segment 5
    - Consider the issues of the use of the central government versus states' rights, the Bank of the United States, excise taxes, Alien and Sedition Acts, foreign policy disagreements, etc.
    - Who supported each group? Who led each group?

12.　............LO 1–5......FP 5, 6, 15, 18, 20 ....pp. 306–308; video segments 2–7
- U.S.-Indian treaties; boundaries established, but usually broken; Indian rights eventually upheld.
- Neutrality in foreign policy; the United States could concentrate on continentalism.
- Censorship during "wartime"? How far can the government go?
- A peaceful transfer of power; creation of a loyal opposition.
- Functions of political parties; in addition to transfer of power, what else happens?

13.　...............LO 4 ....FP 16–18...pp. 316, 323; video segments 5, 6
- Candidates: Who was running for each party?
- Issues: What separated the Federalists and the Republicans?
- Campaign: How were campaigns done in those days?
- Results: Jefferson and Burr end up in a tie; how is this dealt with? What did it mean to the parties? What did it mean to the nation?
- Consider how the United States handles election results without violence; what is the role of the losing candidate and party? What are the alternatives?

14.　.............LO 5.................FP 20 ....video segment 7
- How did the revolution, the Declaration of Independence, the Constitution, and the precedents set in the 1790s give America an identity?
- What role did geography play in this identity?
- How was the concept of freedom defined in this era? How had it changed?
- How were minority groups fitting into the concept of American identity?
- What are the most important elements of revolutionary America still present today?

ENRICHMENT IDEAS

These activities are not required unless your instructor assigns them. They are offered as suggestions to help you learn more about the material presented in this lesson.

1. Imagine yourself to be a Republican newspaper editor after the passage of the Sedition Act of 1798. Write an editorial in which you state your opinion about that legislation and what you plan to do about it.

2. Examine the role of censorship during wartime. In a well-developed essay, describe how and why media access to information has evolved in American history. What limits, if any, do you think should be placed on the media in times of war?

3. Consider the views of the Federalist and Republican political parties and their leaders at the end of the 1790s. In a thoughtful essay, explain how those views are reflected in national politics today (that is, role of the central government, support for business, appeal to which economic class).

4. Research the issue of liquor in the history of relations between the United States and American Indians. Then submit a report in which you describe your findings.

5. The text and the video for this lesson contain political cartoons from the 1790s to help illustrate the temper of the times. Analyze two political cartoons from the 1790s and two from newspapers published in the last three months. Then submit a report (with copies of the cartoons) describing what point of view the cartoons are trying to convey and your opinion about their effectiveness.

SUGGESTED READINGS/RESOURCES

See the "Bibliography" on pages 316–317 of the text if you wish to examine other books and resources related to the material presented in this lesson.

Unit Three

America in Transition
1801-1848
"Manifest Destiny?"

THEME

In 1845, journalist John L. O'Sullivan coined the term "Manifest Destiny" to help justify the latest push by the United States to acquire more land in the west. O'Sullivan's popular phase gave expression to the idea that it was the right of the United States to "possess the whole of the continent which Providence has given us for the development of the great experiment of liberty and . . . self-government entrusted to us." In many ways, the concept of Manifest Destiny carried forward the American vision found in colonial America ("city on a hill") and in revolutionary America ("all men are created equal").

Indeed, during the first half of the nineteenth century, the United States appeared to offer white Americans the chance to shape their own destinies. Thomas Jefferson's vision of a nation of independent small farmers seemed to be secured by the geographical expansion across the continent. Economic changes in the North and West opened up new opportunities for thousands of people. Politicians celebrated the expansion of the vote and the rise of the "common man." Social reformers thought that society might be brought closer to its ideals, if not perfected.

However, tensions and conflict accompanied all these transitions. Most notably, American Indians were pushed even further from inclusion in the promise of America, and slaves experienced no liberty and no opportunity. Finally, the triumph over Mexico in 1848 seemed to fulfill the destiny that O'Sullivan had identified, but it also renewed old questions about whether the nation would live up to its founding principles.

Lesson 13

Jefferson's Vision of America

OVERVIEW

Thomas Jefferson's inauguration as president in 1801 represented a significant transfer of power as well as a vision about the future of America. Unlike Alexander Hamilton, Jefferson saw the independent farmer as the source of true freedom. To secure that freedom and future, agricultural America needed room to expand. The Louisiana Purchase virtually doubled the size of the country, assuring, in Jefferson's mind, an empire of liberty. Shortly thereafter, the Lewis and Clark expedition provided the nation with a glimpse of the wonder and promise of the vast new territory.

Meanwhile, Jefferson and his Republican successors had to deal with the realities of on-going national and international issues. Even though Hamilton and his party died during this time, the Republicans adopted many of his key economic policies. In addition, Chief Justice John Marshall secured Federalist objectives as he established the independence of the Supreme Court.

Foreign crises proved to be even more troublesome than those that had confronted the Federalists in the 1790s, and the United States found itself in a peculiar war with Britain by 1812. That war may have been militarily inconclusive as far as the British were concerned, but there was no doubt that American Indians suffered major losses because of it.

At the end of the War of 1812, most Americans seemed to feel good about the state of the nation and ready to move forward with nationalistic policies. The promise of the West allowed the United States to postpone a day of reckoning about the expansion of slavery, but this sectional issue set off a "fire-bell in the night," warning of danger ahead.

LESSON ASSIGNMENTS

Text: Roark, et al., *The American Promise*, Chapter 10, "Republicans in Power," pp. 320–349, 352

Video: "Jefferson's Vision of America" from the series *Shaping America*

LEARNING OBJECTIVES

This lesson examines the changing political, geographic, and social landscapes of America during the first two decades of the nineteenth century. Upon completing this lesson, you should be able to:

1. Explain the "unfinished quality" of America in the early nineteenth century and how the West factored into the promise of America at that time.

2. Explain Jefferson's vision of America and how republican simplicity, the Louisiana Purchase, the Lewis and Clark expedition, and the West fit into that vision.

3. Explain the causes and consequences of the War of 1812, including the war's effects on the American Indians and the Federalist Party.

4. Describe the status of women in the early nineteenth century.

5. Assess the significant features of nationalism and sectionalism during the "era of good feelings."

LESSON FOCUS POINTS

The following questions are designed to help you get the most benefit from the sources selected for this lesson. For reference purposes, the titles of the video segments are: (1) Introduction, (2) "We Proceeded On," (3) "Tecumseh," and (4) Summary Analysis: ". . . Like a Fire-Bell in the Night."

1. What choices and opportunities did the generation inheriting the revolution have that influenced their role in shaping America? What role would the West play in this process? (video segment 1)

2. What was Gabriel's Rebellion? How was it dealt with? How did it illustrate the ongoing conflict between republican ideals and the reality of slavery? (textbook, pp. 323, 326)

3. What did Jefferson mean by the "revolution of 1800"? What was his vision of republican simplicity? How did Jefferson implement his vision of limited government? (textbook, pp. 322–323, 326–327)

4. What was the significance of John Marshall's decision in *Marbury v. Madison*? (textbook, pp. 327–328)

5. How did the West fit into Jefferson's vision of America? How did widespread land ownership guarantee liberty for white settlers? (textbook, pp. 328–330; video segment 2)

6. How and why did the United States make the Louisiana Purchase? (textbook, pp. 328–329; video segment 2)

7. What was the purpose and the significance of the Lewis and Clark expedition? What can we learn from the Corps of Discovery? (textbook, pp. 329–330; video segment 2)

8. Why did Vice President Aaron Burr fight a duel with Alexander Hamilton? Did he get away with murder? Why was Aaron Burr later charged with treason? (textbook, pp. 324–325)

9. What was the significance of the *Chesapeake* incident? What was important about the Embargo Act of 1807? (textbook, p. 331)

10. Who was Tecumseh? Why did the United States consider him to be a threat? What actions had William Henry Harrison and the United States taken against him and other Indians prior to the outbreak of the War of 1812? (textbook, pp. 321–322, 333–334; video segment 3)

11. Why did the United States go to war with Britain in 1812? Why were the British and Tecumseh fighting against the Americans? (textbook, pp. 333–335; video segment 3)

12. What were the most significant military engagements of the War of 1812? Why were they important? (textbook, pp. 335–336)

13. What were the results of the War of 1812? Did anyone win? What were the effects of the war on the Federalist Party and the American Indians? (textbook, pp. 336–337; video segment 3)

14. How did the status of white women change in the early republic? Who was Jemima Wilkinson and what made her rather unique in that time period? How did Emma Hart Willard affect female education? (textbook, pp. 337–344)

15. What was the "era of good feelings"? How was nationalism reflected in the period after the War of 1812? What is significant about the Adams-Onis Treaty and the Monroe Doctrine? (textbook, pp. 344–349; video segment 4)

16. What was the Missouri Compromise? Why did Jefferson refer to it as a "fire-bell in the night"? (textbook, pp. 346–348; video segment 4)

17. Examine Map 10.5 in the text. Answer the questions posed in the text. (textbook, p. 348)

HISTORICAL EXPERTS INTERVIEWED

Andrew Cayton, Distinguished Professor of History, Miami University, Oxford, OH
Dayton Duncan, Writer, SoVerNet, Walpole, NH
R. David Edmunds, Watson Professor of American History, University of Texas at Dallas, Richardson, TX
Joseph J. Ellis, Professor of History, Mount Holyoke College, South Hadley, MA
Richard White, Margaret Byrne Professor of American History, Stanford University, Stanford, CA

PRACTICE TEST

The following items will help you evaluate your understanding of this lesson. Use the Answer Key at the end of the lesson to check your answers or to locate material related to each question.

Multiple choice: Choose the BEST answer.

1. In the video, Professor Andrew Cayton observes that, in American history, the period from 1800 to 1850 has an "unfinished" quality to it because _____.
   A. many young people living then had choices and opportunities
   B. historians have not focused on those times
   C. transportation systems were not keeping up with the growing market
   D. political leadership seemed confused after the founding fathers died

2. According to Thomas Jefferson, the source of true freedom in America was _____.
   A. the virtuous, independent farmer who owned and worked his land both for himself and for the market
   B. the rising class of mechanics in American cities, single-minded men who allowed no one to push them around
   C. the political party system that had come about in the late eighteenth century
   D. the continuation of property qualifications for voting

3. Events in the Louisiana Territory in 1802 alerted the United States to a potential national security problem as _____.
   A. England was negotiating to buy the territory from France
   B. Spain had turned over the territory to France, then under the rule of powerful expansionist Napoleon Bonaparte
   C. a large confederation of Native Americans had hatched a plan to cross the Mississippi River and attack the United States
   D. a large contingent of slaves from St. Dominique had taken refuge there and were planning to capture New Orleans

4. The purpose of the Lewis and Clark expedition included all of the following objectives EXCEPT _____.
   A. legitimizing a United States claim to California
   B. opening up contact with Indian peoples
   C. looking for a water route across the continent
   D. gathering scientific information

5. Impressment, one of the key issues that led the United States into war with England in 1812, was _____.
   A. the practice of American naval vessels stopping English ships to search for prohibited goods
   B. the practice of the British navy stopping U.S. ships to search for deserters from the Royal Navy and sometimes removing U.S. citizens from the ships along with supposed deserters
   C. the practice of the British navy confiscating U.S. ships on the high seas because His Majesty's navy was experiencing a shortage of vessels
   D. the practice of the U.S. merchant fleet taking or impressing goods from ports in the West Indies when American ship captains were short on funds

6. The Treaty of Ghent ending the War of 1812 _____.
   A. paved the way for an important exchange of territory between the United States and England
   B. settled the ongoing dispute over shipping rights
   C. set up a commission to determine the exact boundary between the United States and Florida
   D. actually settled few of the issues that had led to war

7. A woman in the early republic who owned and conveyed property, made contracts, and initiated lawsuits probably was _____.
   A. friends with influential men in her neighborhood
   B. single
   C. married
   D. a lawyer

8. As part of the Missouri Compromise, _____.
   A. Kansas Territory was open to slavery
   B. Missouri became a free state
   C. a line was drawn to separate free and slave territory
   D. American Indians were removed west of the Mississippi River

9. In 1823, President James Monroe issued what became known as the Monroe Doctrine, a statement that the Americas "_____."
   A. will ultimately come under the rule of one republic, the United States
   B. are henceforth not to be considered as subjects for future colonization by any European power
   C. have no interests in Europe that supercede the Western Hemisphere's domestic tranquility
   D. are destined to become one economic unit with laws and procedures by which Europe must abide

Short Answer: Your answers should be one or two paragraphs long and specifically address the points indicated.

10. How did the Louisiana Purchase and the Adams-Onis Treaty affect the boundaries of the United States?

11. What effect did the Lewis and Clark expedition have on the country? What can we learn from the Corps of Discovery?

Essay Questions: Your answers should be several paragraphs long and express a clear understanding of the points indicated.

12. Describe and explain why Thomas Jefferson looked to the West to fulfill his vision of America. How did he attempt to assure that the West would be accessible? What effects did movement to the West have on American Indians and the question of slavery?

13. Describe and explain the causes and consequences of the War of 1812. How did that war affect American Indians and the Federalist Party?

ANSWER KEY

Answer	Learning Objectives	Focus Points	References
1. A	LO 1	FP 1	video segment 1
2. A	LO 2	FP 5	pp. 328–330; video segment 2
3. B	LO 2	FP 6	pp. 328–329; video segment 2
4. A	LO 2	FP 7	pp. 329–330; video segment 2
5. B	LO 3	FP 11	pp. 333–335; video segment 3
6. D	LO 3	FP 13	pp. 336–337; video segment 3
7. B	LO 4	FP 14	pp. 337–344
8. C	LO 5	FP 16	pp. 346–348; video segment 4
9. B	LO 5	FP 15	pp. 348–349; video segment 4

10. ....LO 2, 5.............FP 6, 15 .... pp. 328–329, 344–348; video segments 2, 4
    • Describe the area acquired from France in the Louisiana Purchase; what areas were not included?
    • How did the Adams-Onis Treaty affect Florida? What was significant about the transcontinental feature of the treaty?

11. ....LO 2.................FP 7.....................................pp. 329–330; video segment 2
    • Why did the expedition whet the appetite for further expansion westward?
    • What did the Corps of Discovery illustrate about diversity? How did it create a sense of wonder about how westward expansion might have proceeded?

12.   .... LO 2, 3, 5 ... FP 3, 5–7, 10, 13, 15–16 .... pp. 321–323, 326–330, 333–334,
       .... pp. 336–337, 344–349; video segments 2–4
   - Why was the independent farmer a key to Jefferson's vision? How could an empire of liberty be maintained?
   - How did the Louisiana Purchase fit into Jefferson's vision? How did the Lewis and Clark expedition facilitate movement westward?
   - How did American Indians, particularly Tecumseh, respond? How did the War of 1812 affect Indians? Where would Indians go?
   - How did having more land in the West affect debates on the future of slavery?

13.   .... LO 3 .... FP 9, 11–13, 15 .... pp. 331, 333–337, 344–349;
       .... video segments 3, 4
   - What were the causes of the war? Consider the diplomatic breakdown, the expansionist desires, and the question of honor.
   - What were the military highlights of the war? What did the treaty ending the war change?
   - Why were American Indians big losers in the war?
   - Why did the Federalist Party lose ground because of the war?
   - Why did the United States have a surge of nationalism after the war?

ENRICHMENT IDEAS

These activities are not required unless your instructor assigns them. They are offered as suggestions to help you learn more about the material presented in this lesson.

1. In the spirit of Lewis and Clark, research the first non-Indian peoples to explore the area in which you live. Then submit a report on your findings, including an evaluation of how the exploration affected the later development of the area.

2. An image of Sacajawea, the Shoshone Indian woman who served as a guide and mediator on the Lewis and Clark expedition, is now found on dollar coins in the United States. Investigate why she was chosen for this honor. What is the process for selecting someone to be on U.S. currency? Who else is being considered? Submit your findings in a well-developed essay.

3. Investigate the respective historical legacies of Thomas Jefferson and Aaron Burr and how those legacies are usually portrayed in American memory. In a well-developed essay, describe your findings. Are the two men and their legacies characterized accurately?

4. Some historians consider the War of 1812 to be an unnecessary war. What do you think? In a thoughtful essay, take a position and defend it.

5. Examine the *Marbury v. Madison* decision by the Supreme Court. In a well-developed essay, explain how and why John Marshall arrived at his decision and evaluate the significance of it.

SUGGESTED READINGS/RESOURCES

See the "Bibliography" on pages 352–353 of the text if you wish to examine other books and resources related to the material presented in this lesson.

Lesson 14

The Market Revolution

OVERVIEW

Both Alexander Hamilton and Thomas Jefferson had quite different visions of what they hoped the United States would become. Each had taken steps to put in place policies and practices which might enable their respective visions to become reality. The generation coming to maturity in the first part of the nineteenth century had the opportunity to give shape to the visions of the founding generation, particularly in the northern and western regions of the country.

It was then and there that a market revolution took place. Spurred by new developments in manufacturing, transportation, and commerce, the American economy was on the move. Factories at Lowell, Massachusetts, and elsewhere initially employed a largely female labor force, which was, at least temporarily, attracted by the possibilities presented. The Erie Canal illustrated new transportation networks facilitating the movement of goods, services, and people. The independent farmers who moved into the midsection of the country expanded the area of agricultural opportunity, and the resulting increase in agricultural production provided the basis for reciprocal growth and opportunities in other areas of the economy. Meanwhile, family and work relationships were evolving toward a pattern that would become quite familiar to many succeeding generations.

In the midst of all these changes, a free-labor economy emerged in the North and West. Based on hard work and the belief in landed independence, this society forged a link between economic and political freedom. While certainly not encompassing everybody, more and more people came to believe that they deserved the opportunity to try to shape their own destiny. By midcentury, this "northern" culture was beginning to be identified with America, even though the southern regions of the country had been pursuing a quite different path to the future. Ultimately, it would take a civil war to see what view would prevail.

LESSON ASSIGNMENTS

Text: Roark, et al., The American Promise, Chapter 10, "Republicans in Power," pp. 338–339; Chapter 11, "The Expanding Republic," pp. 358–366, 375–379; Chapter 12, "The New West and Free North," pp. 395–407

Video: "The Market Revolution" from the series *Shaping America*

Documents:
            "A Mill Worker Describes Her Work and Life," found at the end of this lesson

LEARNING OBJECTIVES

This lesson addresses the question of why a market revolution took place in the North and West and how the resulting free-labor society helped shape America. Upon completing this lesson, you should be able to:

1. Explain the market revolution occurring during the first half of the nineteenth century.

2. Analyze the working conditions and the lives of factory workers during this era.

3. Explain the major developments in the economic and social evolution of the North and West during the first half of the nineteenth century.

4. Explain the major developments in agriculture in the Northwest during this era and how these changes affected the rest of the nation.

5. Assess the promise and reality of the free-labor ideals developing at this time and the long-term significance of these ideals for the American people.

LESSON FOCUS POINTS

The following questions are designed to help you get the most benefit from the sources selected for this lesson. For reference purposes, the titles for the video segments are: (1) Introduction, (2) "The Working Women of Lowell," (3) Short-take: "Progress in Print," (4) "The Big Ditch," (5) Short-take: "Runs Like a Deere," (6) "Moving Westward," and (7) Summary Analysis: "A Free-Labor Economy."

1. What is meant by the term *market revolution*? (textbook, pp. 358–359; video segment 1)

2. Examine Maps 11.1 and 12.1 in the text. What major transportation routes are identified? How would these routes potentially change America? (textbook, pp. 359, 400)

3. How involved was the federal government in supporting transportation and commerce? Why was this politically contentious? (textbook, pp. 359–363)

4. How did the development of the cookstove, steamboat, and telegraph illustrate the promise of technology during this period? Regarding steamboats, how safe was this new mode of transportation? Who was responsible for public safety? (textbook, pp. 338–339, 362–363, 399, 402–403)

5. Why did women enter the factory labor force at this time? What was life like for the women working in the textile mills? How did this experience change their lives? (textbook, pp. 361–365; document; video segment 2)

6. How successful was collective action by workers at this time? How did immigrants affect the labor movement? Who were these immigrants? Why were they coming to America? (textbook, pp. 362–365, 402–407; video segment 2)

7. How did the writings published at Lowell reflect the progress in printing during this era? How did the press affect literacy? In general, how did the press, public life, and popular amusements affect culture? (textbook, pp. 361–364, 375–379; video segment 3)

8. Why was the Erie Canal built? How was it built? How did it affect the movement of goods? What effect did it have on New York City? (textbook, pp. 359–361; video segment 4)

9. How did bankers and lawyers affect the economy during this era? (textbook, p. 365)

10. What explains the emerging boom and bust cycle in the economy? How did the Panic of 1819 illustrate this feature of the economy? (textbook, pp. 365–366)

11. What fundamental changes in American society were associated with the economic and industrial evolution occurring in the North and West during the first half of the nineteenth century? (textbook, p. 397)

12. What factors contributed to increased agricultural production? How and why did the federal government promote agriculture? (textbook, pp. 397–398; video segments 5, 6)

13. How did Jacksonville, Illinois, represent development on the northwestern frontier? Generally, how did developments in agriculture affect manufacturing? (textbook, pp. 398–399; video segment 6)

14. Why were railroads capturing the American imagination by midcentury? How were railroads affecting the economy? (textbook, pp. 399–401; video segment 6)

15. By the mid-nineteenth century, how was the free-labor ideal meshing with reality? How and why was the free-labor economy becoming more associated with America? What did that portend for the future? (textbook, pp. 402–407; video segment 7)

HISTORICAL EXPERTS INTERVIEWED

Joyce Appleby, Professor of History, University of California at Los Angeles, Los Angeles, CA
Thomas Dublin, Professor, State University of New York, Binghamton University, Binghamton, NY
John Steele Gordon, Economic Historian and Author, North Salem, NY
John Majewski, Associate Professor, University of California at Santa Barbara, Santa Barbara, CA

PRACTICE TEST

The following items will help you evaluate your understanding of this lesson. Use the Answer Key at the end of the lesson to check your answers or to locate material related to each question.

Multiple choice: Choose the BEST answer.

1. The market revolution experienced by Americans after the War of 1812 _____.
   A. brought increasing numbers of people out of old patterns of rural self-sufficiency into the wider realm of national market relations
   B. gave rise to a huge factory system that pulled millions from the countryside to labor in the cities
   C. was seen to have limited impact on most Americans, who were relatively poor and not much affected by the economic growth
   D. was hardly revolutionary, as many northerners refused to do business with southern slave masters, whom they regarded as immoral

2. The 1824 Supreme Court decision in *Gibbon v. Ogden* _____.
   A. upheld the practice of states granting monopolies to steam transportation companies
   B. opened the avenues of economic expansion by declaring that navigation on rivers traversing more than one state came under the jurisdiction of the federal government and that state-granted transportation monopolies on such rivers were invalid
   C. set a limit on the number of steamboat companies that could operate on U.S. rivers
   D. instituted strict licensing requirements for all steamboat companies operating on U.S. waterways and thus improved the safety of steamboat travel

3. In the video, Professor Thomas Dublin expresses the view that women workers learned that they could _____.
   A. hardly make enough to pay the boardinghouse rent
   B. publicly protest ill treatment
   C. usually find a future husband in the workforce
   D. lose their paycheck if they remained single

4. Employees of early textile mills in New England were mainly _____.
   A. young women seeking careers in America's expanding economy
   B. young men seeking careers in America's expanding economy
   C. young women seeking a new degree of autonomy in their lives that was difficult to achieve by remaining on the family farm
   D. immigrant families trying to escape the factory system in Europe

5. Beginning around 1840, one of the factors that fueled economic growth in the United States was _____.
   A. Americans moving from farms to cities, where they found jobs working in factories
   B. a decline in family size
   C. a decline in agricultural productivity that forced industrial growth
   D. better tariff rates with England

6. Agricultural productivity in the North and West increased significantly in the late 1830s because of _____.
   A. waterwheels
   B. John Deere's steel plow
   C. the invention of thrashers
   D. the numbers of freed slaves eager for wage-earning work

7. The invention of the telegraph _____.
   A. was a unifying force for the young United States
   B. caused a splintering in the United States as news could spread more rapidly
   C. caused the postal service to flounder
   D. caused an immediate rise in school attendance as people wanted to know how to read

8. Proponents of the free-labor system touted in the North and West in the 1840s and 1850s claimed that the system _____.
   A. opened up doors to all segments of the population
   B. made it possible for hired laborers to become independent landowners
   C. gave slaves compensation for their labor
   D. enforced the Puritan ideal of working hard and saving one's money

Short Answer: Your answers should be one or two paragraphs long and specifically address the points indicated.

9. What did the experience of the working women of Lowell indicate about labor and economic opportunities for women in the first half of the nineteenth century?

10. How did the building of the Erie Canal illustrate the confluence of a vision, public support, and the practical use of labor and technology?

Essay Question: Your answer should be several paragraphs long and express a clear understanding of the points indicated.

11. Describe and explain the significant economic changes that took place in the North and West during the first half of the nineteenth century. How did these changes affect the development of a free-labor ideology in that region of the country? What were the short- and long-term effects of these developments?

ANSWER KEY

	Answer	Learning Objectives	Focus Points	References
1.	A	LO 1	FP 1	pp. 358–359; video segment 1
2.	B	LO 1	FP 3	pp. 359–363
3.	B	LO 2	FP 5	pp. 361–365; document; video segment 2
4.	C	LO 2	FP 5	pp. 361–365; document; video segment 2
5.	A	LO 3	FP 11	p. 397
6.	B	LO 4	FP 12	pp. 397–398; video segments 5, 6
7.	A	LO 1, 3	FP 4	pp. 399, 402–403
8.	B	LO 5	FP 15	pp. 402–407; video segment 7

9. ....LO 2...............FP 5, 6 ....pp. 365, 402–407; document; video segment 2
- Why were women recruited to the mills?
- Why did the women go to work there?
- What were the positive and negative sides to the experience?
- What other types of opportunities were available?

10. ....LO 1, 3...............FP 8 ....pp. 359–361 video segment 4
- Explain the vision of DeWitt Clinton.
- What type of public support became available?
- Who provided the labor?
- How did they overcome barriers?
- What was the result?

11. ....LO 1–5.............FP 1–15 .... pp. 358–366, 375–379, 395–407; video segments 1–7
- What characterized the market revolution?
- Beyond the market, what opportunities were opening up in the region? Why was this happening?
- What is meant by a free-labor ideology? Why did this emerge?
- What were the results of these changes? How would you describe the losses and benefits?
- What was important about linking economic and political freedom in the North?

ENRICHMENT IDEAS

These activities are not required unless your instructor assigns them. They are offered as suggestions to help you learn more about the material presented in this lesson.

1. Imagine yourself to be a working girl at Lowell, Massachusetts, in the 1830s. Write a letter to your family at home in which you describe your daily routine and express your feelings about your life.

2. Imagine that you have enough money to make a round-trip from New York City to New Orleans in 1840, but you refuse to go via the ocean and you want to take a different route each way. Plan a trip using the available means of transportation. Submit your itinerary and include an explanation of why you planned the trip as you did.

3. Imagine yourself to be a merchant in Albany, New York, in 1830. In a well-developed essay, describe how your business and life in the city has been affected by the Erie Canal.

4. Research a modern federal or state-supported public works project in your community. In a thoughtful essay, explain how this project is funded, who is likely to benefit, and what effect the project is likely to have on the community.

5. Research the latest statistics comparing wages for women and men in America. Then submit a report in which you explain your findings. What explains the difference in average earnings?

SUGGESTED READINGS/RESOURCES

See the "Bibliography" on pages 391 and 430–431 of the text if you wish to examine other books and resources related to the material presented in this lesson.

DOCUMENTS

As the United States began to industrialize, a form of labor was to house and work young women in the textile mills. Their days were long and their lives regulated. The experience of a worker, known only as Susan, is recounted here.

As you read this document, focus on answering the following questions:

1. How did she feel about her work and her coworkers?
2. What was her overall view of the factory and work?

"A Mill Worker Describes Her Work and Life" (1844)

Dear Mary:

In my last I told you I would write again, and say more of my life here; and this I will now attempt to do.

I went into the mill to work a few days after I wrote to you. It looked very pleasant at first, the rooms were so light, spacious, and clean, the girls so pretty and neatly dressed, and the machinery so brightly polished or nicely painted. The plants in the windows, or on the overseer's bench or desk, gave a pleasant aspect to things. You will wish to know what work I am doing. I will tell you of the different kinds of work.

There is, first, the carding-room, where the cotton flies most, and the girls get the dirtiest. But this is easy, and the females are allowed time to go out at night before the bell rings—on Saturday night at least, if not on all other nights. Then there is the spinning-room, which is very neat and pretty. In this room are the spinners and doffers. The spinners watch the frames; keep them clean, and the threads mended if they break. The doffers take off the full bobbins, and put on the empty ones. They have nothing to do in the long intervals when the frames are in motion, and can go out to their boarding-houses, or do any thing else that they like. In some of the factories the spinners do their own doffing, and when this is the case they work no harder than the weavers. These last have the hardest time of all—or can have, if they choose to take charge of three or four looms, instead of the one pair which is the allotment. And they are the most constantly confined. The spinners and dressers have but the weavers to keep supplied, and then their work can stop. The dressers never work before breakfast, and they stay out a great deal in the afternoons. The drawers-in, or girls who draw the threads through the harnesses, also work in the dressing-room, and they all have very good wages — better than the weavers who have but the usual work. The dressing-rooms are very neat, and the frames move with a gentle undulating motion which is really graceful. But these rooms are kept very warm, and are disagreeably scented with the "sizing," or starch, which stiffens the "beams," or unwoven webs. There are many plants in these rooms, and it is really a good greenhouse for them. The dressers are generally quite tall girls, and must have pretty tall minds too, as their work requires much care and attention.

I could have had work in the dressing-room, but chose to be a weaver; and I will tell you why. I disliked the closer air of the dressing-room, though I might have become accustomed to that. I could not learn to dress so quickly as I could to weave, nor have work of my own so soon, and should have had to stay with Mrs. C. two or three weeks before I could go in at all, and I did not like to be "lying upon my oars" so long. And, more than this, when I get well learned I can have extra work, and make double wages, which you know is quite an inducement with some.

Well, I went into the mill, and was put to learn with a very patient girl—a clever old maid. I should be willing to be one myself if I could be as good as she is. You cannot think how odd every thing seemed to me. I wanted to laugh at every thing, but did not know what to make sport of first. They set me to threading shuttles, and tying weaver's knots, and such things, and now I have improved so that I can take care of one loom. I could take care of two if I only had eyes in the back part of my head, but I have not got used to "looking two ways of a Sunday" yet.

At first the hours seemed very long, but I was so interested in learning that I endured it very well; and when I went out at night, the sound of the mill was in my ears, as of crickets, frogs, and jewsharps [small musical instrument; it twangs], all mingled together in strange discord. After that it seemed as though cotton-wool was in my ears, but now I do not mind it at all. You know that people learn to sleep with the thunder of Niagara in their ears, and a cotton mill is no worse, though you wonder that we do not have to hold our breath in such a noise.

It makes my feet ache and swell to stand so much, but I suppose I shall get accustomed to that too. The girls generally wear old shoes about their work, and you know nothing is easier; but they almost all say that when they have worked here a year or two they have to procure shoes a size or two larger than before they came. The right hand, which is the one used in stopping and starting the loom, becomes larger than the left; but in other respects the factory is not detrimental to a young girl's appearance. Here they look delicate, but not sickly; they laugh at those who are much exposed, and get pretty brown; but I, for one, had rather be brown than pure white. I never saw so many pretty looking girls as there are here. Though the number of men is small in proportion there are many marriages here, and a great deal of courting. I will tell you of this last sometime.

You wish to know minutely of our hours of labor. We go in at five o'clock; at seven we come out to breakfast; at half-past seven we return to our work, and stay until half-past twelve. At one, or quarter-past one four months in the year, we return to our work, and stay until seven at night. Then the evening is all our own, which is more than some laboring girls can say, who think nothing is more tedious than a factory life.

When I first came here, which was the last of February, the girls ate their breakfast before they went to their work. The first of March they came out at the present breakfast hour, and the twentieth of March they ceased to "light up" the rooms, and come out between six and seven o'clock.

You ask if the girls are contented here: I ask you, if you know of *any one* who is perfectly contented. Do you remember the old story of the philosopher, who offered a field to the person who was contented with his lot; and when one claimed it, he asked him why, if he was so perfectly satisfied, he wanted his field. The girls here are not contented; and there is no disadvantage in their situation which they do not perceive as quickly, and lament as loudly, as the sternest opponents of the factory system do. They would scorn to say they were contented, if asked the question; for it would compromise their Yankee spirit—their pride, penetration, independence, and love of "freedom and equality" to say that they were *contented* with such a life as this. Yet, withal, they are cheerful. I never saw a happier set of beings. They appear blithe in the mill, and out of it. If you see one of them, with a very long face, you may be sure that it is because she has heard bad news from home, or because her beau has vexed her. But, if it is a Lowell trouble, it is because she has failed in getting off as many "sets" or "pieces" as she intended to have done; or because she had a sad "break-out," or "break-down," in her work, or something of that sort.

You ask if the work is not disagreeable. Not when one is accustomed to it. It tried my patience sadly at first, and does now when it does not run well; but, in general, I like it very much. It is easy to do, and does not require very violent exertion, as much of our farm work does. You also ask how I get along with the girls here. Very well indeed.

Dear Mary:

The mill girls are the prettiest in the city. You wonder how they can keep neat. Why not? There are no restrictions as to the number of pieces to be washed in the boarding-house. And, as there is plenty of water in the mill, the girls can wash their laces and muslins and other nice things themselves, and no boarding woman ever refuses the conveniences for starching and ironing. You say too that you do not see how we can have so many conveniences and comforts at the price we pay for board. You must remember that the boarding-houses belong to the companies, and are let to the tenants far below the usual city rent—sometimes the rent is remitted. Then there are large families, so that there are the profits of many individuals. The country farmers are quite in the habit of bringing their produce to the boarding-houses for sale, thus reducing the price by the omission of the market-man's profit. So you see there are many ways by which we get along so well.

You ask me how the girls behave in the mill, and what are the punishments. They behave very well while about their work, and I have never heard of punishments, or scoldings, or anything of that sort. Sometimes an overseer finds fault, and sometimes offends a girl by refusing to let her stay out of the mill, or some deprivation like that; and then, perhaps, there are tears and pouts on her part, but, in general, the tone of intercourse between the girls and overseers is very good—pleasant, yet respectful. When the latter are fatherly sort of men the girls frequently resort to them for advice and assistance about other affairs than their work. Very seldom is this confidence abused; but, among the thousands of overseers who have lived in Lowell, and the tens of thousands of girls who have in time been here, there are legends still told of wrong suffered and committed. "To err is human," and when the frailties of humanity are exhibited by a factory girl it is thought of for worse than are the errors of any other persons.

The only punishment among the girls is dismission from their places. They do not, as many think, withhold their wages; and as for corporal punishment—mercy on me! To strike a female would cost any overseer his place. If the superintendents did not take the affair into consideration the girls would turn out [go on strike], as they did at the Temperance celebration, "Independent day;" and if they didn't look as pretty, I am sure they would produce as deep an impression.

Do you wish to hear anything more about the overseers? Once for all, then, there are many very likely intelligent public-spirited men among them. They are interested in the good movements of the day; teachers in the Sabbath schools; and some have represented the city in the State Legislature. They usually marry among the factory girls, and do not connect themselves with their inferiors either. Indeed, in almost all the matches here the female is superior in education and manner, if not in intellect, to her partner.

The overseers have good salaries, and their families live very prettily. I observe that in almost all cases the mill girls make excellent wives. They are good managers, orderly in their households, and "neat as waxwork." It seems as though they were so delighted to have houses of their own to take care of, that they would never weary of the labor and the care.

"A Mill Worker Describes Her Work and Life" (1844). Excerpts taken from *The Lowell Offering*. June and August 1844, pp. 169–172, 237–240.

Lesson 15

A White Man's Democracy

OVERVIEW

The economic transformations in the North and the movement of settlers westward during the early nineteenth century brought about new opportunities and challenges for many Americans. Meanwhile, politicians were responding to the changing times, and politics and political parties took on a different shape.

Andrew Jackson, the first president from west of the Appalachian Mountains, became closely associated with the spirit of the age and the image of the "common man." However, neither Jackson's personal background nor his presidential decisions were ordinary. His strong actions regarding the nullification crisis, the national bank, and Indian removal were controversial but generally popular with the electorate.

As scholar Richard Ellis observes in the video, historians have difficulty coming to terms with Jackson. On one hand, his appeal attracted a wide following among his constituents. On the other hand, the narrowness of his appeal meant that only white men had a direct role in the democratic process. It would be up to later generations to broaden the meaning of democracy.

LESSON ASSIGNMENTS

Text: Roark, et al., *The American Promise,* Chapter 10, "Republicans in Power,"
          pp. 349–351 and Chapter 11, "The Expanding Republic," pp. 356–358, 366–375, and
          385–393

Video: "A White Man's Democracy" from the series *Shaping America*

LEARNING OBJECTIVES

This lesson examines the major political developments occurring during the 1820s and 1830s. Upon completion of this lesson, you should be able to:

1. Analyze the political democratization of the 1820s and 1830s.

2. Analyze how Andrew Jackson mirrored the changing American society and became a symbol for the era.

3. Explain President Jackson's policies regarding American Indians, particularly in reference to the southeastern tribes.

4. Explain the nullification crisis and Jackson's response to it.

5. Explain Jackson's actions regarding the Bank of the United States.

6. Assess the short- and long-term effects of the political decisions and developments of this era.

LESSON FOCUS POINTS

The following questions are designed to help you get the most benefit from the sources selected for this lesson. For reference purposes, the video segments are: (1) Introduction, (2) "The People's Politician," (3) "The Jackson Presidency," (4) Short-take: "The Panic of 1837," (5) "Trail of Tears," (6) Summary Analysis: "In the Name of Majority Rule."

1. Why was Andrew Jackson an appealing presidential candidate in the 1820s? What distinguishes Jacksonian democracy from Jeffersonian democracy? (textbook, pp. 357–358, 367–368; video segments 1, 2)

2. Why was the outcome of the 1824 presidential election decided by the House of Representatives? From which regions of the country did the respective candidates gain their support? What is important about the "corrupt bargain"? (textbook, pp. 349–351; video segment 2)

3. Why was John Quincy Adams a one-term president? (textbook, p. 351)

4. Starting in 1828, why did voter turnout increase? How did campaign styles change? What new role did the press play in political campaigns? (textbook, pp. 366–368)

5. What scandals and questions of character influenced the presidential election of 1828? Why did Andrew Jackson win? Where did he get his support? What did his victory mean? (textbook, pp. 367–369; video segment 2)

6. What factors explain the emergence of the second-party system? How were the Democrats and Whigs different from each other? What political traditions from the previous party system did each party carry forward? (textbook, pp. 368–369, 390–391; video segment 2)

7. What were Andrew Jackson's core beliefs? What was his agenda as president? (textbook, pp. 368–369; video segment 3)

8. What factors explain Jackson's Indian policy? How did President Jackson and Congress try to implement this policy? What choices did the Indian tribes in the Northwest and Southeast have? (textbook, pp. 369–372; video segment 5)

9. How had the Cherokee Indians adapted to Anglo-American culture? What steps did the Cherokee Indians take to resist removal? (textbook, pp. 371–372; video segment 5)

10. What was the Supreme Court's decision in *Worcester v. Georgia*? How did President Jackson respond to this decision? Why did he respond in this manner? (textbook, p. 371; video segment 5)

11. What decisions finally led to the forced removal of the Cherokee? From what part of the country were the Cherokee and other tribes being removed? Where were they sent? What happened on the Trail of Tears? (textbook, pp. 371–372; video segment 5)

12. What were the short- and long-term effects of Indian removal to the West? (video segment 5)

13. What was the philosophical and political basis for nullification? Why did South Carolina advocate this position by the late 1820s and act upon it in the early 1830s? (textbook, p. 373; video segment 3)

14. How and why did President Jackson respond to the nullification as he did? Why did this situation become a constitutional crisis? What were the results of the crisis? What did the crisis portend? (textbook, p. 373; video segment 3)

15. Why and how did President Jackson dismantle the Bank of the United States? Was this a wise decision? Was it popular? What were the economic and political results? (textbook, pp. 373–375; video segment 3)

16. What were the causes and effects of the panic of 1837? (textbook, pp. 386–390; video segment 4)

17. Why did Martin Van Buren win the presidency in the election of 1836? Why was he a one-term president? (textbook, pp. 385–390)

18. How and why did the political decisions and developments of this era change the nation? What does this teach us? (textbook, pp. 390–391; video segment 6)

HISTORICAL EXPERTS INTERVIEWED

Richard Ellis, Chairman and Professor, Department of History, State University of New York, Buffalo, NY

John Steele Gordon, Economic Historian, Author, North Salem, NY

Theda Perdue, Professor of History, University of North Carolina, Chapel Hill, NC

Harry Watson, Professor of History and Director of Center for the Study of the American South, The University of North Carolina, Chapel Hill, NC

PRACTICE TEST

The following items will help you evaluate your understanding of this lesson. Use the Answer Key at the end of the lesson to check your answers or to locate material related to each question.

Multiple choice: Choose the BEST answer.

1. The changing market and economic conditions in the early nineteenth century _____.
   A. caused more people to take a greater interest in politics
   B. forced the Bank of the United States to lower interest rates
   C. led to lower tariff rates
   D. extended the life of the Federalist Party

2. John Quincy Adams was a one-term president primarily because _____.
   A. he proved to lack a sense of diplomacy
   B. he had not developed the political savvy necessary to survive in America's rough and tumble world of electoral politics
   C. of repeated scandals in his administration
   D. so many congressmen opposed his programs that he wisely chose not to run again

3. In the video, Professor Harry Watson observes that Andrew Jackson's presidential victory in 1828 helped create _____.
   A. the need for greater security at the White House
   B. greater emphasis on campaign finance reform
   C. a dualism in American political culture between the elite and the common people
   D. disillusionment with the corrupt bargains used to gain the presidency

4. In Jacksonian America, the federal government's Indian policy viewed Native Americans as _____.
   A. potential U.S. citizens
   B. people who should move out of the path of white settlement
   C. people who should assimilate into white society
   D. too expensive to relocate and thus better exterminated

5. In the video, Professor Theda Perdue observes that Indian removal _____.
   A. diminished President Jackson's popularity
   B. angered the residents of Oklahoma
   C. helped unify the Cherokee people behind a common cause
   D. was another step toward making the United States a white man's country

6. The most compelling underlying reason why South Carolina argued for nullification in 1828 was _____.
   A. the growing fear among some South Carolinians that Congress was attracting ever larger numbers of northern representatives increasingly hostile to the institution of slavery
   B. that South Carolinians could not afford to pay higher tariffs and needed to protect themselves
   C. that Congress authorized a special tax on slaves, which South Carolinians viewed as discriminatory
   D. that Congress was debating a peacetime conscription law that would have drafted slaves into the military to fight in foreign wars

7. For President Jackson, the Bank of the United States represented _____.
   A. Wall Street domination of the nation's finances
   B. an elite threat to people's liberty
   C. a logical way to control interest rates
   D. a classic example of the spoils system

8. Between 1828 and 1836 the second American party system took shape; it _____.
   A. featured a revival of the Federalists to challenge Jeffersonian Republicans
   B. offered little more than new political labels pasted over old political organizations with the same philosophies and beliefs
   C. was chiefly sectional in nature: Whigs tended to be northerners, and Democrats tended to be southerners
   D. reestablished a fully functioning, national, two-party political system with the appearance of the Whig and Democratic parties

Short Answer: Your answers should be one or two paragraphs long and specifically address the points indicated.

9. How did President Andrew Jackson justify Indian removal?

10. What was at the basis of the nullification crisis? How did this episode escalate the ongoing debate about states' rights?

11. Why was Andrew Jackson so popular with the common man?

Essay Question: Your answer should be several paragraphs long and express a clear understanding of the points indicated.

12. Describe and explain President Andrew Jackson's decisions and actions regarding Indian removal, the nullification crisis, and the bank war. What were the effects of his decisions? How would you rate Jackson as a president?

ANSWER KEY

Answer	Learning Objectives	Focus Points	References
1. A	LO 1	FP 1	pp. 357–358, 367–368; video segments 1, 2
2. B	LO 1	FP 3	p. 351
3. C	LO 2	FP 5	pp. 367–369; video segment 2
4. B	LO 3	FP 8	pp. 369–372; video segment 5
5. D	LO 3, 6	FP 12	video segment 5
6. A	LO 4	FP 13	p. 373; video segment 3
7. B	LO 5	FP 15	pp. 373–375; video segment 3
8. D	LO 6	FP 6	pp. 368–369, 390–391; video segment 2

9. .... LO 3 .... FP 8 .... pp. 369–372; video segment 5

- What were Jackson's views on Indian treaties?
- What did he think of the "civilization" program?
- How could it benefit both Indians and whites?

10. .... LO 4 .... FP 13, 14 .... p. 373; video segment 3

- How and why did nullification challenge federal authority?
- What did President Jackson think about nullification?
- What did Jackson propose to do about it?
- What key idea now became linked to the states' rights ideology?

11. .... LO 2 .... FP 1, 5, 18 .... pp. 357–358, 390–391; video segments 1, 2, 6

- What elements of his personality appealed to and reflected the culture of the times?
- Who generally benefited from Jackson's decisions and actions? Why?

12. .... LO 2–6 .... FP 4–18 .... pp. 366–375, 385–393; video segments 2–6

- Present a clear explanation of each issue specified in the question.
- Be sure to consider the short-term as well as long-term effects.
- What was Jackson's legacy?
- What is your opinion of Jackson?

ENRICHMENT IDEAS

These activities are not required unless your instructor assigns them. They are offered as suggestions to help you learn more about the material presented in this lesson.

1. Imagine yourself to be a member of the Cherokee Nation in the 1830s. In a well-developed essay that you hope to publish in the newspaper, explain your position on the issue of removal to the West.

2. You are a banker in 1837. In a thoughtful essay, describe your perspective on the panic of 1837. Why did this happen? What should be done?

3. You are an advisor to either Andrew Jackson or John C. Calhoun during the nullification crisis. Write a position paper in which you recommend actions to be taken and a defense of those actions.

4. Research a current issue that pits states' rights against the authority of the federal government. Then submit an essay in which you explain the issue and how you think it will be resolved.

5. Examine the rationale for isolating ethnic groups at various times in American history (that is, Indian removal, segregation, Japanese American internment during World War II). Are there similarities in why this occurs? What has the nation learned from these experiences? Compose an essay dealing with these questions.

SUGGESTED READINGS/RESOURCES

See the "Bibliography" on page 391 of the text if you wish to examine other books and resources related to the material presented in this lesson.

Lesson 16

The Slave South

OVERVIEW

Slavery has a long history in America. During the colonial period the southern colonies took on a distinctive identity due, in large part, to the unique characteristics of a slave-labor system. Slavery had existed on a much smaller scale in the North until the revolutionary generation took action to abolish it there. Southern states were not ready to take that step, but some prominent individuals, including George Washington, took action to free their own slaves. Others, like Thomas Jefferson, seemed conflicted over the issue, but they could not bring themselves to act decisively against the "necessary evil" of slavery.

The evils of slavery and the potential conflicts associated with it took on a new dimension in the early nineteenth century. While a market revolution and economic evolution brought about new opportunities and a free-labor ideology in the North and West, slavery became even more entrenched in the South. The expansion of the cotton kingdom brought with it the expansion of the slave empire. But slavery was much more than just part of an economic system. It increasingly dominated southern politics and the social lives of both whites and blacks.

Slaves coped with the system in a variety of ways. Most saw no choice other than to acquiesce publicly and to negotiate private lives for their families and communities. Thousands resisted individually on the job or by running away. A few, most dramatically, engaged in violent rebellion.

By midcentury, political leaders of the slave South had largely closed the region to any discussion about eradicating slavery and were defending the institution as a "positive good." The nation was becoming half slave and half free, and whether a nation so divided could survive would ultimately be answered by a civil war. That war would abolish slavery, but the effects of that institution would continue to shape America for generations.

LESSON ASSIGNMENTS

Text: Roark, et al., *The American Promise*, Chapter 13 "The Slave South,"
            pp. 434–473

Video: "The Slave South" from the series *Shaping America*

Documents:
            "Defending Slavery," pp. 440–441 in the textbook
            "Letter to an English Abolitionist" and "Memories of a Slave Childhood" found at
            the end of this lesson

LEARNING OBJECTIVES

This lesson explains how and why slavery dominated the South in the first half of the nineteenth century and how that affected the shaping of America. Upon completing this lesson, you should be able to:

1. Explain how and why slavery spread across the South in the early nineteenth century.

2. Explain how slavery and the plantation economy affected southern economic, social, and political development.

3. Analyze how slaves and free blacks coped with the conditions existing in the slave South.

4. Assess the short- and long-term significance of the slave South on the shaping of the American nation.

LESSON FOCUS POINTS

The following questions are designed to help you get the most benefit from the sources selected for this lesson. For reference purposes, the titles for the video segments are: (1) Introduction, (2) "Shaped by Slavery," (3) "The Slave World," (4) Short-take: "Quilts and the Underground Railroad," (5) "Runaways and Rebellion," (6) Summary Analysis: "The Long Road."

1. Why was the invention of the cotton gin so important? (textbook, pp. 443–445; video segment 1)

2. What was the relationship between the spread of cotton and the spread of slavery? (textbook, pp. 436–438; video segments 1, 2)

3. Why did non-slaveholding southern whites support slavery? How did the defense of slavery evolve? What role did slavery play in unifying southern whites? Why did southern whites become intensely dedicated to white supremacy? (textbook, pp. 437–442; documents; video segment 2)

4. What characterized the plantation economy? How and why did the plantation economy dominate the South? How did this economy affect the economic and social development of the region? (textbook, pp. 442–448)

5. What was the economic relationship between the South and North? Who profited from the plantation economy? (textbook, pp. 443–448; video segment 1)

6. How did the plantation master manage his plantation? What was paternalism? How did it function in reality? (textbook, pp. 448–450)

7. How often were slaves whipped? What effect did whippings have? (textbook, pp. 452–453)

8. What roles were plantation mistresses expected to play? What did they think of miscegenation? How did the ideal of the mistress mesh with reality? (textbook, pp. 450–451, 454–456)

9. What was a typical day like for a slave? How hard were they worked? At what age did they start working? How did gender and age affect work assignments? What were these assignments? How and why did work conditions vary? (textbook, pp. 456–457; video segment 3)

10. How did slaves cope with daily life? How important were family life and religion to slaves? How did slave families organize themselves? Why was the land important to them? What aspects of Christianity did slaves embrace? Why? (textbook, pp. 457–459; video segment 3)

11. What were the various ways that slaves resisted slavery? How and why were folktales used as a form of resistance? (textbook, pp. 459–461; video segment 3)

12. How could quilts possibly be linked to runaway slaves? (video segment 4)

13. Why did slaves run away? How common were the instances of runaways? Where did they go? What happened when they were apprehended? (textbook, pp. 460–461; video segment 5)

14. Why were organized slave rebellions relatively rare? What did Denmark Vesey attempt to do? What were the results of his efforts? (textbook, pp. 460–461; video segment 5)

15. What prompted Nat Turner's rebellion? How did southern white society react to it? Why did Turner become a hero to some? (textbook, pp. 435–436; video segment 5)

16. What was life like for free blacks in the South? How did free blacks respond to the institution of slavery? (textbook, pp. 461–462)

17. Who were the "plain folk" of the Old South? What was life like for them? What were the differences between the plantation belt yeoman and the upcountry yeoman? How were "poor whites" different from yeomen? What were the hopes and visions of most of these people? How did reality limit their dreams? (textbook, pp. 462–466)

18. Why and how did the minority slaveholding whites gain and wield political power in the South? What political positions were they determined to defend? What effects did this have on politics in the South? How were political parties affected? (textbook, pp. 466–469)

19. In summary, how had slavery shaped the South? How did it affect the nation and its people in the long term? (textbook, pp. 469–470; video segment 6)

HISTORICAL EXPERTS INTERVIEWED

Ira Berlin, Professor of History, University of Maryland, College Park, MD

Raymond Dobard, Ph.D., Professor of Art and Art History, College of Arts and Sciences, Howard University, Washington, DC

Larry Hudson, Associate Professor of History, University of Rochester, Rochester, NY

Dorothy Redford, History Site Manager, Somerset Place Plantation Historic Site, Creswell, NC

James Roark, Samuel Candler Dobbs Professor of American History, Emory University, Atlanta, GA

Loren Schweninger, Professor of History, University of North Carolina at Greensboro, Greensboro, NC

PRACTICE TEST

The following items will help you evaluate your understanding of this lesson. Use the Answer Key at the end of the lesson to check your answers or to locate material related to each question.

Multiple choice: Choose the BEST answer.

1. The cultivation of cotton was well suited to the South because of the _____.
    A. number of slaves
    B. South's climate and geography
    C. number of towns and cities
    D. above-average rainfall

2. The growth in the southern slave population between 1790 and 1860 occurred primarily because of _____.
    A. the importation of slaves from Africa
    B. natural reproduction
    C. miscegenation
    D. buying slaves from the North, where the practice was waning

3. Antebellum southern whites of all classes were unanimous in their commitment to _____.
    A. the teachings of Christianity
    B. white supremacy
    C. keeping cotton their primary source of income
    D. keeping industrial growth to a minimum in the South

4. As late as 1850, there was no public school system in the South because _____.
    A. the South had no money for schools
    B. legislatures failed to provide essential services, and planters saw no need to educate their workforce
    C. Southerners sent their sons and daughters to the North for schooling
    D. Southerners were too involved in making money for themselves

5. African American Christianity, the form of religion created by slaves themselves, _____.
   A. was an interpretation of the Christian message that emphasized justice and salvation to all
   B. delivered the same message taught by white preachers
   C. was a combination of witchcraft and African traditions
   D. emphasized obedience and passive resistance

6. Slaves ran away for all of the following reasons EXCEPT _____.
   A. trouble with owners
   B. realistic chances of making it out of the South
   C. to see loved ones nearby
   D. to pursue freedom

7. The antebellum South's elite class protected slavery by _____.
   A. making sure slaveholders paid higher taxes than other whites to ensure the continued support of the poorer people
   B. trying to keep yeomen farmers and other non-slaveholders from voting
   C. criticizing people who did not own slaves and trying to convince them to join the slaveholding class
   D. stifling the expression of dissenting views

8. Slavery benefited the North by _____.
   A. opening up new jobs for immigrants
   B. providing for growth in trade goods
   C. spurring westward expansion
   D. all of the above

Short Answer: Your answers should be one or two paragraphs long and specifically address the points indicated.

9. How did slaves create a culture that sustained their lives in meaningful ways? How and why did this culture survive the abolition of slavery?

10. Why did Nat Turner lead a slave rebellion in Virginia in 1831? What meaning did Turner and the rebellion have for both blacks and whites?

Essay Question: Your answer should be several paragraphs long and express a clear understanding of the points indicated.

11. Describe and explain how slavery affected the economic, social, and political development of the South during the first half of the nineteenth century. Why did slavery become the essential difference between the North and the South? What are the long-term effects of slavery?

ANSWER KEY

Answer	Learning Objectives	Focus Points	References
1. B	LO 1	FP 2	pp. 436–438; video segments 1, 2
2. B	LO 1	FP 2	pp. 436–438; video segments 1, 2
3. B	LO 2	FP 3	pp. 437–442; documents; video segment 2
4. B	LO 2, 4	FP 4, 9	pp. 442–448, 456–457; video segment 3
5. A	LO 3	FP 10	pp. 457–459; video segment 3
6. B	LO 3	FP 13	pp. 460–461 video segment 5
7. D	LO 2	FP 18	pp. 466–469
8. B	LO 4	FP 5	pp. 443–448; video segment 1
9.	LO 3	FP 10	pp. 457–459; video segment 3

- Consider how slaves could "negotiate" work and living conditions, including use of land.
- What roles did the family and religion play?
- How did they use folktales and music?
- Be sure to give a reasoned opinion on how and why elements of the slave's culture survived the abolition of slavery.

10.	LO 3	FP 15	pp. 435–436; video segment 5

- Who was Nat Turner and what prompted his actions?
- How did whites react to the immediate threat? What did they do to prevent future rebellions?
- How did blacks view Turner?

11.	LO 1–4	FP 1–19	pp. 435–473; video segments 1–6

- Consider how and why slavery spread across the South and what that meant to the southern economy.
- What effects did slavery have on race relations and the class system in the South?
- How and why did the plantation aristocracy dominate southern politics? What interests were they sure to support?
- Consider how the South differed from the North. Why is slavery at the basis of these differences?
- How has slavery affected America since its abolition?

ENRICHMENT IDEAS

These activities are not required unless your instructor assigns them. They are offered as suggestions to help you learn more about the material presented in this lesson.

1. Imagine yourself to be a slave in 1830. Describe why you are organizing a slave rebellion, what you hope to accomplish, and how you plan to succeed. How are you going to convince others to join you?

2. Read the book *Slaves in the Family* by Edward Ball. Then write a report in which you explain what you learned from the reading.

3. Research the major issues raised by the *Amistad* affair. Then submit a report in which you describe the episode and the significance of the outcome.

4. The South became quite militant in its defense of slavery. Research how the founding of military schools (e.g., The Citadel) reflected this militancy. Submit a report on your findings.

5. Read *The Diary of Mary Chesnut* and then submit an essay in which you reflect on what you have learned from that reading.

6. Read *Somerset Homecoming* by Dorothy Spruill Redford and then submit an essay in which you describe what you learned from that book.

SUGGESTED READINGS/RESOURCES

See the "Bibliography" on pages 470–471 of the text if you wish to examine other books and resources related to the material presented in this lesson.

DOCUMENTS

James Henry Hammond, a South Carolinian politician and owner of a substantial plantation, vigorously defended the South's peculiar institution. In this letter to an English abolitionist, he clearly outlined his views.

As you read this document, focus on answering the following questions:

1. Did Hammond find any evil in slavery? How were the slaveholders responsible for their slaves?
2. How did he argue that slavery was the backbone of a republican government?
3. How did abolitionists influence slaveholders?

"Letter to an English Abolitionist," (1845) by James Henry Hammond

You will say that man cannot hold *property in man*. The answer is, that he can and *actually does* hold property in his fellow all the world over, in a variety of *forms, and has always done so*.

If you were to ask me whether I am an advocate of Slavery in the abstract, I should probably answer, that I am not, according to my understanding of the question. I do not like to deal in abstractions. It seldom leads to any useful ends. There are few universal truths. I do not now remember any single moral truth universally acknowledged. . . . Justice itself is impalpable as an abstraction, and abstract liberty the merest phantasy that ever amused the imagination. This world was made for man, and man for the world as it is. We ourselves, our relations with one another and with all matter, are real, not ideal. I might say that I am no more in favor of Slavery in the abstract, than I am of poverty, disease, deformity, idiocy, or any other inequality in the condition of the human family; that I love perfection, and think I should enjoy a millennium such as God has promised. But what would that amount to? A pledge that I would join you to set about eradicating those apparently inevitable evils of our nature, in equalizing the condition of all mankind, consummating the perfection of our race, and introducing the millennium? By no means. To effect these things, belongs exclusively to a higher power. And it would be well for us to leave the Almighty to perfect his own works and fulfil his own covenants. Especially, as the history of the past shows how entirely futile all human efforts have proved, when made for the purpose of aiding Him in carrying out even his revealed designs, and how invariably he has accomplished them by unconscious instruments, and in the face of human expectation. Nay more, that every attempt which has been made by fallible man to extort from the world obedience to his "abstract" notions of right and wrong, has been invariably attended with calamities dire, and extended just in proportion to the breadth and vigor of the movement. On Slavery in the abstract, then, it would not be amiss to have as little as possible to say. Let us contemplate it as it is. And thus contemplating it, the first question we have to ask ourselves is, whether it is contrary to the will of God, as revealed to us in his Holy Scriptures—the only certain means given us to ascertain his will. If it is, then Slavery is a sin. And I admit at once that every man is bound to set his face against it, and to emancipate his slaves, should he hold any.

Let us open these Holy Scriptures. [Hammond goes on to cite several instances from the Scriptures as biblical justification for slavery.] It is impossible to suppose that Slavery is contrary to the will of God. I think, then, I may safely conclude, and I firmly believe, that American Slavery is not only not a sin, but especially commanded by God through Moses, and approved by Christ through his apostles. And here I might close its defence; for what God ordains, and Christ sanctifies, should surely command the respect and toleration of man.

I endorse without reserve the much abused sentiment . . . that "Slavery is the corner-stone of our republican edifice;" while I repudiate, as ridiculously absurd, that much lauded but nowhere accredited dogma of Mr. Jefferson, that "all men are born equal." No society has ever yet existed . . . without a natural variety of classes. The most marked of these must, in a country like ours, be the rich and the poor, the educated and the ignorant. It will scarcely be disputed that the very poor have less leisure to prepare themselves for the proper discharge of public duties than the rich; and that the ignorant are wholly unfit for them at all. In all countries save ours, these two classes, or the poor rather, who are presumed to be necessarily ignorant, are by law expressly excluded from all participation in the management of public affairs. In a Republican Government this cannot be done. Universal suffrage, though not essential in theory, seems to be in fact a necessary appendage to a republican system. Where universal suffrage obtains, it is obvious that the government is in the hands of a numerical majority; and it is hardly necessary to say that in every part of the world more than half the people are ignorant and poor. Though no one can look upon poverty as a crime, and we do not here generally regard it as any objection to a man in his individual capacity, still it must be admitted that it is a wretched and insecure government which is administered by its most ignorant citizens, and those who have the least at stake under it. Though intelligence and wealth have great influence here, as everywhere, in keeping in check reckless and unenlightened numbers, yet it is evident to close observers, if not to all, that these are rapidly usurping all power in the non-slaveholding States, and threaten a fearful crisis in republican institutions there at no remote period. In the slaveholding States, however, nearly one-half of the whole population, and those the poorest and most ignorant, have no political influence whatever, because they are slaves. Of the other half, a large proportion are both educated and independent in their circumstances, while those who unfortunately are not so, being still elevated far above the mass, are higher toned and more deeply interested in preserving a stable and well ordered government, than the same class in any other country. Hence, Slavery is truly the "corner-stone" and foundation of every well designed and durable "republican edifice."

But the question is, whether free or slave labor is cheapest to us in this country, at this time, situated as we are. And it is decided at once by the fact that we cannot avail ourselves of any other than slave labor. We neither have, nor can we procure, other labor to any extent, or on anything like the terms mentioned. We must, therefore, content ourselves with our dear labor, under the consoling reflection that what is lost to us, is gained to humanity; and that, inasmuch as our slave costs us more than your free man costs you, by so much is he better off. Slavery is rapidly filling up our country with a hardy and healthy race, peculiarly adapted to our climate and productions, and conferring signal political and social advantages on us as a people.

Failing in all your attempts to prove that [slavery] is sinful in its nature, immoral in its effects, a political evil, and profitless to those who maintain it, you appeal to the sympathies of mankind, and attempt to arouse the world against us by the most shocking charges of tyranny and cruelty. You begin by a vehement denunciation of "the irresponsible power of one man over his fellow men." I deny that the power of the slave-holder in America is "irresponsible." He is responsible to God. He is responsible to the world. He is responsible to the community in which he lives, and to the laws under which he enjoys his civil rights. Those laws do not permit him to kill, to maim, or to punish beyond certain limits, or to overtask, or to refuse to feed and clothe his slave. In short, they forbid him to be tyrannical or cruel. Still, though a slaveholder, I freely acknowledge my obligations as a man; and that I am bound to treat humanely the fellow-creatures whom God has entrusted to my charge. I feel, therefore, somewhat sensitive under the accusation of cruelty, and disposed to defend myself and fellow-slaveholders against it. It is certainly the interest of all, and I am convinced that it is also the desire of every one of us, to treat our slaves with proper kindness. It is necessary to our deriving the greatest amount of profit from them. Of this we are all satisfied.

Slaveholders are no more perfect than other men. They have passions. Some of them, as you may suppose, do not at all times restrain them. Neither do husbands, parents and friends. And in each of these relations, as serious suffering as frequently arises from uncontrolled passions, as ever does in that of master and slave. I have no hesitation in saying that our slaveholders are kind masters, as men usually are kind husbands, parents and friends—as a general rule, kinder. A bad master—he who overworks his slaves, provides ill for them, or treats them with undue severity—loses the esteem and respect of his fellow-citizens to as great an extent as he would for the violation of any of his social and most of his moral obligations.

Of late years we have been not only annoyed, but greatly embarrassed in this matter, by the abolitionists. We have been compelled to curtail some privileges; we have been debarred from granting new ones. In the face of discussions which aim at loosening all ties between master and slave, we have in some measure to abandon our efforts to attach them to us, and control them through their affections and pride. We have to rely more and more on the power of fear. We must, in all our intercourse with them, assert and maintain strict mastery, and impress it on them that they are slaves. This is painful to us, and certainly no present advantage to them. But it is the direct consequence of the abolition agitation. We are determined to continue masters, and to do so we have to draw the rein tighter and tighter day by day to be assured that we hold them in complete check. How far this process will go on, depends wholly and solely on the abolitionists. When they desist, we can relax. We may not before . . . . I assure you that my sentiments, and feelings, and determinations, are those of every slaveholder in this country.

Now I affirm, that in Great Britain the poor and laboring classes of your own race and color, not only your fellow-beings, but your *fellow-citizens*, are more miserable and degraded, morally and physically, than our slaves; to be elevated to the actual condition of whom, would be to these, your *fellow-citizens*, a most glorious act of *emancipation*. And I also affirm, that the poor and laboring classes of our older free States would not be in a much more enviable condition, but for our Slavery. [Hammond then quotes from a British report giving examples of the terrible working conditions experienced by some free laborers in England.]

It is shocking beyond endurance to turn over your records, in which the condition of your laboring classes is but too faithfully depicted. Could our slaves but see it, they would join us in lynching the abolitionists, which, by the by, they would not now be loth to do. We never think of imposing on them such labor, either in amount or kind. We never put them to *any work*, under ten, more generally at twelve years of age, and then the very lightest. Destitution is absolutely unknown—never did a slave starve in America; while in moral sentiments and feelings, in religious information, and even in general intelligence, they are infinitely the superiors of your operatives. When you look around you, how dare you talk to us before the world of Slavery? For the condition of your wretched laborers, you, and every Briton who is not one of them, are responsible before God and man. If you are really humane, philanthropic, and charitable, here are objects for you. Relieve them. Emancipate them. Raise them from the condition of brutes, to the level of human beings—of American slaves, at least.

The American slaveholders, collectively or individually, ask no favors of any man or race who tread the earth. In none of the attributes of men, mental or physical, do they acknowledge or fear superiority elsewhere. They stand in the broadest light of the knowledge, civilization and improvement of the age, as much favored of heaven as any of the *sons of* Adam. They cannot be flattered, duped, nor bullied out of their rights or their propriety.

James Henry Hammond, "Letter to an English Abolitionist" (1845), reprinted in Drew Gilpin Faust, *The Ideology of Slavery: Proslavery Thought in the Antebellum South, 1830–1860* (Baton Rouge: Louisiana State University Press, 1981); 172–204.

This was the recollection of an elderly woman of her youth spent in slavery. She recalled how the tensions between the white leaders on the plantation and the slaves often erupted into violence.

As you read this document, focus on answering the following questions:

1. According to the speaker, where were the profits in slavery?
2. What impressions of her childhood are gleaned from her recollection?

"Memories of a Slave Childhood"

[The] overseer . . . went to my father one morning and said, "Bob, I'm gonna whip you this morning." Daddy said, "I ain't done nothing," and he said, "I know it, I'm gonna whip you to keep you from doing nothing," and he hit him with that cowhide — you know it would cut the blood out of you with every lick if they hit you hard — and daddy was chopping cotton, so he just took up his hoe and chopped right down on that man's head and knocked his brains out. Yes'm, it killed him, but they didn't put colored folks in jail then, so when old Charlie Merrill, the nigger trader, come along they sold my daddy to him, and he carried him way down in Mississippi. Ole Merrill would buy all the time, buy and sell niggers just like hogs. They sold him Aunt Phoebe's little baby that was just toddling long, and Uncle Dick — that was my mammy's brother.
 The way they would whip you was like they done my oldest sister. They tied her, and they had a place just like they're gonna barbecue a hog, and they would strip you and tie you and lay you down. . . . Old Aunt Fanny had told marster that my sister wouldn't keep her dress clean, and that's what they was whipping her 'bout. So they had her down in the cellar whipping her, and I was real little. I couldn't say "Big Sis," but I went and told Mammy. "Old Marster's got 'Big Jim' down there in the cellar beating her," and mammy got out of bed and went in there and throwed Aunt Fan out the kitchen door, and they had to stop whipping Big Sis and come and see about Aunt Fan. You see, she would tell things on the others, trying to keep from getting whipped herself. I seed mistress crack her many a time over the head with a broom, and I'd be so scared she was gonna crack me, but she never did hit me, 'cept slap me when I'd turn the babies over. I'd get tired and make like I was sleep, and would ease the cradle over and throw the baby out. I never would throw mammy's out, though. Old Miss would be setting there just knitting and watching the babies; they had a horn and every woman could tell when it was time to come and nurse her baby by the way they would blow the horn. The white folks was crazy 'bout their nigger babies, 'cause that's where they got their profit. When I'd get tired, I would just ease that baby over and Mistress would slap me so hard; I didn't know a hand could hurt so bad, but I'd take the slap and get to go out to play. She would slap me hard and say, "Git on out of here and stay till you wake up," and that was just what I wanted, 'cause I'd play then.

"Memories of a Slave Childhood" Excerpts taken from *Unwritten History of Slavery: Autobiographical Accounts of Negro Ex-Slaves* by O. S. Egypt, J. Masuoka, and C. S. Johnson. Social Science Source Documents No.1 (Fisk University, Social Science Institute, 1946), pp. 113–117, 276–279. Reprinted by permission of Fisk University Special Collections. Also excerpted from *The Female Experience: An American Documentary* edited by Gerda Lemer. (Indianapolis: Bobbs-Merrill, 1977), pp. 11–14.

Lesson 17

Perfecting America

OVERVIEW

The idea of trying to form a more perfect society in America had a long history before the nineteenth century began. To paraphrase one historian, America was the only country founded by those who were seeking perfection ("city on a hill"; "all men are created equal"; "a more perfect union") and then tried to improve upon it!

What did happen amidst the expanding opportunities in the early nineteenth century was that a new burst of religious enthusiasm compelled a new generation of Americans to seek their version of perfection. For some, like the Shakers and the Mormons, this meant following a vision toward a communal lifestyle removed from the temptations of the rest of society. For others, inspired by the belief that individuals could shape their own destinies and improve the lives of those less fortunate or able, it meant undertaking a variety of initiatives to bring about what they envisioned as a better way of life. Social reformers sought to promote temperance, improve health care, and broaden public education. Abolitionists defined slavery as a sin that must be purged. Women's rights activists pointed out that all men *and women* were created equal.

Like those coming before and after, the social reformers of the mid-nineteenth century faced real limits when trying to implement their visions of a perfect America. However, they did illustrate what was needed to bring about social change, and they inspired later generations to continue the pursuit of an American dream.

LESSON ASSIGNMENTS

Text: Roark, et al., *The American Promise,* Chapter 11, "The Expanding Republic," pp. 375–385, and Chapter 12, "The New West and Free North," pp. 409–412, 424–430

Video: "Perfecting America" from the series *Shaping America*

Documents:
    "On Conversion" and "Declaration of Sentiments" found at the end of this lesson

LEARNING OBJECTIVES

This lesson describes the causes and consequences of the religious and social reform movements occurring during the first half of the nineteenth century. Upon completing this lesson, you should be able to:

1. Analyze the cultural shifts taking place in American society during the 1820s through the 1840s.

2. Explain the major developments in American religion at this time.

3. Examine the important social reform movements of the era, particularly those involving abolition and women's rights.

4. Assess the short- and long-term effects of the social and cultural changes which occurred during this era.

LESSON FOCUS POINTS

The following questions are designed to help you get the most benefit from the sources selected for this lesson. For reference purposes, the titles for the video segments are: (1) Introduction, (2) "Paradise on Earth," (3) "I am the Revelation," (4) "An Affront in the Eyes of God," (5) "Ar'n't I a Woman," and (6) Summary Analysis: ". . . A Restorer of Truth and Goodness."

1. How and why did the doctrine of "separate spheres" develop in the 1820s and 1830s? What did this mean in the lives of men, women, and the family? (textbook, pp. 375–378)

2. How and why did the education and training of youth change in the 1820s and 1830s? What new anxieties arose about the morals of youth? Why? (textbook, pp. 378–379)

3. Who were Sarah and Angelina Grimké? How did they reflect the spirit of the times? (textbook, p. 385; video segment 1)

4. What is meant by the Second Great Awakening? How did it start and why did it spread? How would you describe and explain what happened at camp meetings? (textbook, pp. 379–380; video segment 2)

5. Who was Charles Grandison Finney? How does he explain his conversion? How did he exemplify the religious currents of the time? (textbook, pp. 379–380; document)

6. What is the millennium? How is a belief in the millennium connected to religious communes? (video segment 2)

7. Who were the Shakers? What characterized their lifestyle? What is their significance? (video segment 2)

8. What explains the development of the Church of Jesus Christ of Latter-Day Saints during the 1830s and 1840s? What beliefs and practices separated Mormons from other Christians? Why did they migrate to Utah? (textbook, pp. 409–412; video segment 2)

9. How is the religious enthusiasm present in the early and mid-nineteenth century connected to social reform movements of the era? Why do women emerge as reformers? How do Catherine Beecher and Dorothea Dix represent this? (textbook, pp. 380–381; video segment 3)

10. What explains the emergence of the temperance movement? How and why did the temperance issue move from moral suasion to a political agenda? What were the results of this movement? (textbook, p. 381; video segment 3)

11. What was the "moral reform" movement? What effects did it have? (textbook, p. 381)

12. What was transcendentalism? How did it reflect American individualism? What writers are associated with this movement? (textbook, pp. 424–425)

13. Why did so many utopian communities form during the 1840s? What beliefs characterized the Fourierist and Oneida communities? (textbook, pp. 424–425)

14. How and why did the antislavery movement become more radical in the 1830s and 1840s? What roles did William Lloyd Garrison and Frederick Douglass play in the movement? What did their working relationship illustrate? (textbook, pp. 381–385; video segment 4)

15. What roles did David Walker and Elijah Lovejoy play in the abolition movement? How important were women in the movement? What did Maria Stewart, Sojourner Truth, and Harriet Tubman do? (textbook, pp. 381–385, 426–430; video segment 4)

16. How and why did the women's rights movement evolve from other reform movements? Who were the prominent women's rights advocates? How did they challenge social norms? (textbook, pp. 425–426; video segment 5)

17. What happened at the Seneca Falls meeting? How did the Declaration of Sentiments describe the conditions of women in 1848? What was the significance of the meeting and the Declaration? (textbook, pp. 425–426; document; video segment 5)

18. In summary, what effects did the cultural, religious, and social reform movements of this era have on the shaping of America? What does this teach us about social change? (textbook, all pages; video, all segments)

HISTORICAL EXPERTS INTERVIEWED

Paul Benson, Professor of Humanities, Mountain View College, Dallas, TX

Richard Blackett, Moores Professor of History and African American Studies, University of Houston, Houston, TX

Jon Butler, Coe Professor of History, Yale University, New Haven, CT

Kathryn Sklar, Distinguished Professor of History, State University of New York, Binghamton, NY

James Stewart, James Wallace Professor of History, Macalester College, St. Paul, MN

PRACTICE TEST

The following items will help you evaluate your understanding of this lesson. Use the Answer Key at the end of the lesson to check your answers or to locate material related to each question.

Multiple choice: Choose the BEST answer.

1. After 1815, the idea of separate spheres with separate duties for men and women was strengthened by the fact that _____.
    A. most women went to work in the newly established mills and factories
    B. an experiment in which males and females had attended the same colleges and gone on to similar jobs proved unsuccessful
    C. most men worked at home and separation of men from women was necessary to avoid discord and distraction
    D. work was newly disconnected from the home and evaluated by the amount of cash it generated

2. The Second Great Awakening _____.
    A. was a philosophical offshoot of the market revolution emphasizing the pitfalls of a society run by bankers and lawyers
    B. brought forth an outpouring of evangelical religious fervor that offered salvation to anyone willing to eradicate individual sin and accept faith in God's grace
    C. constituted a second wave in a temperance movement that had failed in its first attempt
    D. was the spiritual component accompanying the second-party system

3. In the video, Professor Jon Butler observes that part of Joseph Smith's success in establishing the Mormon movement stemmed from _____.
    A. his ability to cut through some of the religious confusion of the era
    B. widespread support for practicing polygamy
    C. the availability of free land in Utah
    D. all of the above

4. Alcohol consumption in Jacksonian America was _____.
   A. characterized by moderate drinking
   B. widespread, rising, and often tended toward abusive amounts
   C. very low due to the increased safety of urban drinking water sources
   D. confined to persons over eighteen years of age

5. Within the antislavery movement, what made immediate emancipation so radical was that it _____.
   A. rejected Christian teachings
   B. sought funding from overseas
   C. endorsed imprisonment for slaveowners
   D. accepted African Americans as fully equal humans

6. The Seneca Falls convention of 1848 advocated _____.
   A. women's rights and suffrage
   B. better sanitary conditions to curb the rising infant mortality rate
   C. prohibition of intoxicating beverages
   D. the abolition of slavery

7. The social reform movements of the 1830s through the 1850s teach us that to bring about social change in America you must do all of the following EXCEPT _____.
   A. agitate
   B. reach across racial divides
   C. have a vision
   D. engage in violence

Short Answer: Your answers should be one or two paragraphs long and specifically address the points indicated.

8. What do the Shakers and the Mormons illustrate about cultural life in the first half of the nineteenth century?

9. How and why was the women's rights movement of the 1840s connected to the religious and abolitionist movements of the era?

10. How and why did the abolition movement become more radical in the 1830s and 1840s? Why is it important that it did?

Essay Question: Your answer should be several paragraphs long and express a clear understanding of the points indicated.

11. How and why did social reform movements, especially those relating to abolition and women's rights, emerge and develop out of the religious and cultural ferment of the early and mid-nineteenth century? What effects did these movements have on shaping America? What did that era teach us about social change?

ANSWER KEY

Answer	Learning Objectives	Focus Points	References
1. D	LO 1	FP 1	pp. 375–378
2. B	LO 2	FP 4	pp. 379–380; video segment 2
3. A	LO 2	FP 8	pp. 409–412; video segment 2
4. B	LO 3	FP 10	p. 381; video segment 3
5. D	LO 3	FP 14	pp. 381–385; video segment 4
6. A	LO 3	FP 17	pp. 425–426; document; video segment 5
7. D	LO 4	FP 18	all pages and all video segments

8. ....LO 1, 2...........FP 6, 7, 8 .... pp. 409–412; video segment 2
   - What cultural changes encouraged the development of new religions?
   - How and why did each group arrange its community as it did?
   - What was the significance of each group?

9. ....LO 2, 3.....FP 3, 9–11, 15–16 ....pp. 385, 380–385, 425–430; .... video segments 1, 3, 4
   - How and why did religion help some women get out of their normal sphere?
   - What roles did women play in the abolition movement? How were they treated?
   - What connections did women make between slaves and their own status?

10. ....LO 3, 4...........FP 14–15 ....pp. 381–385, 426–430
    - Why was immediate emancipation considered radical?
    - Why was defining slavery as a sin important?
    - How did the abolitionists challenge the United States to live up to its principles?

11. ....LO 1–4............FP 1–18 ....pp. 375–385, 409–412, 424–430; .... video segments 1–6
    - Consider the economic, social, and political changes occurring at the time.
    - Why did evangelical religious enthusiasm spread relatively quickly?
    - Why and how did people think they could perfect society?
    - How does temperance, moral reform, care for the insane, etc., have a moral basis?
    - How does abolition appear radical? How does it define slavery?
    - What factors influenced women to become organized in their own behalf?
    - What were the long-term effects of these movements?
    - What does it take to bring about social change?

ENRICHMENT IDEAS

These activities are not required unless your instructor assigns them. They are offered as suggestions to help you learn more about the material presented in this lesson.

1. Imagine yourself to be a young man or woman in western New York in the 1830s and 1840s. You are swept up by the religious ferment of the times and decide to join a religious commune. In a well-developed essay, explain why you have made this decision, what type of commune you are joining, and what you hope to accomplish.

2. Research the history of William Miller, the religious movement that he started in the 1840s, and the effects of this movement. Then submit an essay in which you describe your findings.

3. Research the life of Sylvester Graham. In a well-developed essay, describe what you discovered about Graham and the effect that he had on food products in the United States.

4. Some people argue that you cannot legislate morality. In a thoughtful essay, explain how the abolition movement, the temperance movement, and anti-abortion/free-choice movements all have attempted to affect moral behavior by using the law. What have been the results of their efforts? What are your conclusions?

5. Research the life and work of Margaret Fuller. Then submit an essay in which you describe her role in the transcendentalist movement.

SUGGESTED READINGS/RESOURCES

See the "Bibliography" on page 391 and pages 430–431 of the text if you wish to examine other books and resources related to the material presented in this lesson.

DOCUMENTS

Charles G. Finney, a leading revivalist of the second quarter of the nineteenth century, was especially prominent in urban areas of the United States. His conversion was so overwhelming he gave up his legal practice and took the Gospel to the people. Finney explained his conversion, and, in essence, spoke for thousands that came under the influence of the Second Great Awakening.

As you read this document, focus on answering the following questions:

1. What physical and mental changes did Finney undergo?
2. How did his life change?

"On Conversion" (1821) by Charles Grandison Finney

On a Sunday evening in the autumn of 1821 I made up my mind that I would settle the question of my soul's salvation at once, that if it were possible I would make my peace with God.

During Monday and Tuesday my convictions increased, but still it seemed as if my heart grew harder. I could not shed a tear. I could not pray.

Tuesday night I had become very nervous, and in the night a strange feeling came over me as if I were about to die. I knew that if I did I would sink down to hell, but I quieted myself as best I could until morning. At an early hour I started for the office. But just before I arrived at the office, it seemed as if an inward voice confronted me with questions like these: "What are you waiting for? Did you not promise to give your heart to God? And what are you trying to do? Are you endeavoring to work out a righteousness of your own?"

Just at this point the whole question of Gospel salvation opened to my mind in a manner most marvelous. I think I then saw, as clearly as I ever have in my life, the reality and fullness of the atonement of Christ. I saw that his work was a finished work, and that instead of having, or needing, any righteousness of my own to recommend me to God, I had to submit to the righteousness of God through Christ. Gospel salvation seemed to be an offer to be accepted, and that it was full and complete. All that was necessary on my part was my own consent to give up my sins and accept Christ. Salvation was not achieved by my own works, but was to be found entirely in the Lord Jesus Christ, who presented himself before me as my God and my Savior.

Without being distinctly aware of it, I had stopped in the street right where the inward voice seemed to arrest me. How long I remained in that position I cannot say. But after this distinct revelation had stood for some little time before my mind, the question seemed to be, "Will you accept it now, today?"

I replied, "Yes, I will accept it today, or I will die in the attempt."

The thought was pressing me of the rashness of my promise that I would give my heart to God that day or die in the attempt. It seemed to me as if that was binding upon my soul, and yet I was going to break my vow. A great sinking and discouragement came over me, and I felt almost too weak to stand upon my knees.

Just at this moment I again thought I heard someone approach me, and I opened my eyes to see whether it were so. But right there the revelation of my pride was distinctly shown to me as the great difficulty that stood in the way. An overwhelming sense of my wickedness in being ashamed to have a human being see me on my knees before God took such powerful possession of me that I cried at the top of my voice and exclaimed that I would not leave that place if all the men on earth and all the devils in hell surrounded me. "What!" I said, "such a degraded sinner as I am, on my knees confessing my sins to the great and holy God, ashamed to have any human being find me on my knees endeavoring to make my peace with my offended God!" The sin appeared awful, infinite. It broke me down before the Lord.

Just at that point this passage of scripture seemed to drop into my mind with a flood of light: "Then shall you go and pray unto me, and I will hearken to you. Then shall you seek me and find me, when you shall search for me with all your heart."

I instantly seized hold of this with my heart. I had intellectually believed the Bible before, but never had the truth been in my mind that faith was a voluntary trust instead of an intellectual state. I was as conscious of trusting at that moment in God's truthfulness as I was of my own existence. Somehow I knew that that was a passage of scripture, though I do not think I had ever read it. I knew that it was God's word, and God's voice, as it were, that spoke to me.

I cried to him, "Lord, I take Thee at Thy word. Now Thou knowest that I do search for Thee with all my heart, and that I have come here to pray to Thee; and Thou hast promised to hear me."

But how was I to account for the quiet of my mind? I tried to recall my convictions, to get back again the load of sin under which I had been laboring. But all sense of sin, all consciousness of present sin or guilt, had departed from me. I said to myself, "What is this, that I cannot arouse any sense of guilt in my soul, as great a sinner as I am?" I tried in vain to make myself anxious about my present state. I was so quiet and peaceful that I tried to feel concerned about that, lest it should be a result of my having grieved the Spirit away. But take any view of it I would, I could not be anxious at all about my soul and about my spiritual state. The repose of my mind was unspeakably great. I cannot describe it in words. The thought of God was sweet to my mind, and the most profound spiritual tranquillity had taken full possession of me. This was a great mystery, but it did not distress or perplex me.

[That evening] There was no fire and no light in this back room; nevertheless it appeared to me as if it were perfectly light. As I went in and shut the door after me, it seemed as if I met the Lord Jesus Christ face to face. It seemed to me that I saw him as I would see any other man. He said nothing, but looked at me in such a manner as to break me right down at his feet. It seemed to me a reality that he stood before me, and I fell down at his feet and poured out my soul to him. I wept aloud like a child and made such confessions as I could with my choked words. It seemed to me that I bathed his feet with my tears, and yet I had no distinct impression that I touched him.

I must have continued in this state for a good while, but my mind was too much absorbed with the interview to remember anything that I said. As soon as my mind became calm enough I returned to the front office and found that the fire I had made of large wood was nearly burned out. But as I turned and was about to take a seat by the fire, I received a mighty baptism of the Holy Spirit. Without any expectation of it, without ever having the thought in my mind that there was any such thing for me, without any memory of ever hearing the thing mentioned by any person in the world, the Holy Spirit descended upon me in a manner that seemed to go through me, body and soul. I could feel the impression, like a wave of electricity, going through and through me. Indeed it seemed to come in waves of liquid love, for I could not express it in any other way. It seemed like the very breath of God. I can remember distinctly that it seemed to fan me, like immense wings.

No words can express the wonderful love that was spread abroad in my heart. I wept aloud with joy and love. I literally bellowed out the unspeakable overflow of my heart. These waves came over me, and over me, and over me, one after the other, until I remember crying out, "I shall die if these waves continue to pass over me." I said, "Lord, I cannot bear any more," yet I had no fear of death.

In this state I was taught the doctrine of justification by faith as a present experience. That doctrine had never taken possession of my mind. I had never viewed it distinctly as a fundamental doctrine of the Gospel. Indeed, I did not know at all what it meant in the proper sense. But I could now see and understand what was meant by the passage, "Being justified by faith, we have peace with God through our Lord Jesus Christ." I could see that the moment I believed, while up in the woods, all sense of condemnation had entirely dropped out of my mind, and that from that moment I could not feel a sense of guilt or condemnation by any effort I could make. My sense of guilt was gone, my sins were gone, and I do not think I felt any more sense of guilt than if I never had sinned.

This was just the revelation I needed. I felt myself justified by faith, and, so far as I could see, I was in a state in which I did not sin. Instead of feeling that I was sinning all the time, my heart was so full of love that it overflowed. My cup ran over with blessing and with love. I could not feel that I was sinning against God, nor could I recover the least sense of guilt for my past sins. Of this experience of justification I said nothing to anybody at the time.

"On Conversion (1821)" Taken from *The Autobiography of Charles Finney*, condensed and edited by Helen Wessel, pp. 13–25. Copyright 1977.

Elizabeth Cady Stanton (1815–1902) played a major role in drafting the Declaration that was presented at the convention at Seneca Falls, New York, in 1848. The Declaration is possibly the most significant document in the history of U.S. women.

As you read this document, focus on answering the following questions:

1. What are the most significant demands in the document?
2. Did the Declaration deny or uphold the view of women's moral superiority?
3. In what ways did the Declaration speak for all women?
4. In what ways did it reflect the particular experience of white middle-class women?

"Declaration of Sentiments" (1848) by Elizabeth Cady Stanton

When, in the course of human events, it becomes necessary for one portion of the family of man to assume among the people of the earth a position different from that which they have hitherto occupied, but one to which the laws of nature and of nature's God entitle them, a decent respect to the opinions of mankind requires that they should declare the causes that impel them to such a course.

We hold these truths to be self-evident: that all men and women are created equal; that they are endowed by their Creator with certain inalienable rights; that among these are life, liberty and the pursuit of happiness; that to secure these rights governments are instituted, deriving their just powers from the consent of the governed. Whenever any form of government becomes destructive of these ends, it is the right of those who suffer from it to refuse allegiance to it, and to insist upon the institution of a new government, laying its foundation on such principles, and organizing its powers in such form, as to them shall seem most likely to effect their safety and happiness. Prudence, indeed, will dictate that governments long established should not be changed for light and transient causes; and accordingly all experience has shown that mankind are more disposed to suffer, while evils are sufferable, than to right themselves by abolishing the forms to which they are accustomed. But when a long train of abuses and usurpations, pursuing invariably the same object, evinces a design to reduce them under absolute despotism, it is their duty to throw off such government, and to provide new guards for their future security. Such has been the patient sufferance of the women under this government, and such is now the necessity which constrains them to demand the equal station to which they are entitled.

The history of mankind is a history of repeated injuries and usurpations on the part of man toward woman, having in direct object the establishment of an absolute tyranny over her. To prove this, let facts be submitted to a candid word.

He has never permitted her to exercise her inalienable right to the elective franchise.

He has compelled her to submit to laws, in the formation of which she had no voice.

He has withheld from her rights which are given to the most ignorant and degraded men—both natives and foreigners.

Having deprived her of this first right of a citizen, the elective franchise, thereby leaving her without representation in the halls of legislation, he has oppressed her on all sides.

He has made her, if married, in the eye of the law, civilly dead.

He has taken from her all right in property, even to the wages she earns.

He has made her, morally, an irresponsible being, as she can commit many crimes with impunity, provided they be done in the presence of her husband. In the covenant of marriage, she is compelled to promise obedience to her husband, he becoming, to all intents and purposes, her master, the law giving him power to deprive her of her liberty, and to administer chastisement.

He has so framed the laws of divorce, as to what shall be the proper causes, and in case of separation, to whom the guardianship of the children shall be given, as to be wholly regardless of the happiness of women—the law, in all cases, going upon a false supposition of the supremacy of man, and giving all power into his hands.

After depriving her of all rights as a married woman, if single, and the owner of property, he has taxed her to support a government which recognizes her only when her property can be made profitable to it.

He has monopolized nearly all the profitable employments, and from those she is permitted to follow, she receives but a scanty remuneration. He closes against her all the avenues to wealth and distinction which he considers most honorable to himself. As a teacher of theology, medicine, or law, she is not known.

He has denied her the facilities for obtaining a thorough education, all colleges being closed against her.

He allows her in Church, as well as in State, but a subordinate position, claiming Apostolic authority for her exclusion from the ministry, and, with some exceptions, from any public participation in the affairs of the Church.

He has created a false public sentiment by giving to the world a different code of morals for men and women, by which the moral delinquencies which exclude women from society are not only tolerated, but deemed of little account in man.

He has usurped the prerogative of Jehovah himself, claiming it as his right to assign for her a sphere of action, when that belongs to her conscience and to her God.

He has endeavored, in every way he could, to destroy her confidence in her own powers, to lessen her self-respect, and to make her willing to lead a dependent and abject life.

Now, in the view of this entire disfranchisement of one-half of the people of this country, their social and religious degradation, in view of the unjust laws above mentioned, and because women do feel themselves aggrieved, oppressed, and fraudulently deprived of their most sacred rights, we insist that they have immediate admission to all the rights and privileges which belong to them as citizens of the United States.

In entering upon the great work before us, we anticipate no small amount of misconception, misrepresentation, and ridicule; but we shall use every instrumentality within our power to effect our object. We shall employ agents, circulate tracts, petition the State and National legislatures, and endeavor to enlist the pulpit and the press on our behalf. We hope this Convention will be followed by a series of Conventions embracing every part of the country .

From "Declaration of Sentiments," ed. Elizabeth Cady Stanton, Susan B. Anthony, and Matilda J. Gage, in *History of Woman Suffrage* (Rochester: Charles Mann, 1881), I: 67–94.

Lesson 18

Moving Westward

OVERVIEW

For generations, white Americans from both the North and South moved westward in pursuit of opportunities. By the 1830s and 1840s, the westward expansion of the American people had brought them once again into territory claimed by other people and nations. It was then that the term *manifest destiny* became the latest justification for this march across the continent, spreading the benefits of American culture. National boundaries, expanded earlier in the century by the Louisiana Purchase and the Adams-Onis Treaty, would soon include the Oregon country, California, Texas, and areas in between.

In the process of this westward movement, the United States went to war with Mexico in 1846. Although the events which sparked the war were controversial, the decisiveness of the American victory was not in question. The treaty ending that war recognized new United States borders and acknowledged the rights of the Mexican nationals, now known as "Mexican Americans," who chose to stay in American territory. Even today, the effects of the U.S.-Mexican War and the Treaty of Guadalupe Hidalgo continue to resonate with people on both sides of the border.

The year 1848 provides a useful time to pause and reflect on how and why the United States had taken shape during the first half of the nineteenth century. The last segment of the video accompanying this lesson should help place that era in perspective. Just as the geographic boundaries of the United States had changed, the boundaries of American freedom and identity were also being redrawn.

LESSON ASSIGNMENTS

Text: Roark, et al., *The American Promise*, Chapter 12 "The New West and Free North," pp. 407–424

Video: "Moving Westward" from the series *Shaping America*

Documents:

"Sumner Assails the Texas Grab" and "A Mexican View" found at the end of this lesson

LEARNING OBJECTIVES

This lesson is about how and why the United States expanded its geographic borders in the 1840s and how that affected the American people. In addition, you will be asked to reflect upon how American identity, freedom, and equality were shaped in the first half of the nineteenth century. Upon completing this lesson, you should be able to:

1. Explain the concept of manifest destiny and how that term came to justify American expansionism in the 1840s.

2. Explain American interests in the Oregon country and how disputes with Britain in that region were resolved.

3. Analyze the causes and consequences of the U.S.-Mexican War.

4. Describe the geographic expansion of the United States from 1801–1848 and how the United States acquired this territory.

5. Assess how American identity and the concepts of freedom and equality had been shaped during the first half of the nineteenth century.

LESSON FOCUS POINTS

The following questions are designed to help you get the most benefit from the sources selected for this lesson. For reference purposes, the titles for the video segments are: (1) Introduction, (2) "Oregon Fever," (3) "We Must Have Texas," (4) "The U.S.-Mexican War," (5) Unit Close: "Manifest Destiny?"

1. What was meant by the term *manifest destiny*? How did it provide "an ideological shield" for American westward expansion in the 1840s? How are the concepts conveyed by the term linked backward and forward in American history? (textbook, pp. 407–408; video segment 1)

2. Why did Americans want to go to Oregon? How did they get there? What hardships did they endure in migrating? What did the settlers find when they got there? How did men and women cope with the conditions? (textbook, pp. 408–411; video segment 2)

3. What characterized the lifestyles of Plains Indians? How did the Anglo migration westward affect these Indians? How and why did the policy of placing Indians on reservations begin? (textbook, pp. 408–411)

4. How and why did Americans become interested in the Mexican borderlands of New Mexico, Texas, and California? (textbook, pp. 411–414; video segment 2)

5. Why and how did the Mexican government recruit Anglo-Americans to Texas? Why did Texans revolt against Mexico? How were they able to win independence? Why was Texas' annexation to the United States postponed? (textbook, pp. 413–416; video segment 3)

6. How were the developments in California in this period similar and different from those in Texas? (textbook, p. 414)

7. How did John Tyler become president? How did his decisions affect the Whig Party? What actions did President Tyler take on the question of Texas' annexation? (textbook, pp. 414–415)

8. What roles did the annexation of Texas and Oregon play in the 1844 presidential election? Why did James K. Polk win? What was important about his victory? (textbook, pp. 415–416)

9. Why did President Polk pursue peaceful compromise with Britain in Oregon and war with Mexico in Texas? (textbook, pp. 415–417; video segments 2, 3)

10. How did the U.S.-Mexican War begin? Who provoked whom? Who opposed the war? Why? (textbook, pp. 416–417; video segment 4)

11. How and why did the United States defeat Mexico? (textbook, pp. 417–420; video segment 4)

12. What were the terms of the Treaty of Guadalupe Hidalgo? (textbook, p. 420; video segment 4)

13. What were the short- and long-term consequences of the U.S.-Mexican War for Mexico and the United States? (textbook, pp. 420–424; video segment 4)

14. In summary, how did the United States acquire each major piece of new territory between 1801 and 1848? Use Map 12.5 in the text for reference. What were the consequences of this geographic expansion? (textbook, p. 420; comprehensive, Lessons 13–18)

15. In addition to geographic changes, how did America change economically, politically, and socially between 1801 and 1848? What was the legacy of this period, particularly in regard to American identity and the concepts of freedom and equality? (video segment 5; comprehensive, Lessons 13–18)

HISTORICAL EXPERTS INTERVIEWED

Ernesto Chavez, Assistant Professor, University of Texas at El Paso, El Paso, TX

R. David Edmunds, Watson Professor of American History, University of Texas at Dallas, Richardson, TX

Eric Foner, Professor of History, Columbia University, New York City, NY

David Gutierrez, Associate Professor, University of California at San Diego, La Jolla, CA

James Oliver Horton, Benjamin Banneker Professor of American Civilization and History, The George Washington University, Washington, DC

Robert Johannsen, J. G. Randall Distinguished Professor of History Emeritus, University of Illinois Urbana-Champaign, Champaign, IL

Linda Kerber, May Brodbeck Professor in the Liberal Arts and Professor of History, University of Iowa, Iowa City, IA

Chet Orloff, Director, Oregon Historical Society, Portland, OR

PRACTICE TEST

The following items will help you evaluate your understanding of this lesson. Use the Answer Key at the end of the lesson to check your answers or to locate material related to each question.

Multiple choice: Choose the BEST answer.

1. In 1845, New York journalist and expansionist John L. O'Sullivan coined the term *manifest destiny* which meant _____.
    A. the United States should expand into Canada and Mexico
    B. Americans were destined by a higher power to create a worldwide empire
    C. the United States should take advantage of economic turmoil in Europe to gain new markets
    D. Americans had the God-given right to expand their superior civilization across the country

2. In the video, historian Chet Orloff observes that the Oregon Trail experience _____.
    A. most often ended in failure
    B. reinforced the idea of moving west to start over again
    C. actually benefited the Indian peoples in the region
    D. was extremely dangerous when Britain had claims to the area

3. How was President Polk able to add Oregon to U.S. holdings?
    A. He annexed it without approval by the British.
    B. He authorized military action.
    C. He recommended a continued joint occupation with Britain.
    D. He renewed an old offer to divide Oregon along the forty-ninth parallel, and the British accepted.

4. In 1829, Mexico issued an emancipation proclamation in Texas because _____.
   A. it hoped to discourage any further American settlers from coming to the area
   B. the Texans were asking for independence
   C. the Mexicans were opposed to slavery on their land
   D. Santa Anna had a change of heart and decided the area was better off undeveloped

5. Just prior to James K. Polk's taking office in 1845, President Tyler was successful in obtaining the annexation of Texas by _____.
   A. passage of a joint resolution of Congress, admitting Texas as the fifteenth slave state
   B. Senate approval of a treaty to annex Texas
   C. negotiating with Mexican officials
   D. sending John Slidell to Mexico to buy Texas freedom from the Mexicans

6. In the video, Professor Robert Johannsen points out that one reason American military efforts in the U.S.-Mexican War had support at home was because most Americans _____.
   A. advocated the expansion of slavery
   B. saw the war as a fight between a republic and a dictatorship
   C. wanted to settle in the Southwest
   D. desired easier access to the California gold fields

7. The Mexican War ended with the 1848 Treaty of Guadalupe Hidalgo, which stipulated that _____.
   A. Mexico agreed that the Nueces River was the Texas boundary
   B. Mexico agreed to pay $15 million to American citizens for claims against Mexico
   C. Mexico agreed to give up Wyoming and Idaho
   D. Mexico gave up claims to Texas and ceded the provinces of New Mexico and California to the United States

8. In the video, Professor Eric Foner observes that, during the 1840s, the abolition and women's movements were _____.
   A. uniting in their support for the Republican Party
   B. convincing states to support equal rights amendments
   C. losing ground to more radical political groups
   D. demanding that freedom be a universal entitlement

Short Answer: Your answers should be one or two paragraphs long and specifically address the points indicated.

9. Define the term *manifest destiny*. How is this concept linked to earlier "missionary" ideas in American history? How was the term an "intellectual shield" for American expansionism?

10. Why were the disputes between Britain and the United States in the Oregon Country settled peacefully? How were they settled?

11. Do you think President James K. Polk provoked war with Mexico in 1846 or was he defending U.S. territory at the time? Explain.

12. How did the United States' annexation of the Southwest affect Mexicans who had been living in that region?

Essay Questions: Your answers should be several paragraphs long and express a clear understanding of the points indicated.

13. Describe and explain how the United States acquired each major piece of new territory between 1801 and 1848. What were the consequences of this geographic expansion?

14. How and why did the meaning of freedom in America change in the period from 1801 to 1848? How did American Indians, women, and African Americans fit into the spectrum of American freedom and identity? In what way was a Mexican American identity present?

ANSWER KEY

Answer	Learning Objectives	Focus Points	References
1. D	LO 1	FP 1	pp. 407–408; video segment 1
2. B	LO 2	FP 2	pp. 408–411; video segment 2
3. D	LO 2	FP 9	pp. 415–417; video segments 2, 3
4. A	LO 3	FP 5	pp. 413–416; video segment 3
5. A	LO 3	FP 7	pp. 414–415
6. B	LO 3	FP 11	pp. 417–420; video segment 4
7. D	LO 3, 4	FP 12, 13	pp. 420–424; video segment 4
8. D	LO 5	FP 15	comprehensive, Lessons 13–18; video segment 5

9. ....LO 1.................FP 1 ....pp. 407–408; video segment 1
    *   What noble ideas are being spread across the continent?
    *   How does it connect to the Puritan mission and the Revolutionary ideals?
    *   How would the idea help avert criticism of expansionism?

10. ....LO 2................FP 2, 9 .... pp. 408–411, 415–417; video segments 2, 3
    *   What else was concerning the United States at the same time?
    *   What attitudes did the Americans have toward the British?
    *   Where was the boundary drawn? Why there?

11. ....LO 3.................FP 10...pp. 416–417; video segment 4
    *   What was the incident that sparked the war?
    *   Take a stand on the actions taken.
    *   Explain your position.

12. ....LO 3.............FP 12, 13...pp. 420–424; video segment 4
    *   What did the Treaty of Guadalupe Hidalgo say about these people?
    *   What happened to the property rights involved?
    *   What sort of cultural adaptation occurred in the short term?

13. ....LO 4.................FP 14....................................p. 420; comprehensive, Lessons 13–18
- Consider the Louisiana Purchase and the Adams-Onis Treaty. What areas were acquired? How did Oregon become part of the United States?
- How and why was Texas annexed?
- What territories were acquired in the Mexican Cession?
- Consider the positive and negative effects.

14. ....LO 5.................FP 15...................comprehensive, Lessons 13–18; video segment 5
- Consider how the free-labor concept emerged during this time.
- Did political freedom change for white men?
- How did the status of American Indians change? How could they maintain an identity?
- How were women challenging limits on their freedom?
- How did the status of African Americans deny freedom? What was their identity?
- What occurred to affect Mexican Americans?

ENRICHMENT IDEAS

These activities are not required unless your instructor assigns them. They are offered as suggestions to help you learn more about the material presented in this lesson.

1. Imagine yourself to be a top official in the Mexican government in 1829. Write a position paper explaining your concerns about developments in Texas and what you propose to do about them.

2. Henry David Thoreau expressed his opposition to the Mexican American war by refusing to pay taxes. He was arrested and imprisoned briefly, an experience that formed the basis for an essay entitled "Civil Disobedience." Read the essay and then write a report in which you summarize the essay. Why did he take the position that he did? Do you agree with him?

3. Watch the film entitled "The U.S.-Mexican War," produced by KERA (Dallas). Then submit a report in which you summarize how that film broadened your understanding of that war.

4. Imagine yourself to be a Mexican national who owns land in the area of New Mexico at the time of the signing of the Treaty of Guadalupe Hidalgo. In a well-developed essay, explain the choices that you have and what course of action you are going to take.

SUGGESTED READINGS/RESOURCES

See the "Bibliography" on pages 430–431 of the text if you wish to examine other books and resources related to the material presented in this lesson.

DOCUMENTS

The Abolitionist Charles Sumner drafted this resolution and the Massachusetts Legislature passed it in opposition to the U.S.-Mexican War. It reflected the views of many northerners who strongly opposed the war because they saw it as a means to acquire more slave territory.

1. In what ways is this resolution accurate in describing the outbreak of the war?
2. Did it verge on treason? Why or why not?

"Sumner Assails the Texas Grab" (1847)

The history of the annexation of Texas cannot be fully understood without reverting to the early settlement of that province by citizens of the United States.

Mexico, on achieving her independence of the Spanish Crown, by a general ordinance worthy of imitation by all Christian nations, had decreed the abolition of human slavery within her dominions, embracing the province of Texas. . . .

At this period, citizens of the United States had already begun to remove into Texas, hardly separated, as it was, by the River Sabine from the slaveholding state of Louisiana. The idea was early promulgated that this extensive province ought to become a part of the United States. Its annexation was distinctly agitated in the Southern and Western states in 1829; and it was urged on the ground of the strength and extension it would give to the "Slave Power," and the fresh market it would open for the sale of slaves.

The suggestion of this idea had an important effect. A current of emigration soon followed from the United States. Slaveholders crossed the Sabine with their slaves, in defiance of the Mexican ordinance of freedom. Restless spirits, discontented at home, or feeling the restraint of the narrow confines of our country, joined them; while their number was swollen by the rude and lawless of all parts of the land, who carried to Texas the love of license which had rendered a region of justice no longer a pleasant home to them. To such spirits, rebellion was natural.

It soon broke forth. At this period the whole [Texan] population, including women and children, did not amount to twenty thousand; and, among these, most of the older and wealthier inhabitants still favored peace. A Declaration of Independence, a farcical imitation of that of our fathers, was put forth, not by persons acting in a Congress or in a representative character, but by about ninety individuals—all, except two, from the United States—acting for themselves, and recommending a similar course to their fellow citizens. In a just cause the spectacle of this handful of adventurers, boldly challenging the power of Mexico, would excite our sympathy, perhaps our admiration. But successful rapacity, which seized broad and fertile lands while it opened new markets for slaves, excites no sentiment but that of abhorrence.

The work of rebellion sped. Citizens of the United States joined its fortunes, not singly, but in numbers, even in armed squadrons. Our newspapers excited the lust of territorial robbery in the public mind. Expeditions were openly equipped within our own borders. Advertisements for volunteers summoned the adventurous, as to patriotic labors. Military companies, with officers and standards, directed their steps to the revolted province.

During all this period the United States were at peace with Mexico. A proclamation from our government, forbidding these hostile preparations within our borders, is undeniable evidence of their existence, while truth compels us to record its impotence in upholding the sacred duties of neutrality between Mexico and the insurgents. . . .

The Texan flag waved over an army of American citizens. Of the six or eight hundred who won the [decisive] battle of San Jacinto, scattering the Mexican forces and capturing their general [Santa Anna], not more than fifty were citizens of Texas having grievances of their own to redress on that field.

The victory was followed by the recognition of the independence of Texas by the United States; while the new state took its place among the nations of the earth. . . .

Certainly our sister republic [Mexico] might feel aggrieved by this conduct. It might justly charge our citizens with disgraceful robbery, while, in seeking extension of slavery, they repudiated the great truths of American freedom.

Meanwhile Texas slept on her arms, constantly expecting new efforts from Mexico to regain her former power. The two combatants regarded each other as enemies. Mexico still asserted her right to the territory wrested from her, and refused to acknowledge its independence.

Texas turned for favor and succor to England. The government of the United States, fearing it might pass under the influence of this power, made overtures for its annexation to our country. This was finally accomplished by joint resolutions of Congress, in defiance of the Constitution [?], and in gross insensibility to the sacred obligations of amity with Mexico, imposed alike by treaty and by justice, "both strong against the deed." The Mexican minister regarded it as an act offensive to his country, and, demanding his passport, returned home.

Old South Leaflets (1904), Vol. 6, no. 132, pp. 10–11, 30–31

In this elementary survey of Mexican history, Mexicans gave their account of the war and treaty which followed it. They bitterly resented losing almost half of their territory.

As you read this document, focus on answering the following questions:

1. What were the weaknesses of Mexican resistance to American military advances?
2. What issues remained most difficult for the Mexicans to accept?

"A Mexican View" (1935)

In the war with the United States, and in the military operations incidental thereto, we are unable to find a single outstanding figure to represent the defense of Mexico, in the form of a hero or military leader. Invasion first of all took place from the north, and the American troops defeated our armies, not beneath them in courage, but due to inferior organization, armaments, and high command. The classes that controlled material resources, and the groups at the head of the political situation, failed to rise to the occasion in that desperate situation.

A chronicle of the march of invasion makes painful reading. Our soldiers were defeated at Matamoros, at Resaca de Guerrero, and Monterrey, in spite of the sacrifices of the troops.

When one follows, event by event, the military operations and the political happenings of this period, one's feelings are harrowed by the details.

In this swift historical sketch, we shall be content to mention, if no great captain representative of defense, the youthful heroes who saved the honor of Mexico: the cadets of the Military College [at Chapultepec], who fell on September 13, 1847, when the school was stormed by the invading troops, then on the point of occupying the capital of the Republic. The glorious deaths of Francisco Marquez, Agustin Melgar, Juan Escutia, Fernando Montes de Oca, Vicente Suarez, and Juan de la Barrera, in an unequal contest, without hope, crushed by an overwhelming force, are as it were a symbol and image of this unrighteous war.

To Mexico, the American invasion contains a terrible lesson. In this war we saw that right and justice count but little in contests between one people and another, when material force, and organization, are wanting.

A great portion of Mexico's territory was lost because she had been unable to administer and settle those regions, and handed them over to alien colonization [Texas].

There is no principle nor law that can sanction spoliation. Only by force was it carried out, and only by force or adroit negotiation could it have been avoided. That which Spain had been unable to colonize, and the [Mexican] Republic to settle, was occupied by the stream of Anglo-American expansion.

The war of 1847 is not, so far as Mexico is concerned, offset by anything but the courage of her soldiers. At Matamoros, at Resaca de Guerrero, at La Angostura [Buena Vista], at Vera Cruz, at Cerro Gordo, at Padierna, at Churubusco, and at Chapultepec, victory was won by a well-organized and instructed General Staff; by longer-range rifles and cannon, better-fed soldiers, abundance of money and ammunition, and of horses and wagons. . . .

The American invasion cost Mexico the total loss of Texas, whose boundaries were, without the slightest right, brought down to the Rio Grande; the Province of New Mexico and Upper California; and an outpouring of blood, energy, and wealth, offset only by material compensation in the amount of fifteen million pesos, by way of indemnity.

Alfonso Teja Zabre, *Guide to the History of Mexico* (Mexico: Ministry of Foreign Affairs, 1935), pp. 299–304, passim.

Unit Four

America in Crisis
1848-1877
"A New Birth of Freedom?"

THEME

When the U.S.-Mexican War began, the essayist Ralph Waldo Emerson turned prophet. He wrote, "The United States will conquer Mexico, but it will be as the man who swallows the arsenic which brings him down in turn. Mexico will poison us." That war immediately reopened the divisive issue of the expansion of slavery into the territories. This was not a new issue, but this time the attempts to compromise it would ultimately fail.

During the 1850s, conflicts over the issues centering on slavery proved to be irrepressible. Resistance to the Fugitive Slave Law of 1850 dramatized the issue of freedom, and abolitionists pounded away at the moral evil of the South's "peculiar institution." The opening of Kansas and Nebraska territories to the possibilities of slavery led to bloodshed on the plains and in the halls of Congress. National political parties splintered, and a northern sectional party emerged with a position diametrically opposed to the ruling of the Supreme Court in its Dred Scott decision. When the Republicans won the presidential election of 1860, southern secessionists proceeded to attempt to dissolve the United States of America. And the war came.

The Civil War tested, as Abraham Lincoln would say at Gettysburg in 1863, whether a nation "conceived in Liberty, and dedicated to the proposition that all men are created equal" could long endure. In that same address, Lincoln called for the nation to seek "a new birth of freedom." The results of the Civil War preserved the Union and brought about the abolition of slavery, but freedom remained contested territory during Reconstruction. By the time of the nation's centennial in 1876, Americans had much to celebrate and many challenges to face. The generation living then, like those before and afterward, would build upon the past as they shaped their future.

Lesson 19

Crisis and Compromise

OVERVIEW

As the American people approached the midpoint of the nineteenth century, the geographical boundaries of the United States resembled those recognized today. However, the ties that bind the American people together in a union were then being threatened by sectional divisions based on slavery.

The cotton economy reached out of the South, but the institution of slavery did not. People living in New York, Charleston, and St. Louis were increasingly drawn into the emotional political debate about the future of slavery in America. Some politicians, as before, looked westward in hopes of finding ways to skirt the issue. Residents in the areas of Santa Fe and Portland were experiencing transitions associated with becoming part of the United States, but the changes in the San Francisco area were even more dramatic. There the rush of people in pursuit of gold propelled California to seek admission to the United States as a free state.

When the U.S. Senate eyed "the forbidden fruit" of California, they saw poison. John C. Calhoun trembled at the possibility that the slave power might be losing its control. Daniel Webster and Henry Clay, as he did before, sought compromise. William H. Seward labeled any compromise with slavery "radically wrong." Into this breach moved young Stephen Douglas, who managed to garner majority approval for pieces of legislation that together became known as the Compromise of 1850. Secession and possible war had been averted. But how long could such a compromise last?

LESSON ASSIGNMENTS

Text: Roark, et al., *The American Promise,* Chapter 12, "The New West and Free North," pp. 422–423, and Chapter 14, "The House Divided," pp. 474–481

Video: "Crisis and Compromise" from the series *Shaping America*

Documents:

     "California Diary, 1849–1850" and "Union and Freedom without Compromise" found at the end of this lesson

---

LEARNING OBJECTIVES

This lesson is about the state of the nation in 1850, why a crisis faced the union at that time, and how that crisis was addressed by political compromise. Upon completing this lesson, you should be able to:

1. Describe the state of the nation in 1850, particularly as reflected in six geographical areas surrounding New York, Charleston, St. Louis, Santa Fe, Portland, and San Francisco.

2. Explain how the issue of slavery in the territories had been dealt with prior to the late 1840s.

3. Discuss the three major philosophical positions on the issue of slavery in the territories.

4. Analyze the presidential election of 1848.

5. Explain the background, issues, terms, and consequences of the Compromise of 1850.

LESSON FOCUS POINTS

The following questions are designed to help you get the most benefit from the sources selected for this lesson. For reference purposes, the titles for the video segments are: (1) Introduction, (2) "The United States in 1850," (3) "The Compromise of 1850," and (4) Summary Analysis: "The Only Thing of Substance . . ."

1. What factors divided the North and the South by 1850? Why had these divisions taken place? (video segment 1)

2. What characterized life in the following areas in 1850: New York, Charleston, St. Louis, Santa Fe, Oregon, and San Francisco? (textbook, pp. 422–423; document; video segment 2)

3. How had the issue of slavery in the territories been dealt with in the Northwest Ordinance, the Constitution, the Louisiana Purchase, the Missouri Compromise, and the annexation of Texas? (textbook, p. 476)

4. Who was David Wilmot? What was the Wilmot Proviso? On what precedent did this proposal rest? Who supported the proviso? Why? (textbook, pp. 476–478)

5. Why were white Southerners so vehement in opposition to the Wilmot Proviso? What arguments did John C. Calhoun put forward to justify the expansion of slavery? (textbook, p. 478)

6. What was meant by "popular sovereignty"? Why did Lewis Cass and other proponents think that this concept might be an acceptable middle ground? (textbook, p. 478)

7. Who were the candidates in the 1848 presidential election? What positions did they take on the issue of slavery in the territories? (textbook, p. 479)

8. What were the results of the 1848 presidential election? What did the election results say about slavery in the territories? What did the election portend for political parties? (textbook, p. 479)

9. How did the California gold rush help precipitate a political crisis by 1850? What was significant about the possible admission of California as a free state? (textbook, pp. 479–480; video segments 2 and 3)

10. Besides the California question, what other issues were on the table during the Senate debate in 1850? (textbook, pp. 479–480; video segment 3)

11. Who were the major players in the "Great Debate" in the Senate? What were their positions on the issues? (textbook, pp. 479–481; document; video segment 3)

12. What were the major provisions of the Compromise of 1850? How and why were these agreements reached? (textbook, p. 481; video segments 3, 4)

13. What did the North and South give up in the Compromise of 1850? What did each section gain? Why was the compromise not a true compromise at all? (textbook, p. 481; video segment 4)

14. In the end, what was important about the Compromise of 1850? What was the "poison pill" that it contained? (video segment 4)

HISTORICAL EXPERTS INTERVIEWED

Joyce Appleby, Professor of History, University of California at Los Angeles, Los Angeles, CA
Robert Archibald, President, Missouri Historical Society, St. Louis, MO
Eric Foner, Professor of History, Columbia University, New York City, NY
Charles Fracchia, President, San Francisco Historical Society, San Francisco, CA
Deena Gonzalez, Professor of History/Chicano/a Studies, Pomona College, Claremont, CA
Michael Holt, Professor of History, University of Virginia, Charlottesville, VA
Frances Levine, Division Head of Arts and Sciences, Santa Fe Community College, Santa Fe, NM
John Majewski, Associate Professor, University of California at Santa Barbara, Santa Barbara, CA
Chet Orloff, Director, Oregon Historical Society, Portland, OR
Jonathan Poston, Director of Museums and Preservation Initiatives, Historic Charleston Foundation, Charleston, SC
James Roark, Samuel Candler Dobbs Professor of American History, Emory University, Atlanta, GA

PRACTICE TEST

The following items will help you evaluate your understanding of this lesson. Use the Answer Key at the end of the lesson to check your answers or to locate material related to each question.

Multiple choice: Choose the BEST answer.

1. In 1850, New York City was _____.
   A. a hotbed of abolitionist activity
   B. losing business to Albany
   C. closely involved with the well-being of the South
   D. the eastern terminus for the transcontinental railroad

2. In referring to Santa Fe in 1850, Professor Deena Gonzalez uses the story of Gertrudes Barcelo to illustrate _____.
   A. opportunities available in a time of transition
   B. discrimination against women of Mexican origin
   C. resistance to the United States takeover
   D. attempts to destroy the pueblo people

3. As the battle over the expansion of slavery intensified in the 1840s, Senator Lewis Cass of Michigan proposed the doctrine of "popular sovereignty," a measure that would allow _____.
   A. a popular election of Supreme Court justices to decide whether territories might sanction slavery
   B. a national referendum on the issue of slavery expansion
   C. the people who settled the territories to decide whether they wanted slavery
   D. a special congressional commission to decide slavery's fate in the territories

4. To reunite their party, the Whig strategy in the presidential campaign of 1848 was to run a _____.
   A. slaveholder and denounce abolitionists
   B. military hero and remain silent on the issue of slavery
   C. wealthy Southerner who opposed slavery
   D. Southerner who advocated admitting California as a slave state

5. Southerners feared the admission of California as a free state because they _____.
   A. wanted to use San Francisco as a slave-trading center
   B. believed in upholding the terms of the Missouri Compromise
   C. knew Mexican Americans were in positions of power there
   D. would lose the balance of power in the U.S. Senate

6. In the video, Professor Michael Holt supports the view that the Compromise of 1850
    _____.
    A. conceded too much to the South
    B. averted a civil war for a decade
    C. should have balanced California's admission with a slave state
    D. left too many issues unresolved

Short Answer: Your answers should be one or two paragraphs long and specifically address the points indicated.

7. Why and how was New York state somewhat divided on the issue of slavery in 1850?

8. How did the views of David Wilmot, John C. Calhoun, and Lewis Cass articulate three distinct positions on the issue of slavery in the territories? Why did each take the position that he did?

Essay Question: Your answer should be several paragraphs long and express a clear understanding of the points indicated.

9. Describe and explain the background, issues, terms, and consequences of the Compromise of 1850.

ANSWER KEY

Answer	Learning Objectives	Focus Points	References
1. C	LO 1	FP 2	video segment 2
2. A	LO 1	FP 2	video segment 2
3. C	LO 3	FP 6	p. 478
4. B	LO 4	FP 7	p. 479
5. D	LO 5	FP 9	pp. 479–480; video segments 2, 3
6. B	LO 5	FP 14	video segment 4

| 7. | LO 1 | FP 2 | video segment 2 |

*   What was going on in upstate New York regarding slavery?
*   Why did New York City have less enthusiasm for abolition?

| 8. | LO 3 | FP 4–6 | pp. 476–478 |

*   Who was Wilmot? Why did he want to keep slavery out of the territories? How did he propose to do that?
*   Who was Calhoun? On what basis did he think that slaves could not be kept out of the territories? Why is there some irony in his position?
*   Who was Cass? What did "popular sovereignty" mean? Why was it a middle ground?

9. ....LO 2, 5.............FP 1–14 ....pp. 422–423, 476–481; document; video segments 1–4
    - Background: How had the issue of slavery in the territories been dealt with previously? What prompted the "Great Debate" in 1850?
    - Issues: Why was California's admission as a free state important? What should be done with the other territory acquired from Mexico? What was the border dispute between Texas and New Mexico? Why were fugitive slaves in general and the slave trade in Washington, D.C., issues?
    - Terms: What agreement was reached on the above issues?
    - Consequences: What did each side gain or lose? What was the poison pill in the agreement? Why was it important?

ENRICHMENT IDEAS

These activities are not required unless your instructor assigns them. They are offered as suggestions to help you learn more about the material presented in this lesson.

1. Imagine yourself to be a U.S. Senator from the state of Missouri in 1850. Write the text of a speech that articulates your views on the fugitive slave and slave-trade provisions of the proposed Compromise of 1850.

2. Imagine yourself to be the editor of a newspaper published in either New York City or Charleston. Write an editorial in which you explain your position on the Compromise of 1850.

3. Research the boundary dispute between Texas and New Mexico in the 1840s. Then submit a well-developed essay in which you explain the dispute and how and why it was resolved in the Compromise of 1850.

4. What elements are necessary to reach a true compromise? What process must leaders go through to reach compromise on difficult issues? In a thoughtful essay, address those questions and use an example from the recent history to illustrate your points.

SUGGESTED READINGS/RESOURCES

See the "Bibliography" on pages 506–507 of the text if you wish to examine other books and resources related to the material presented in this lesson.

DOCUMENTS

Gold fever struck many men in the 1840s. Walter Colton, a local resident, kept a diary of what he observed as the fever struck the Monterey, California, area.

As you read this document, focus on answering the following questions:

1. How were people affected by the gold fever? How did it upset social and domestic arrangements?
2. How did the gold rush illustrate the free-labor system?
3. Did the gold fever influence white's attitudes toward other racial and ethnic groups?

"California Diary, 1849–1850" by Walter Colton

Monday, May 29 [1849]. Our town was startled out of its quiet dreams to-day, by the announcement that gold had been discovered on the American Fork. The men wondered and talked, and the women too; but neither believed.

Monday, June 5. Another report reached us this morning from the American Fork. The rumor ran, that several workmen, while excavating for a millrace, had thrown up little shining scales of a yellow ore, that proved to be gold; that an old Sonoranian, who had spent his life in gold mines, pronounced it the genuine thing. Still the public incredulity remained, save here and there a glimmer of faith.

Tuesday, June 6. Being troubled with the golden dream, I determined to put an end to the suspense, and dispatched a messenger this morning to the American Fork. He will have to ride, going and returning, some four hundred miles, but his report will be reliable. We shall then know whether this gold is a fact or a fiction.

Tuesday, June 20. My messenger sent to the mines, has returned with specimens of the gold; he dismounted in a sea of upturned faces. As he drew forth the yellow lumps from his pockets, and passed them around among the eager crowd, the doubts, which had lingered till now, fled. All admitted they were gold, except one old man, who still persisted they were some Yankee invention, got up to reconcile the people to the change of flag. The excitement produced was intense; and many were soon busy in their hasty preparations for a departure to the mines. The family who had kept house for me caught the moving infection. Husband and wife were both packing up; the blacksmith dropped his hammer, the carpenter his plane, the mason his trowel, the farmer his sickle, the baker his loaf, and the tapster his bottle. All were off for the mines, some on horses, some on carts, and some on crutches, and one went in a litter. An American woman, who had recently established a boarding-house here, pulled up stakes, and was off before her lodgers had even time to pay their bills. Debtors ran, of course. I have only a community of women left, and a gang of prisoners, with here and there a soldier, who will give his captain the slip at the first chance. I don't blame the fellow a whit; seven dollars a month, while others are making two or three hundred a day! [T]hat is too much for human nature to stand.

Tuesday, July 18. Another bag of gold from the mines, and another spasm in the community. It was brought down by a sailor from Yuba river, and contains a hundred and thirty-six ounces. It is the most beautiful gold that has appeared in the market. My carpenters, at work on the schoolhouse, on seeing it, threw down their saws and planes, shouldered their picks, and are off for the Yuba. Three seamen ran from the Warren, forfeiting their four years' pay; and a whole platoon of soldiers from the fort left only their colors behind.

Thursday, Aug. 16. Four citizens of Monterey are just in from the gold mines on Feather River, where they worked in company with three others. They employed about thirty wild Indians, who are attached to the rancho owned by one of the party. They worked precisely seven weeks and three days, and have divided seventy-six thousand eight hundred and forty-four dollars,—nearly eleven thousand dollars to each. Let me introduce a man, well known to me, who has worked on the Yuba river sixty-four days, and brought back, as the result of his individual labor, five thousand three hundred and fifty-six dollars. Let me introduce another townsman, who has worked on the North Fork fifty-seven days, and brought back four thousand five hundred and thirty-four dollars. Is not this enough to make a man throw down his leger and shoulder a pick?

Tuesday, Aug. 28. The gold mines have upset all social and domestic arrangements in Monterey; the master has become his own servant, and the servant his own lord. The millionaire is obliged to groom his own horse, and roll his wheelbarrow; and the hidalgo—in whose veins flows the blood of all the Cortes—to clean his own boots! Here is lady L—, who has lived here seventeen years, the pride and ornament of the place, with a broomstick in her jewelled hand! And here is lady B— with her daughter—all the way from "old Virginia," where they graced society with their varied accomplishments—now floating between the parlor and kitchen, and as much at home in the one as the other! And here is lady S—, whose cattle are on a thousand hills, lifting, like Rachel of old, her bucket of water from the deep well! And here is lady M. L—, whose honeymoon is still full of soft seraphic light, unhouseling a potatoe, and hunting the hen that laid the last egg. And here am I, who have been a man of some note in my day, loafing on the hospitality of the good citizens, and grateful for a meal, though in an Indian's wigwam. Why, is not this enough to make one wish the gold mines were in the earth's flaming centre, from which they sprung?

Saturday, Sept. 16. All distinctions indicative of means have vanished; the only capital required is muscle and an honest purpose. I met a man to-day from the mines in patched buckskins, rough as a badger from his hole, who had fifteen thousand dollars in yellow dust, swung at his back. And there is more where this came from. His rights in the great domain are equal to yours, and his prospects of getting it out vastly better. With these advantages, he bends the knee to no man, but strides along in his buckskins, a lord of earth by a higher prescriptive privilege than what emanates from the partiality of kings. Clear out of the way with your crests, and crowns, and pedigree trees, and let this democrat pass.

Wednesday, Oct. 18. We are camped in the centre of the gold mines, in the heart of the richest deposits which have been found, and where there are many hundred at work. I have taken some pains to ascertain the average per man that is got out; it must be less than half an ounce per day. It might be more were there any stability among the diggers; but half their time is consumed in what they call prospecting; that is, looking up new deposits. An idle rumor, or more surmise, will carry them off in this direction or that, when perhaps they gathered nothing for their weariness and toil. I have never met with one who had the strength of purpose to resist these roving temptations.

Thursday, Oct. 19. All the gold-diggers through the entire encampment, were shaken out of their slumbers this morning by a report that a solid pocket of gold had been discovered in a bend of the Stanislaus. In half an hour a motley multitude, covered with crowbars, pickaxes, spades, rifles, and washbowls, went streaming over the hills in the direction of the new deposits. You would have thought some fortress was to be stormed, or some citadel sapped. The most curious feature in this business is, that out of a regiment of gold-hunters, where the utmost apparent confusion prevails, the absence of two men should be noticed. But the motions of every man are watched. Even when he gathers up his traps, takes formal leave, and is professedly bound home, he is tracked for leagues. No disguise can avail him; the most successful war-stratagem would fail here.

Thursday, Nov. 2. Quite a sensation was produced among the gold-diggers this morning by the arrival of a wagon from Stockton, freighted with provisions and a barrel of liquor. The former had been getting scarce, and the latter had long since entirely given out. The prices of the first importation were—flour, two dollars a pound; sugar and coffee, four dollars; and the liquor, which was nothing more nor less than New England rum, was twenty dollars the quart. But few had bottles: every species of retainer was resorted to; some took their quart cups, some their coffee-pots, and others their sauce-pans; while one fellow, who had neither, offered ten dollars to let him suck with a straw from the bung. All were soon in every variety of excitement, from prattling exhilaration, to roaring inebriety. Some shouted, some danced, and some wrestled: a son of Erin poured out his soul on the beauties of the Emerald isle; a German sung the songs of his father-land; a Yankee apostrophized the mines, which swelled in the hills around; an Englishman challenged all the bears in the mountain glens to mortal combat; and a Spaniard, posted aloft on a beetling crag, addressed the universe.

Wednesday, Nov. 8. Some fifty thousand persons are drifting up and down these slopes of the great Sierra, of every hue, language, and clime, tumultuous and confused as a flock of wild geese taking wing at the crack of a gun, or autumnal leaves strown on the atmospheric tides by the breath of the whirlwind. All are in quest of gold; and, with eyes dilated to the circle of the moon, rush this way and that, as some new discovery, or fictitious tale of success may suggest. Some are with tents, and some without; some have provisions, and some are on their last ration; some are carrying crowbars; some pickaxes and spades; some wash-bowls and cradles; some hammers and drills, and powder enough to blow up the rock of Gibraltar. Such a mixed and motley crowd—such a restless, roving, rummaging, ragged multitude, never before roared in the rookeries of man. Each great camping-ground is denoted by the ruins of shovels and shanties, the bleaching bones of the dead, disinhumed by the wolf, and the skeleton of the culprit, still swinging in the wind, from the limb of a tree, overshadowed by the raven.

Monday, May 14 [1850]. Much has been said of the amounts of gold taken from the mines by Sonoranians, Chilians, and Peruvians, and carried out of the country. As a general fact, this apprehension and alarm is without any sound basis. Not one pound of gold in ten, gathered by these foreigners, is shipped off to their credit: it is spent in the country for provisions, clothing, and in the hazards of the gaming table. It falls into the hands of those who command the avenues of commerce, and ultimately reaches our own mints. I have been in a camp of five hundred Sonoranians, who had not gold enough to buy a month's provisions—all had gone, through their improvident habits, to the capacious pockets of the Americans. To drive them out of California, or interdict their operations, is to abstract that amount of labor from the mines, and curtail proportionably the proceeds. If gold, slumbering in the river banks and mountains of California, be more valuable to us than when stamped into eagles and incorporated into our national currency, then drive out the Sonoranians: but if you would have it here and not there, let those diggers alone. When gold shall begin to fail, or require capital and machinery, you will want these hardy men to quarry the rocks and feed your stampers; and when you shall plunge into the Cinnabar mountains, you will want them to sink your shafts and kindle fires under your great quicksilver retorts. They will become the hewers of wood and drawers of water to American capital and enterprise. But if you want to perform this drudgery yourself, drive out the Sonoranians, and upset that cherished system of political economy founded in a spirit of wisdom and national justice.

Wednesday, June 20. The causes which exclude slavery from California lie within a nut-shell. All here are diggers, and free white diggers wont dig with slaves. They know they must dig themselves: they have come out here for that purpose, and they wont degrade their calling by associating it with slave-labor: self-preservation is the first law of nature. They have nothing to do with slavery in the abstract, or as it exists in other communities; not one in ten cares a button for its abolition, nor the Wilmot proviso either: all they look at is their own position; they must themselves swing the pick, and they wont swing it by the side of negro slaves. That is their feeling, their determination, and the upshot of the whole business. An army of half a million, backed by the resources of the United States, could not shake their purpose. Of all men with whom I have ever met, the most firm, resolute, and indomitable, are the emigrants into California. They feel that they have got into a new world, where they have a right to shape and settle things in their own way. No mandate, unless it comes like a thunder-bolt straight out of heaven, is regarded. They walk over hills treasured with the precious ores; they dwell by streams paved with gold; while every mountain around soars into the heaven. All these belong to them; they walk in their midst; they feel their presence and power, and partake of their grandeur. Think you that such men will consent to swing the pick by the side of slaves? Never! While the stream owns its source, or the mountain its base. You may call it pride, or what you will, but *there* it is—deep as the foundations of our nature, and unchangeable as the laws of its divine Author.

Walter Colton, *Three Years in California* (1850; new ed. 1949; reprint, Temecula, California: Reprint Services Corp., 1992), pp. 242–375.

During the debates over the Compromise of 1850, the abolitionist Salmon P. Chase argued against the passage of the bill. His long opposition to the continuation of slavery gave his position a deep emotional intensity.

As you read this document, focus on answering the following questions:

1. How did he invoke a sense of patriotism to his cause?
2. What changed the slavery issue for the worse?

"Union and Freedom without Compromise" (1850) by Salmon P. Chase

I think, Mr. President, that two facts may now be regarded as established: First that in 1787 the national policy in respect to slavery was one of restriction, limitation, and discouragement. Second that it was generally expected that under the action of the State Governments slavery would gradually disappear from the States.

Such was the state of the country when the Convention met to frame the Constitution of the United States. The framers of the Constitution acted under the influence of the general sentiment of the country. Some of them had contributed in no small measure to form that sentiment. Let us examine the instrument [the Constitution] in its light, and ascertain the original import of its language.

What, then, shall we find in it? The guaranties so much talked of? Recognition of property in men? Stipulated protection for that property in national territories and by national law? No, sir: nothing like it.

We find, on the contrary, extreme care to exclude these ideas from the Constitution. Neither the word "slave" nor "slavery" is to be found in any provision. There is not a single expression which charges the National Government with any responsibility in regard to slavery. No power is conferred on Congress either to establish or sustain it. The framers of the Constitution left it where they found it, exclusively within and under the jurisdiction of the States. Wherever slaves are referred to at all in the Constitution, whether in the clause providing for the apportionment of representation and direct taxation [Article I, section 2], or in that stipulating for the extradition of fugitive from service [the "fugitive slave" clause, Article IV, section 2], or in that restricting Congress as to the prohibition of importation or migration [Article I, section 9], they are spoken of, not as persons held as property, but as persons held to service, or having their condition determined, under State laws. We learn, indeed from the debates in the Constitutional Convention that the idea of property in men was excluded with special solicitude.

Unhappily, the original policy of the Government and the original principles of the Government in respect to slavery did not permanently control its action. A change occurred—almost imperceptible at first but becoming more and more marked and decided until nearly total. It was natural, though it does [not] seem to have been anticipated, that the unity of the slave interest strengthened by this accession of political power, should gradually weaken the public sentiment and modify the national policy against slavery. Mr. President, I have spoken freely of slave State ascendency in the affairs of this Government, but I desire not to be misunderstood. I take no sectional position. The supporters of slavery are the sectionalists. Freedom is national; slavery only is local and sectional.

What have been the results of the subversion of the original policy of slavery restriction and discouragement instead of slavery being regarded as a curse, a reproach, a blight, an evil, a wrong, a sin, we are now told that it is the most stable foundation of our institutions; the happiest relation that labor can sustain to capital; a blessing to both races this is a great change, and a sad change. If it goes on, the spirit of liberty must at length become extinct, and a despotism will be established under the forms of free institutions. There can be no foundation whatever for the doctrine advanced that an equilibrium between the slaveholding and non-slaveholding sections of our country has been, is, and ought to be, an approved feature of our political system. I shall feel myself supported by the precepts of the sages of the Revolutionary era, by the example of the founders of the Republic, by the original policy of the Government, and by the principles of the Constitution.

Excerpt taken from *Union and Freedom, without Compromise, Speech of Mr. Chase of Ohio, on Mr. Clay's Compromise Resolutions* by Salmon P. Chase. (Washington, D.C.: Buell and Blanchard, 1850).

Lesson 20

Irrepressible Conflicts

OVERVIEW

Developments taking place in the 1850s are critical to understanding why the people of the United States would ultimately experience a gruesome civil war. As historian Richard Blackett observes, a "triangle of disasters," all involving the persistent issue of slavery, shattered the Compromise of 1850 and led to irrepressible conflicts.

Implementation of the Fugitive Slave Act in the early 1850s aroused deep emotions, and abolitionists and slave catchers dramatized the moral issues involved. Resistance to the federal law involved both violence and appeals to a "higher law." Meanwhile, abolitionist literature heightened awareness about the evils inherent in the slave system.

Stephen Douglas may have hoped that the passage of the Kansas-Nebraska Act in 1854 would resolve the issue of slavery in the territories, but that legislation unleashed a torrent of violence and invective. As blood flowed in Kansas and on the floor of the United States Senate, political rhetoric sharpened and political party realignment indicated a further erosion of a middle ground. If popular sovereignty would not work, what choices were left?

After the Supreme Court's 1857 decision in the *Dred Scott* case, compromise seemed legally impossible. By ruling that slaves were property and that slaveholders could take them wherever they wanted, the Court affirmed the belief that the Constitution was a proslavery document. Besides, the "slave power" now appeared to be in total control of the national government. In order to change that, more radical action would be needed.

LESSON ASSIGNMENTS

Text: Roark, et al., *The American Promise,* Chapter 14, "The House Divided," pp. 481–499

Video: "Irrepressible Conflicts" from the series *Shaping America*

Documents:
            "The Fugitive Slave Act of 1850" found at the end of this lesson

LEARNING OBJECTIVES

This lesson explains how and why the conflicts surrounding the Fugitive Slave Act, the Kansas-Nebraska Act, and the *Dred Scott* decision threatened the national unity of the United States of America. Upon completing the lesson, you should be able to:

1. Explain the controversy surrounding the enforcement of the Fugitive Slave Act.

2. Assess the effect of abolitionist literature and activities in the 1850s.

3. Analyze the reasons for and the results of the Kansas-Nebraska Act.

4. Describe how sectional interests were affecting elections and political parties in the 1850s.

5. Explain the *Dred Scott* decision and its consequences.

6. Assess how choices made and actions taken between 1850 and 1857 had moved the nation toward a more intense division between the North and South.

LESSON FOCUS POINTS

The following questions are designed to help you get the most benefit from the sources selected for this lesson. For reference purposes, the titles for the video segments are: (1) Introduction, (2) "A Higher Law," (3) Short-take: "Uncle Tom's Cabin," (4) "Bleeding Kansas," (5) Short-take: "A New Party," (6) "Dred Scott," (7) Summary Analysis: "Revolutions Never Go Backward."

1. What were the terms of the Fugitive Slave Act of 1850? Why was enforcement of the act so controversial? How was the act resisted? What was meant by a "higher law" doctrine? (textbook, pp. 481–484; documents; video segment 2)

2. How did the arrest of Anthony Burns in Boston in 1854 illustrate the tension brought about by the Fugitive Slave Act? (video segment 2)

3. Why was *Uncle Tom's Cabin* so popular in the North? What did Southerners think about it? How influential was this book on shaping attitudes toward slavery? What other pieces of abolitionist literature affected public opinion in the 1850s? How important was this in the coming of the Civil War? (textbook, pp. 484–485; video segment 3)

4. Why did Franklin Pierce win the presidential election of 1852? Why was the Gadsden Purchase made? Where was it? (textbook, pp. 485–486)

5. What were Stephen Douglas' motives for introducing the Kansas-Nebraska Act? What were the terms of this legislation? How did it affect Indian peoples in the region? Why did the act include a repeal of the Missouri Compromise line? (textbook, pp. 485–487; video segment 4)

6. Examine Map 14.3 on page 487 of the text. Answer the questions posed there. (textbook, p. 487)

7. Why did the Kansas-Nebraska Act prompt a restructuring of the political party system? Why did the Whig Party die? What was important about that? Why did some northern Democrats have difficulty with the Kansas-Nebraska Act? (textbook, pp. 487, 490–491; video segments 4 and 5)

8. What explains the emergence of the American (Know-Nothing) Party? Why was this party short-lived? (textbook, pp. 490–493)

9. Why was the Republican Party successful in attracting supporters in the North? How successful were the Republicans in the 1856 presidential election? What did this portend? (textbook, pp. 491–493; video segment 5)

10. How did the events associated with "Bleeding Kansas" affect that area and the rest of the nation? (textbook, pp. 496–497; video segment 4)

11. Why did "popular sovereignty" fail in Kansas? What was the significance of that failure? (textbook, pp. 496–497; video segment 4)

12. Who was Dred Scott? On what grounds did he sue for his freedom? (textbook, pp. 497–499; video segment 6)

13. What was the majority decision in the Dred Scott case? Why did Chief Justice Taney and the majority make this ruling? What did the minority dissent claim? (textbook, pp. 497–499; video segment 6)

14. What did the *Dred Scott* decision mean to African Americans? How did it affect the issue of slavery in the territories? How did the decision affect the Republican and Democratic parties? (textbook, pp. 497–499; video segment 6)

15. In summary, why and how had the nation moved toward greater division between the North and the South between 1850 and 1857? What choices were available to the American people by the end of 1857? (textbook, pp. 481–499; video segments 1–7)

HISTORICAL EXPERTS INTERVIEWED

Richard Blackett, Moores Professor of History and African American Studies, University of Houston, Houston, TX

Paul Finkelman, Chapman Distinguished Professor and Professor of Law, University of Tulsa, Tulsa, OK

Robert Johannsen, J. G. Randall Distinguished Professor of History Emeritus, University of Illinois at Urbana-Champaign, Champaign, IL

PRACTICE TEST

The following items will help you evaluate your understanding of this lesson. Use the Answer Key at the end of the lesson to check your answers or to locate material related to each question.

Multiple choice: Choose the BEST answer.

1. As part of the Compromise of 1850, the Fugitive Slave Act _____.
   A. was designed to operate in conjunction with personal liberty laws
   B. pleased Northerners weary of the increasing numbers of runaway slaves in their communities
   C. was the least controversial component of the agreement
   D. placed the force of the federal government behind Southerners seeking the return of runaway slaves

2. Harriet Beecher Stowe's *Uncle Tom's Cabin* (1852) influenced Northerners' attitude toward slavery _____.
   A. by including some of the first-ever research yielding scientific evidence of the effects of slavery on those enslaved
   B. because it was a compelling novel and a vehicle for a stirring moral indictment of slavery
   C. by arguing that the North was in no way responsible for the institution of slavery
   D. by suggesting that the federal government should free slaves by paying the fair market value for them

3. As a result of the 1854 Kansas-Nebraska Act, _____.
   A. the nation once again had only one functioning political party
   B. the Whigs gained new strength and vitality
   C. the nation witnessed the rise of a new two-party system
   D. the Democrats came to dominate northern politics

4. When the first territorial legislature in Kansas met, it _____.
   A. voted to settle the slavery issue peacefully
   B. voted to secede from the union
   C. enacted tough proslavery laws and prompted the organization of a rival government
   D. voted to repeal the Fugitive Slave Act within the territorial boundaries

5. In the 1857 *Dred Scott* decision, the U.S. Supreme Court ruled that _____.
   A. Dred Scott could not claim violation of his constitutional rights because he was not a citizen of the United States
   B. the Missouri Compromise was constitutional
   C. black people in the United States could be declared citizens under certain circumstances
   D. Congress had the power to prohibit slavery in the territories

6. In the video, Professor Richard Blackett observes that the events of the mid-1850s
   _____.
   A. radicalized many Northerners
   B. illustrated the weakness of the abolitionists
   C. solidified Democratic Party unity
   D. all of the above

Short Answer: Your answers should be one or two paragraphs long and specifically address the points indicated.

7. What role did violence play in shaping public opinion and public policy in the period of 1850–1857? Describe two examples to support your answer.

8. Why did Stephen Douglas support the concept of popular sovereignty? Why did popular sovereignty fail in Kansas?

9. Why did the national party system break down in the 1850s? What was important about that?

Essay Question: Your answer should be several paragraphs long and express a clear understanding of the points indicated.

10. Describe and explain how and why the conflicts surrounding the Fugitive Slave Act of 1850, the Kansas-Nebraska Act, and the *Dred Scott* decision threatened the national unity of the United States of America.

ANSWER KEY

Answer	Learning Objectives	Focus Points	References
1. D	LO 1	FP 1	pp. 481–484; document; video segment 2
2. B	LO 2	FP 3	pp. 484–485; video segment 3
3. C	LO 3, 4	FP 7	pp. 487, 490–491; video segments 4, 5
4. C	LO 3	FP 11	pp. 496–497; video segment 4
5. A	LO 5	FP 13	pp. 497–499; video segment 6
6. A	LO 6	FP 15	pp. 481–499; video segments 1–7

7.	LO 1–3	FP 1, 2, 10	pp. 481–484, 496–497; video segments 2, 4

- Consider how violent action sharpened the growing division over slavery.
- How much violence was used in resisting the Fugitive Slave Act? What happened in Boston in particular?
- What types of violence were associated with "Bleeding Kansas"? What were the effects?

8.   ....LO 3...............FP 5, 11 ....pp. 485–487, 496–497; video segment 4
   - Consider Douglas' party, the interests he represented, and his goals.
   - Why would popular sovereignty be attractive?
   - Explain what happened in Kansas that led to failure of the concept there.

9.   ....LO 3, 4...............FP 7, 9 .... pp. 487, 490–493; video segments 4, 5
   - Why did the Whig Party practically disappear during the decade?
   - What area and positions did the Republican Party represent?
   - What stresses were being placed on the Democratic Party?
   - What happens when sectional interests are paramount?

10.   ....LO 1–6............FP 1–15 .... pp. 481–499; video segments 1–7
   - Why did the Fugitive Slave Act heighten tensions? How was it resisted? How were sectional interests affected?
   - Why was the Kansas-Nebraska Act so controversial? What happened as a result?
   - What did the *Dred Scott* decision say? What choices were left for those opposed to the expansion of slavery?
   - Consider how the Compromise of 1850 was breaking down. What was dividing the nation?

ENRICHMENT IDEAS

These activities are not assigned unless your instructor assigns them. They are offered as suggestions to help you learn more about the material presented in this lesson.

1. If you live in an area where abolitionist activity took place in the 1850s, research what happened. Then submit an essay in which you describe your findings and assess the effects of the activity.

2. Imagine yourself to be a free black or a fugitive slave in the early 1850s. Write a letter to a close friend in which you describe what actions you are going to take to avoid capture and possible return to a slave state.

3. Imagine yourself to be a newspaper editor in Baltimore, Maryland, in 1856. Write an editorial in which you take a stand on the caning of Senator Charles Sumner.

4. In a well-developed essay, explain how and why the "higher law" doctrine has been used to justify acts of civil disobedience in your lifetime.

5. Consider the role of third parties today. In a thoughtful essay, explain what these parties are trying to accomplish. How do they measure success? Do you think any of them will become a major political party?

SUGGESTED READINGS/RESOURCES

See the "Bibliography" on pages 506–507 of the text if you wish to examine other books and resources related to the material presented in this lesson.

DOCUMENTS

One of the elements of the Compromise of 1850 was a much stricter Fugitive Slave Act. The provisions of this act became the most despised element of the compromise for northern opponents.

As you read this document, focus on answering the following questions:

1. What rights were the accused slaves denied?
2. Is support of this measure in keeping with the South's strong support of states' rights?

The Fugitive Slave Act of 1850

Be it enacted by the Senate and House of Representatives of the United States of America in congress assembled, . . .

SEC. 6. And be it further enacted, That when a person held to service or labor in any State or Territory of the United States, has heretofore or shall hereafter escape into another State or Territory of the United States, the person or persons to whom such service or labor may be due, or his, her, or their agent or attorney, duly authorized, by power of attorney, in writing, acknowledged and certified under the seal of some legal officer or court of the State or Territory in which the same may be executed, may pursue and reclaim such fugitive person, either by procuring a warrant from some one of the courts, judges, or commissioners aforesaid, of the proper circuit, district, or county, for the apprehension of such fugitive from service or labor, or by seizing and arresting such fugitive, where the same can be done without process, and by taking, or causing such person to be taken, forthwith before such court, judge, or commissioner, whose duty it shall be to hear and determine the case of such claimant in a summary manner. . . In no trial or hearing under this act shall the testimony of such alleged fugitive be admitted in evidence; and the certificates in this and the first [fourth] section be mentioned, shall be conclusive of the right of the person or persons in whose favor granted, to remove such fugitive to the State or Territory from which he escaped, and shall prevent all molestation of such person or persons by any process issued by any court, judge, magistrate, or other person whomsoever.

SEC. 7. And be it further enacted, That any person who shall knowingly and willingly obstruct, hinder, or prevent such claimant, his agent or attorney, or any person or persons lawfully assisting him, her, or them, from arresting such a fugitive from service or labor, either with or without process as aforesaid, or shall rescue, or attempt to rescue, such fugitive from service or labor, from the custody of such claimant, his or her agent or attorney, or other person or persons lawfully assisting as aforesaid, when so arrested, pursuant to the authority herein given and declared; or shall aid, abet, or assist such person so owing service or labor as aforesaid, directly or indirectly, to escape from such claimant, his agent or attorney, or other person or persons legally authorized as aforesaid; or shall harbor or conceal such fugitive, so as to prevent the discovery and arrest of such person, after notice or knowledge of the fact that such person was a fugitive from service or labor as aforesaid, shall, for either of said offences, be subject to a fine not exceeding one thousand dollars, and imprisonment not exceeding six months. . . and shall moreover forfeit and pay, by way of civil damages to the party injured by such illegal conduct, the sum of one thousand dollars, for each fugitive so lost as aforesaid.

SEC. 9. And be it further enacted, That, upon affidavit made by the claimant of such fugitive, his agent or attorney, after such certificate has been issued, that he has reason to apprehend that such fugitive will be rescued by force from his or their possession before he can be taken beyond the limits of the State in which the arrest is made, it shall be the duty of the officer making the arrest to retain such fugitive in his custody, and to remove him to the State whence he fled, and there to deliver him to said claimant, his agent, or attorney. And to this end, the officer aforesaid is hereby authorized and required to employ so many persons as he may deem necessary to overcome such force, and to retain them in his service so long as circumstances may require. The said officer and his assistants, while so employed, to receive the same compensation, and to be allowed the same expenses, as are now allowed by law for transportation of criminals, to be certified by the judge of the district within which the arrest is made, and paid out of the treasury of the United States.

"The Fugitive Slave Act of 1850." Taken from *Statutes at Large*, vol. 9, pp. 462ff.

Lesson 21

The Union Collapses

OVERVIEW

Even though the Dred Scott decision had validated the extreme southern position on the issue of slavery in the territories, those who held the opposite view were not about to concede. The Republicans had shown strength in the 1856 elections, and, if they could expand their northern base and nominate an exceptional candidate, victory was possible in the presidential race of 1860.

Enter Abraham Lincoln. He burst upon the national political scene in 1858 when he ran against the incumbent Democrat Stephen Douglas for a seat in the U.S. Senate. At the beginning of that campaign, Lincoln challenged prevailing attitudes in his "House Divided" speech. Then, during a series of debates with Douglas, Lincoln proved to be sound on Republican principles and an adept campaigner. Even though he lost the race for the Senate, Lincoln was now poised to seek an even higher office.

Meanwhile, the violence often accompanying the ongoing national debate over slavery escalated in the fall of 1859, when the fanatical abolitionist John Brown attacked the federal arsenal at Harpers Ferry, Virginia. Brown's quick conviction on treason charges and subsequent execution created a martyr for northern abolitionists and aroused fears in the South that the Republicans were ready to unleash more assaults on slavery.

Raging emotions spilled over into the election year of 1860, when Lincoln and the Republicans achieved a remarkable victory. Seven states in the lower South quickly proceeded to enact ordinances of secession. Thus, even before Abraham Lincoln took office as president of the United States, the Union itself had collapsed. As the new president finished his inaugural address, the stage was set for war.

LESSON ASSIGNMENTS

Text: Roark, et al., *The American Promise,* Chapter 12, "The New West and Free North," pp. 395–396, and Chapter 14, "The House Divided," pp. 474–476, 482–483, and 499–509

Video: "The Union Collapses" from the series *Shaping America*

Documents:

    "The Lincoln-Douglas Debates" and "The Trial of John Brown" found at the end of this lesson

---

LEARNING OBJECTIVES

This lesson explains how Abraham Lincoln emerged as a national politician and how and why his election to the presidency in 1860 led to the collapse of the Union in 1861. After completing this lesson, you should be able to:

1. Explain the emergence of Abraham Lincoln as a major national political figure.

2. Analyze the Lincoln-Douglas debates.

3. Explain John Brown's raid on Harpers Ferry and its effects on the nation.

4. Analyze the presidential election of 1860.

5. Explain the secession of seven southern states during the winter of 1860–1861.

6. Analyze why compromise failed between 1850 and 1861.

LESSON FOCUS POINTS

The following questions are designed to help you get the most benefit from the sources selected for this lesson. For reference purposes, the titles for the video segments are: (1) Introduction, (2) "Mr. Lincoln," (3) Short-take: "Mathew Brady," (4) "John Brown," (5) "Election and Secession," (6) Summary Analysis: "The Stage for War."

1. What was Abraham Lincoln's family background? How successful was he by 1858? (textbook, pp. 395–396, 499–501; video segment 2)

2. What was Abraham Lincoln's political background? How had his political views been shaped? Why did he become a Republican in 1856? What were his political convictions by 1858, particularly in reference to slavery? (textbook, pp. 499–501; video segment 2)

3. Why is Lincoln's "House Divided" speech considered a turning point in his political career? (textbook, p. 500; video segment 2)

4. How did the economy and the events in Kansas intrude on the Illinois senatorial election of 1858? (textbook, pp. 500–501)

5. Why did Lincoln and Douglas have a series of debates? What was the central issue of the debates? What was Lincoln trying to accomplish during these debates? (textbook, pp. 500–501; video segment 2)

6. What was important about the "Freeport Doctrine"? (textbook, pp. 500–501; document; video segment 2)

---

7. Why did Lincoln lose the Senate election to Douglas? What did he gain? (textbook, p. 501; video segment 2)

8. Why was the Cooper Union speech an important one in Lincoln's political career? (video segment 2)

9. What were daguerreotypes? What was important about Mathew Brady's famous photograph of Lincoln? (textbook, pp. 482–483, 503; video segment 3)

10. Why did John Brown organize a raid on Harpers Ferry? Why did Brown fail to accomplish his immediate objective? (textbook, pp. 474–476; video segment 2)

11. How and why was John Brown's hanging turned into a major event? Was he crazy? Was he a traitor? Was he a martyr? What did the South think of his exploits? (textbook, pp. 501–502; document; video segment 4)

12. Why did the Democratic party split into three factions prior to the presidential election of 1860? Who were the candidates of each faction and what did they stand for? How did the split among the Democrats open the way for Republican victory? (textbook, pp. 502–504; video segment 5)

13. How did the Republicans broaden their political base in 1860? Why did they choose Lincoln as their nominee for president? (textbook, pp. 503–504; video segment 5)

14. Why was the presidential election of 1860 unique in American politics? What was at stake? Why did Lincoln win? What did the results indicate about the political state of the nation? (textbook, p. 504; video segment 5)

15. Why did the states in the lower South proceed to secede from the Union during the winter of 1860–61? What was the historical and philosophical basis for the idea of secession? To what extent were Southerners united on the issue of secession? (textbook, pp. 504–506; video segment 5)

16. What did President Buchanan and Congress propose to do about secession during the winter of 1860–1861? What was President-elect Lincoln's position on the issue? How did Lincoln address the issue at his inauguration? (textbook, pp. 505–506; video segment 5)

17. In summary, why had compromise failed between 1850 and 1861? Was the coming Civil War inevitable? (textbook, p. 506; video segment 6)

HISTORICAL EXPERTS INTERVIEWED

Paul Finkelman, Chapman Distinguished Professor and Professor of Law, University of Tulsa, Tulsa, OK

Robert Johannsen, J. G. Randall Distinguished Professor of History Emeritus, University of Illinois at Urbana-Champaign, Champaign, IL

Michael Johnson, Professor of History, Johns Hopkins University, Baltimore, MD

Howard Jones, University Research Professor and Chairman, University of Alabama, Tuscaloosa, AL

James McPherson, Professor of History, Princeton University, Princeton, NJ

James Roark, Samuel Candler Dobbs Professor of American History, Emory University, Atlanta, GA

PRACTICE TEST

The following items will help you evaluate your understanding of this lesson. Use the Answer Key at the end of the lesson to check your answers or to locate material related to each question.

Multiple choice: Choose the BEST answer.

1. In the mid-1850s Abraham Lincoln's search for a political home was based on his _____.
   A. commitment to the abolition of slavery everywhere in the United States
   B. belief that nothing short of an armed confrontation would settle the slavery issue in the country
   C. desire to fight the *Dred Scott* decision
   D. opposition to the extension of slavery in the United States

2. Abraham Lincoln's "House Divided" speech was important because it _____.
   A. stated his opposition to secession in vivid language
   B. helped him emerge as a national opponent to Stephen Douglas
   C. foreshadowed his position fortifying Fort Sumter
   D. enabled him to gain the presidential nomination on the first ballot

3. Seeking to capitalize on the central issue of the debates, slavery and freedom, Stephen A. Douglas tried to depict Abraham Lincoln as _____.
   A. an abolitionist and color-blind egalitarian who loved blacks
   B. uninformed on some of the key issues pertinent to their debates
   C. an avid supporter of the Fugitive Slave Act
   D. pandering to public sentiment when he insisted that slavery was wrong

4. The precise objectives of John Brown's assault on Harpers Ferry, Virginia, in 1859 remain hazy, but most believe he wanted to _____.
    A. steal arms from the arsenal to take back to New England
    B. set up a training camp for militant abolitionists
    C. initiate a slave insurrection
    D. shut down the federal arsenal so it could no longer manufacture weapons

5. Democrats meeting in Charleston, South Carolina, in 1860 to choose a presidential candidate wound up _____.
    A. agreeing unanimously on Stephen A. Douglas
    B. splitting the party into Southern and Northern wings
    C. selecting Jefferson Davis as their candidate
    D. deadlocking over their choice for seventy-two ballots

6. The slave states of the upper South were not as quick to secede from the Union after Lincoln's election because _____.
    A. they generally believed that secession was an ill-considered idea
    B. they had great difficulty in getting together a quorum of legislators to debate the issue
    C. the U.S. army had already assembled on the north bank of the Potomac River as a persuasive deterrent to secession.
    D. they simply did not have the same stake in slavery as did the states in the Deep South.

7. In the video, several historians state the view that _____.
    A. better political leadership could have avoided the Civil War
    B. greater freedom for blacks in the South was inevitable
    C. some kind of conflict between the sections seemed certain to happen
    D. stronger efforts should have been made to compromise the issues in 1861

Short Answer: Your answers should be one or two paragraphs long and specifically address the points indicated.

8. Explain Abraham Lincoln's views on slavery prior to the outbreak of the Civil War.

9. Explain why the Lincoln-Douglas debates were significant in 1858 and in 1860.

10. Why would Abraham Lincoln give some credit to Mathew Brady for his victory in the 1860 election? What does this say about elections in general?

11. Do you think it is fair to say that John Brown fired the "first shots" of the Civil War at Harpers Ferry in 1859? Why or why not?

12. Why did Abraham Lincoln win the presidential election of 1860?

Essay Questions: Your answers should be several paragraphs long and express a clear understanding of the points indicated.

13. How and why had the United States moved to the brink of a Civil War between 1858 and 1861? Was the Civil War inevitable?

14. Looking at the period from 1850 to 1861, analyze the key developments that led to the failure of compromise.

15. During the winter of 1860–1861, seven southern states seceded from the Union. Explain the development of this idea and process from the 1780s to 1861.

ANSWER KEY

Answer	Learning Objectives	Focus Points	References
1. D	LO 1	FP 2	pp. 499–501; video segment 2
2. B	LO 1	FP 3	p. 500; video segment 2
3. A	LO 2	FP 5, 7	pp. 500–501; video segment 2
4. C	LO 3	FP 10	pp. 474–476; video segment 4
5. B	LO 4	FP 12	pp. 502–504; video segment 5
6. D	LO 5	FP 15	pp. 504–506; video segment 5
7. C	LO 6	FP 17	p. 506; video segment 6

8. ....LO 1............FP 1, 2, 3, 5 ....pp. 395–396, 499–501; video segment 2
   - How did his family background and work experience affect his outlook?
   - What did his membership in the Whig and then Republican parties mean in this regard?
   - Why was he so opposed to the *Dred Scott* decision and popular sovereignty?

9. ....LO 2, 4.........FP 5, 6, 7, 14 .... pp. 500–501, 504; document; video segments 2, 5
   - What was Lincoln trying to accomplish in the debates?
   - What was important about the Freeport Doctrine?
   - What happened as a result of the debates in 1858?
   - How is the Illinois senate race connected to the presidential election in 1860?

10. ....LO 4..............FP 9, 14 ....pp. 482–483; 503–504; video segment 5
    - Who is Mathew Brady and what did he do?
    - What effect did Brady's action have on the election?
    - How important is image in elections? Why is it important?

11.   ....LO 3.............FP 10, 11 .... pp. 474–476, 501–502; document, video segment 4
- What exactly did Brown do?
- What were the reactions from the North and the South to Brown's actions and his hanging?
- What is your opinion? Why do you hold that view?

12.   ....LO 4.............FP 12–14 ....pp. 502–504; video segment 5
- Why was Lincoln a strong candidate? Who were his opponents?
- What issues attracted voters to Lincoln?
- What sort of campaign did Lincoln undertake? What did he have to do to win?
- What do the election results demonstrate about our electoral system?

13.   ....LO 2–5.............FP 4–16 .... pp. 474–476, 500–506; video segments 2–5
- What was the significance of the Lincoln-Douglas debates?
- What role did John Brown's raid and execution have on emotions and beliefs?
- What was the importance of the 1860 presidential election?
- Why was secession a threat to the United States?

14.   ....All LOs .... All FPs..Comprehensive of Lessons 20, 21
- What was the most controversial part of the Compromise of 1850? What issues did this arouse?
- What role did the abolitionists play in the 1850s?
- Why was the Kansas-Nebraska Act so significant?
- What effect did "Bleeding Kansas" have on the nation?
- What was the significance of the *Dred Scott* decision?
- Why were the Lincoln-Douglas debates important?
- Why were the actions of John Brown critical?
- Why did the presidential election of 1860 lead to a secession movement?

15.   ....All LOs .... All FPs..Comprehensive of Lessons 20, 21
- Was the Constitution a compact between states or a compact between the people of all the states?
- How did the Virginia and Kentucky Resolutions affect the concept of states' rights?
- Why did the nullification crisis of the 1830s escalate the development of secessionist thought?
- How and why did the leaders of the secessionist movement finally proceed to act in 1860–1861?

ENRICHMENT IDEAS

These activities are not required unless your instructor assigns them. They are offered as suggestions to help you learn more about the material presented in this lesson.

1. Imagine yourself to be a voter in the 1860 presidential election. In a well-developed essay, explain why you voted for the candidate of your choice.

2. Examine Map 14.5 on page 504 of the textbook. Then submit a thoughtful essay in which you explain why different areas of the country supported each of the candidates in the 1860 presidential election.

3. Imagine yourself to be an editor for a major newspaper in 1859. Write an editorial in which you either defend or condemn John Brown.

4. Imagine yourself to be a southern politician during the winter of 1860–1861. Write a thoughtful position paper in which you defend your vote for or against secession of your state.

5. Research the photos and images of Abraham Lincoln circulated during the 1860 presidential election. Then submit a well-documented essay in which you analyze how those images may have affected the outcome of the election.

6. Abraham Lincoln still holds a special place in the American memory and among American historians. Read the article "How I Met Lincoln," published in *American Heritage* magazine in July/August 1999, and then write a review of that article. What are your thoughts about Mr. Lincoln?

7. John Brown was not able to initiate a massive slave uprising. In a thoughtful essay, examine why this attempt and others prior to the Civil War were not successful.

8. Read Stephen Benet's epic poem "John Brown's Body." How does this poem influence the memory of John Brown? Submit your thoughts in a well-developed essay, citing passages from the poem as appropriate.

SUGGESTED READINGS/RESOURCES

See the "Bibliography" on pages 506–507 of the textbook if you wish to examine other books and resources related to the material presented in this lesson.

DOCUMENTS

Abraham Lincoln was nominated to run against Stephen Douglas in the 1858 senatorial race in Illinois. In order to improve his chances to win the necessary support, Lincoln challenged the better-known Douglas to series of debates. Douglas accepted and the two men squared off at seven different sites all across the state of Illinois. Douglas espoused views that made him unacceptable to the Deep South when he attempted to gain the presidential nomination of the Democratic Party in 1860. Just as importantly, Lincoln created a moderate position on slavery that appealed to many Northerners. Although Lincoln lost the senate seat, the debates propelled him toward the presidential nomination in 1860.

As you read this document, focus on answering the following questions:

1. What did Southerners find most objectionable in Douglas's positions? In Lincoln's?
2. How was Lincoln a moderate on the slave and race issues (in his own time)?

"The Lincoln-Douglas Debates" (1858)

Lincoln's Opening Speech

As to the first one, in regard to the fugitive slave law, I have never hesitated to say, and I do not now hesitate to say, that I think, under the Constitution of the United States, the people of the southern states are entitled to a congressional fugitive slave law. Having said that, I have had nothing to say in regard to the existing fugitive slave law further than that I think it should have been framed so as to be free from some of the objections that pertain to it, without lessening its efficiency. And inasmuch as we are not now in an agitation in regard to an alteration or modification of that law, I would not be the man to introduce it as a new subject of agitation upon the general question of slavery.

     In regard to the other question of whether I am pledged to the admission of any more slave states into the Union, I state to you very frankly that I would be exceedingly sorry ever to be put in a position of having to pass upon that question. I should be exceedingly glad to know that there would never be another slave state admitted into the Union; . . . but I must add, that if slavery shall be kept out of the territories during the territorial existence of any one given territory, and then the people shall, having a fair chance and a clear field, when they come to adopt the constitution, do such an extraordinary thing as to adopt a slave constitution, uninfluenced by the actual presence of the institution among them, I see no alternative, if we own the country, but to admit them into the Union.

     The fourth one is in regard to the abolition of slavery in the District of Columbia. In relation to that, I have my mind very distinctly made up. I should be exceedingly glad to see slavery abolished in the District of Columbia. . . . I believe that Congress possesses the constitutional power to abolish it. Yet as a member of Congress, I should not with my present views, be in favor of *endeavoring* to abolish slavery in the District of Columbia, unless it would be upon these conditions. First, that the abolition should be gradual. Second, that it should be on a vote of the majority of qualified voters in the District, and third, that compensation should be made to unwilling owners. With these three conditions, I confess I would be exceedingly glad to see Congress abolish slavery in the District of Columbia, and, in the language of Henry Clay, "sweep from our Capital that foul blot upon our nation."

My answer as to whether I desire that slavery should be prohibited in all the territories of the United States is full and explicit within itself, and cannot be made clearer by any comments of mine. So I suppose in regard to the question of whether I am opposed to the acquisition of any more territory unless slavery is first prohibited therein, my answer is such that I could add nothing by way of illustration, or making myself better understood, than the answer which I have placed in writing.

I now proceed to propound to the Judge the interrogatories, as far as I have framed them. The first one is —

Question 1. If the people of Kansas shall, by means entirely unobjectionable in all other respects, adopt a state constitution, and ask admission into the Union under it, *before* they have the requisite number of inhabitants according to the English Bill—some ninety-three thousand—will you vote to admit them?

Question 2. Can the people of a United States territory, in any lawful way, against the wish of any citizen of the United States, exclude slavery from its limits prior to the formation of a state constitution?

Question 3. If the Supreme Court of the United States shall decide that states can not exclude slavery from their limits, are you in favor of acquiescing in, adopting and following such decision as a rule of political action?

Question 4. Are you in favor of acquiring additional territory, in disregard of how such acquisition may affect the nation on the slavery question?

Douglas's Reply

In a few moments I will proceed to review the answers which he has given to these interrogatories; but in order to relieve his anxiety I will first respond to those which he has presented to me.

First, he desires to know if the people of Kansas shall form a constitution by means entirely proper and unobjectionable and ask admission into the Union as a state, before they have the requisite population for a member of Congress, whether I will vote for that admission. In reference to Kansas; it is my opinion, that as she has population enough to constitute a slave state, she has people enough for a free state. I will not make Kansas an exceptional case to the other states of the Union. ("Sound," and "hear, hear.") I hold it to be a sound rule of universal application to require a territory to contain the requisite population for a member of Congress, before it is admitted as a state into the Union. I made that proposition in the Senate in 1856, and I renewed it during the last session, in a bill providing that no territory of the United States should form a constitution and apply for admission until it had the requisite population.

The next question propounded to me by Mr. Lincoln is, can the people of a territory in any lawful way against the wishes of any citizen of the United States; [sic] exclude slavery from their limits prior to the formation of a state constitution? I answer emphatically, as Mr. Lincoln has heard me answer a hundred times from every stump in Illinois, that in my opinion the people of a territory can, by lawful means, exclude slavery from their limits prior to the formation of a state constitution. Mr. Lincoln knew that I had answered that question over and over again. He heard me argue the Nebraska Bill on that principle all over the state in 1854, in 1855 and in 1856, and he has no excuse for pretending to be in doubt as to my position on that question. It matters not what way the Supreme Court may hereafter decide as to the abstract question whether slavery may or may not go into a territory under the Constitution, the people have the lawful means to introduce it or exclude it as they please, for the reason that slavery cannot exist a day or an hour anywhere, unless it is supported by local police regulations. Those police regulations can only be established by the local legislature, and if the people are opposed to slavery they will elect representatives to that body who will by unfriendly legislation effectually prevent the introduction of it into their midst. If, on the contrary, they are for it, their legislation will favor its extension. Hence, no matter what the decision of the Supreme Court may be on that abstract question, still the right of the people to make a slave territory or a free territory is perfect and complete under the Nebraska Bill. I hope Mr. Lincoln deems my answer satisfactory on that point.

The third question which Mr. Lincoln presented is, if the Supreme Court of the United States shall decide that a state of this Union cannot exclude slavery from its own limits will I submit to it? I am amazed that Lincoln should ask such a question. Yes, a school boy does know better. Mr. Lincoln's object is to cast an imputation upon the Supreme Court. He knows that there never was but one man in America, claiming any degree of intelligence or decency, who ever for a moment pretended such a thing. It is true that the Washington *Union*, in an article published on the 17th of last December, did put forth that doctrine, and I denounced the article on the floor of the Senate.

The fourth question of Mr. Lincoln is, are you in favor of acquiring additional territory in disregard as to how such acquisition may affect the Union on the slavery question? This question is very ingeniously and cunningly put.

The Black Republican creed lays it down expressly, that under no circumstances shall we acquire any more territory unless slavery is first prohibited in the country. I ask Mr. Lincoln whether he is in favor of that proposition. Are you (addressing Mr. Lincoln) opposed to the acquisition of any more territory, under any circumstances, unless slavery is prohibited in it? That he does not like to answer. When I ask him whether he stands up to that article in the platform of his party, he turns, Yankee-fashion, and without answering it, asks me whether I am in favor of acquiring territory without regard to how it may affect the Union on the slavery question. I answer that whenever it becomes necessary, in our growth and progress to acquire more territory, that I am in favor of it, without reference to the question of slavery, and when we have acquired it, I will leave the people free to do as they please, either to make it slave or free territory, as they prefer. It is idle to tell me or you that we have territory enough. Our fathers supposed that we had enough when our territory extended to the Mississippi River, but a few years' growth and expansion satisfied them that we needed more, and the Louisiana territory, from the west branch of the Mississippi, to the British possessions, was acquired. Then we acquired Oregon, then California and New Mexico. We have enough now for the present, but this is a young and a growing nation. It swarms as often as a hive of bees, and as new swarms are turned out each year, there must be hives in which they can gather and make their honey.

"The Lincoln-Douglas Debates" (1858). Taken from *Political Speeches and Debates of Abraham Lincoln and Stephen Douglas, 1854–1861* edited by Alonzo T. Jones. (Battle Creek, Michigan, 1895).

Among the most controversial figures in the antebellum period was John Brown. This violent abolitionist, who killed in Kansas and fled the territory, emerged again in Harpers Ferry, Virginia, in 1859. Following his taking of the arsenal, he was captured and tried for treason, for which he was executed.

As you read this document, focus on answering the following questions:

1. What were John Brown's stated intentions for his attack on Harpers Ferry?
2. What were his feelings about what he had done?

"The Trial of John Brown" (1859)

The clerk then asked Mr. Brown whether he had anything to say why sentence should not be pronounced upon him.

> Mr. Brown immediately rose, and in a clear, distinct voice, said: I have, may it please the Court, a few words to say. In the first place, I deny everything but what I have all along admitted, of a design on my part to free slaves. I intended certainly to have made a clean thing of that matter, as I did last winter when I went into Missouri, and there took slaves without the snapping of a gun on either side, moving them through the country, and finally leaving them in Canada. I designed to have done the same thing again on a larger scale. That was all I intended to do. I never did intend murder or treason, or the destruction of property, or to excite or incite the slaves to rebellion, or to make insurrection. I have another objection, and that is that it is unjust that I should suffer such a penalty. Had I interfered in the manner which I admit, and which I admit has been fairly proved—for I admire the truthfulness and candor of the greater portion of the witnesses who have testified in this case—had I so interfered in behalf of the rich, the powerful, the intelligent, the so-called great, or in behalf of any of their friends, either father, mother, brother, sister, wife, or children, or any of that class, and suffered and sacrificed what I have in this interference, it would have been all right, and every man in this Court would have deemed it an act worthy of reward rather than punishment. This Court acknowledges, too, as I suppose, the validity of the law of God. I see a book kissed, which I suppose to be the Bible, or at least the New Testament, which teaches me that all things whatsoever I would that men should do to me, I should do even so to them. It teaches me further to remember them that are in bonds as bound with them. I endeavored to act up to that instruction. I say I am yet too young to understand that God is any respecter of persons. I believe that to have interfered as I have done, as I have always freely admitted I have done in behalf of His despised poor, is no wrong, but right. Now, if it is deemed necessary that I should forfeit my life for the furtherance of the ends of justice, and mingle my blood further with the blood of my children and with the blood of millions in this slave country whose rights are disregarded by wicked, cruel, and unjust enactments, I say let it be done. Let me say one word further. I feel entirely satisfied with the treatment I have received on my trial. Considering all the circumstances, it has been more generous than I expected. But I feel no consciousness of guilt. I have stated from the first what was my intention, and what was not. I never had any design against the liberty of any

person, nor any disposition to commit treason or excite slaves to rebel or make any general insurrection. I never encouraged any man to do so, but always discouraged any idea of that kind. Let me say also in regard to statements made by some of those who were connected with me, I fear it has been stated by some of them that I have induced them to join me, but the contrary is true. I do not say this to injure them, but as regretting their weakness. Not one but joined me of his own accord, and the greater part at their own expense. A number of them I never saw, and never had a word of conversation with till the day they came to me, and that was for the purpose I have stated. Now, I am done.

While Mr. Brown was speaking, perfect quiet prevailed, and when he had finished the Judge proceeded to pronounce sentence upon him. After a few primary remarks, he said, that no reasonable doubt could exist of the guilt of the prisoner, and sentenced him to be hung in public, on Friday, the 2nd of December next.

Mr. Brown received his sentence with composure.

"The Trial of John Brown" (1859). Excerpt taken from *The Life, Trial and Execution of Captain John Brown...* (New York: R. M. Dewitt, 1859), pp. 94–95.

Lesson 22

And the War Came

OVERVIEW

The Civil War holds a special place in American memory. Battlefield sites, historical markers, books, websites, and family histories are just some of the reminders of the conflict that tested the very survival of the nation. In this and the subsequent two lessons, we will examine why the war was fought, how the war was conducted, how it affected the home fronts, why the North won, and what that meant in the shaping of America.

In his second inaugural address, President Abraham Lincoln reflected on the beginning of the Civil War four years earlier: "Both parties deprecated war; but one of them would *make* war rather than let the nation survive; and the other would *accept* war rather than let it perish. And the war came."

The Civil War fundamentally transformed the United States. But at the time of the first shots fired at Fort Sumter in 1861, it was far from clear what would happen in the ensuing conflict. Political and military leaders made choices that brought thousands of people into harm's way. Individuals had to choose if they were going to fight for a cause that might take the last full measure of devotion.

At the beginning of the war, politicians, military officers, soldiers, and most people at home expected to win and hoped that the victory might be relatively easy. However, it did not take long for the reality of battle to drive home the point that this was going to be a long and costly struggle. In the eastern theater of the war, General Robert E. Lee and other Confederate generals scored enough victories to prevent any significant Union penetration into the South. Meanwhile, in the western theater, General Ulysses S. Grant demonstrated his capacity to direct Union successes, but the Confederacy still controlled traffic up and down the Mississippi River. Thus, by the end of 1862, the war seemed to have reached a stalemate, a condition that might have placed the Confederacy of the verge of an ultimate victory.

LESSON ASSIGNMENTS

Textbook: Roark, et al., *The American Promise*, Chapter 15, "The Crucible of War,"
             pp. 510–524

Video: "And the War Came" from the series *Shaping America*

Documents:
             "Fort Sumter Inflames the North" (1861) and "Fort Sumter Inspirits the South"
             (1861) found at the end of this lesson

LEARNING OBJECTIVES

This lesson examines the significant political, economic, social, and military developments during the early stages of the Civil War. Upon completing this lesson, you should be able to:

1. Explain the decisions made by Abraham Lincoln and Jefferson Davis regarding Fort Sumter in April 1861 and the effects of those decisions.

2. Analyze why soldiers fought in the Civil War.

3. Assess the relative strengths and weaknesses of each side at the start of the war.

4. Explain the major developments in the military and diplomatic theaters of the war during 1861–62.

LESSON FOCUS POINTS

The following questions are designed to help you get the most benefit from the sources selected for this lesson. For reference purposes, the video segments are: (1) Introduction, (2) "Fort Sumter," (3) "Why They Fought," (4) Short-take: "Two Generals," (5) "Bull Run to Fredericksburg," and (6) Summary Analysis: "On the Verge."

1. Why was Fort Sumter so important to the Union and the Confederacy in April 1861? What choices did President Lincoln have regarding Fort Sumter? Why did he choose the course of action that he did? (textbook, pp. 513–514; video segment 2)

2. What choices did President Davis have? Why did he pursue the option that he did? Did Lincoln "force" the South to fire the first shots of the war? Why or why not? (textbook, p. 513; video segment 2)

3. Why did Major Anderson surrender Fort Sumter? (video segment 2)

4. How did both the North and the South respond to the fall of Fort Sumter? (textbook, pp. 514–515; documents; video segment 3)

5. Why did the slave states of Delaware, Maryland, Kentucky, and Missouri stay in the Union? What was important about that? How and why did West Virginia come into existence? (textbook, pp. 514–515; video segment 3)

6. What were the various classes of white Southerners fighting for? Why did they shy away from naming slavery as the cause of their fight? What were the long-term effects of this? (textbook, pp. 515–517; video segment 3)

7. Why did Northerners fight? Why didn't they just let the South go? (textbook, pp. 515–517; video segment 3)

---

8. What were the strengths and weaknesses of the North and of the South? (textbook, pp. 515–518; video segment 3)

9. How and why did the South expect to win? How did cotton fit into the South's calculations for victory? What was the South's war strategy? (textbook, pp. 515–518; video segment 3)

10. How and why did the North expect to win? What did the North have to do to win? What was the North's strategy for victory? In what way did both sides miscalculate what would happen? (textbook, pp. 515–518; video segment 3)

11. What challenges did the Lincoln and Davis administrations face in mobilizing for war? How successful were they in meeting the challenges? How did Abraham Lincoln and Jefferson Davis compare as war leaders? (textbook, pp. 517–518)

12. How did Generals Ulysses S. Grant and Robert E. Lee compare as military leaders? (video segment 4)

13. Examine Map 15.2 on page 519 of the textbook. What does that map tell you about the progress of the war in 1861 to 1862? (textbook, p. 519)

14. What was meant by the "eastern theater" of the war? What was important about this theater of war? How decisive were the battles fought there during 1861 to 1862? Why was Lincoln frustrated with many of his generals? How and why did Robert E. Lee become commander of the Confederate forces? (textbook, pp. 519–521; video segment 5)

15. What was meant by the "western theater" of the war? What was important about this theater? What major battles were fought there during 1861–62? Why was the battle of Shiloh Church significant? What qualities had Ulysses S. Grant demonstrated in this theater of war? (textbook, pp. 522–523; video segment 5)

16. How effective was the naval blockade of the South? What were the diplomatic goals of each side in the war? Why did cotton diplomacy fail the South? Why did European countries shy away from recognizing the Confederacy? (textbook, pp. 523–524)

17. How did the war stand at the end of 1862? (textbook, pp. 521–524; video segment 6)

HISTORICAL EXPERTS INTERVIEWED

Gary Gallagher, John L. Nau III Professor of History, University of Virginia, Charlottesville, VA
James McPherson, Professor of History, Princeton University, Princeton, NJ

PRACTICE TEST

The following items will help you evaluate your understanding of this lesson. Use the Answer Key at the end of the lesson to check your answers or to locate material related to each question.

Multiple choice: Choose the BEST answer.

1. In the video, Professor James McPherson refers to Lincoln's choice of action regarding Fort Sumter as a _____.
   A. miscalculation
   B. stroke of genius
   C. recognition of Southern claims
   D. provocation to Great Britain

2. Typically, Northerners viewed secession as _____.
   A. an attack on the best government on earth and a severe challenge to the rule of law
   B. constitutionally viable but impractical
   C. too expensive and therefore illegal
   D. a concept they wished they had thought of first

3. When considering the wartime leadership offered by Abraham Lincoln and Jefferson Davis, a central irony emerges in that _____.
   A. neither man was very committed to the efforts he embarked on
   B. Jefferson Davis made grandiose public statements about what the Confederate States of American might be able to accomplish but privately believed that the South never had a chance
   C. Abraham Lincoln brought little political experience to his presidency yet rose to the occasion to become a masterful leader, while Jefferson Davis, a seasoned politician, proved to be a relatively ineffectual chief executive
   D. while Lincoln successfully shepherded the nation through an awful war, he struggled with his own misgivings about America's form of republicanism

4. In the video, Professor Gary Gallagher states that the key to victory in the Civil War for each side was _____.
   A. conquering the other's territory
   B. gaining diplomatic recognition from Great Britain
   C. establishing an effective railway system
   D. maintaining the support of the civilian population

5. The first battle at Manassas (or Bull Run), in July 1861, is significant because it _____.
   A. disheartened Northerners to the extent that men stopped volunteering for the army
   B. demonstrated that Americans were in for a real war, one that would be neither quick nor easy
   C. was a bloodbath in which thousands of men died
   D. had an instant sobering effect on Southerners, who realized they would have to beef up their troops to have a chance at winning the war

6. After the battle at Shiloh Church, Tennessee, in April 1862, General Ulysses S. Grant

   _____.
   A. believed the war would ruin the nation forever
   B. gave up all idea of saving the Union except by complete conquest
   C. seriously questioned the war aims of the Lincoln administration
   D. believed that God had made it clear which side he supported in the conflict

Short Answer: Your answers should be one or two paragraphs long and specifically address the points indicated.

7. Do you think that President Abraham Lincoln forced the South to fire the first shots of the Civil War? Why or why not?

8. Why did Southerners generally avoid saying that they were fighting the war to maintain slavery? What were the effects of taking this position?

9. What did the South have to do to win the war? What did the North have to do?

10. Compare and contrast the military leadership of Generals Ulysses S. Grant and Robert E. Lee.

Essay Question: Your answer should be several paragraphs long and express a clear understanding of the points indicated.

11. Describe and explain the advantages and disadvantages of each side at the beginning of the Civil War. How did the major battles fought in 1861–1862 illustrate each side's strengths and weaknesses? What was the status of the war at the end of 1862?

ANSWER KEY

Answer	Learning Objectives	Focus Points	References
1. B	LO 1	FP 1, 2	pp. 513–514; video segment 2
2. A	LO 2	FP 7	pp. 515–517; video segment 3
3. C	LO 3	FP 11	pp. 517–518
4. D	LO 3	FP 9, 10	pp. 515–518; video segment 3
5. B	LO 4	FP 14	pp. 519–521; video segment 5
6. B	LO 4	FP 15	pp. 522–523; video segment 5
7.	LO 1	FP 1	pp. 513–514; video segment 2

   • What did Lincoln do?
   • What choices did the South have?
   • Take a position and defend it.

8. ....LO 2..................FP 6..pp. 515–517; video segment 3
   - What reasons did they give for fighting?
   - To what extent was their way of life dependent on slavery?
   - How would this appeal to non-slaveholders?
   - Would this make the cause more noble?
   - How would this affect southern attitudes after the war?

9. ....LO 3..............FP 8–10..pp. 515–518; video segment 3
   - Explain the advantages, challenges, and strategy of each side.
   - Consider the importance of maintaining civilian support.

10. ....LO 4.................FP 12...video segment 4
   - What was Grant's greatest talent as a commander?
   - What was Lee's greatest talent?
   - What quality of leadership did they both have in common?

11. ....LO 3, 4.............FP 4–17.................pp. 514–524; documents; video segments 3, 4, 5
   - Consider resources, geography, and civilian and military leadership.
   - Consider the battles of Bull Run, Forts Henry and Donelson, Shiloh, Antietam, and Fredericksburg.
   - Evaluate the relative positions of each side at this point in the war.

ENRICHMENT IDEAS

These activities are not required unless your instructor assigns them. They are offered as suggestions to help you learn more about the material presented in this lesson.

1. Imagine yourself to be an advisor to either President Lincoln or President Davis. Write a position paper in which you recommend a course of action regarding the situation at Fort Sumter. Be sure to include an analysis of the likely outcomes of the action that you are recommending.

2. Imagine yourself as a young man living in Kentucky at the start of the Civil War. Write a letter to your parents in which you explain your decision to fight for the Union or the Confederacy.

3. Research the issue of secession in our times, for example, in Chechnya, Kosovo, Quebec, or elsewhere. Select one area and then write an essay explaining how and why the region is seeking independence. How is the "mother country" responding? Explain any parallels with the Civil War in America.

SUGGESTED READINGS/RESOURCES

See the "Bibliography" on pages 548–549 of the textbook if you wish to examine other books and resources related to the material presented in this lesson.

DOCUMENTS

South Carolina officials, in consultation with the new Confederate government, decided to fire on Fort Sumter in April of 1861. Lincoln responded by calling forth the forces of the Union to put down rebellion. In response to Lincoln's call for troops, the South began arming itself. The undecided slave states were left with the difficult option of joining their fellow slave states or remaining loyal to the Union.

As you read this document, focus on answering the following questions:

1. How did John Adams Dix react to the firing on Fort Sumter?
2. What was the reaction of the editorial in the *Daily Richmond Examiner*?

"Fort Sumter Inflames the North" (1861)

On Sunday, April 14 [1861], the fact became known that Fort Sumter had surrendered. The excitement created by the bombardment of that fortress and its magnificent defense by Anderson was prodigious. The outrage on the government of the United States thus perpetrated by the authorities of South Carolina sealed the fate of the new-born Confederacy and the institution of slavery.

Intelligent Southerners at the North were well aware of the consequences which must follow. In the city of New York a number of prominent gentlemen devoted to the interests of the South, and desirous to obtain a bloodless dissolution of the Union, were seated together in anxious conference, studying with intense solicitude the means of preserving the peace. A messenger entered the room in breathless haste with the news: "General Beauregard has opened fire on Fort Sumter!" The persons whom he thus addressed remained a while in dead silence, looking into each other's pale faces; then one of them, with uplifted hands, cried, in a voice of anguish, "My God, we are ruined!"

The North rose as one man. The question had been asked by those who were watching events, "How will New York go?" There were sinister hopes in certain quarters of a strong sympathy with the secession movements; dreams that New York might decide on cutting off from the rest of the country and becoming a free city. These hopes and dreams vanished in a day. The reply to the question how New York would go was given with an energy worthy of herself.

Morgan Dix, *Memoirs of John Adams Dix* (New York: Harper and Brothers, 1883), vol. 2, p. 9.

"Fort Sumter Inspirits the South" (1861)

The news of the capture of Fort Sumter was greeted with unbounded enthusiasm in this city. Everybody we met seemed to be perfectly happy. Indeed, until the occasion we did not know how happy men could be. Everybody abuses war, and yet it has ever been the favorite and most honored pursuit of men; and the women and children admire and love war ten times as much as the men. The boys pulled down the stars and stripes from the top of the Capitol (some of the boys were sixty years old), and very properly run [sic] up the flag of the Southern Confederacy in its place. What the women did we don't precisely know, but learned from rumor that they praised South Carolina to the skies, abused Virginia, put it to the Submissionists hot and heavy with their two-edged swords, and wound up the evening's ceremonies by playing and singing secession songs until fifteen minutes after twelve on Saturday night. The boys exploded an infinite number of crackers; the price of tar has risen 25 percent, and sky-rockets and Roman candles can be had at no price, the whole stock in trade having been used up Saturday night. We had great firing of cannon, all sorts of processions, an infinite number of grandiloquent, hifaluting speeches, and some drinking of healths, which has not improved healths; for one half the people we have met since are hoarse from long and loud talking, and the other half have a slight headache, it may be, from long and patriotic libations.

Daily Richmond Examiner, April 15, 1861, in W. J. Kimball, *Richmond in Time of War* (Boston: Houghton Mifflin, 1960), p. 4.

Lesson 23

Home Fronts

OVERVIEW

During 1861–1862, the realities of the Civil War began to hit home. It was clear this war was not going to be resolved quickly on the battlefields, and its effects would change the course of the nation and its people.

Among those most affected were African Americans. President Abraham Lincoln's initial reluctance to take any bold steps to alter the status of slaves gave way to the needs of war and the desire to transform the nature of the conflict. With Lincoln's decisions to issue the Emancipation Proclamation and to authorize the use of black troops, the war now became a war of liberation as well as a war to preserve the Union.

On the home fronts, both the Union and Confederate governments grappled with the challenges of sustaining the war effort. This led to centralization of power, and, given the eventual outcome of the war, northern initiatives on economic and social policies had lasting effects. Drafting men to fight brought resistance in both sections, especially when the wealthy could evade the call, but each side armed hundreds of thousands of troops. As their husbands and brothers went off to do battle, women worried and had to assume new roles. Hardship was especially acute in the South, the area where most of the fighting took place. As slavery began disintegrating from within and the presence of black troops became more important to northern successes, the resolve of white Southerners approached its ultimate test.

In the video accompanying this lesson, a brief segment on "digital history" emphasizes the point that access to primary source material relating to the Civil War is voluminous and expanding. As with other sources, the challenge is to incorporate and evaluate this material in an attempt to gain a fuller understanding of the Civil War and how it shaped America.

LESSON ASSIGNMENTS

Text: Roark, et al., *The American Promise,* Chapter 15, "The Crucible of War,"
        pp. 511–512, 524–539

Video: "Home Fronts" from the series *Shaping America*

LEARNING OBJECTIVES

This lesson examines how and why decisions made and actions taken on the home fronts affected the Civil War and how the war affected the home fronts. Upon completing this lesson, you should be able to:

1. Analyze the issuance of the Emancipation Proclamation and its effects.

2. Explain the role of African Americans in the Civil War.

3. Describe the effects of the war on the home fronts of the South and the North.

4. Examine how we learn about history in general and the Civil War in particular.

5. Analyze how developments on the home fronts affected the progress of the war.

LESSON FOCUS POINTS

The following questions are designed to help you get the most benefit from the sources selected for this lesson. For reference purposes, the titles of the video segments are: (1) Introduction, (2) "Emancipation," (3) "The War at Home – The North," (4) "The War at Home – The South," (5) Short-take: "Digital History," and (6) Summary Analysis: "The Center of the Struggle."

1. Why was President Lincoln's original position on emancipation very cautious? What sort of pressure did Frederick Douglass and other abolitionists put on Lincoln? How did Congress engage this issue? What did slaves do to force emancipation onto the political agenda? Why was an attempt at colonization unsuccessful? (textbook, pp. 511–512, 524–528; video segment 2)

2. Why did Lincoln finally issue the Emancipation Proclamation? What did it actually do? Who criticized the proclamation? Why? How did the proclamation transform the nature of the Civil War? (textbook, pp. 528–529; video segment 2)

3. What roles did African Americans play in the military at the beginning of the war? Why were these roles limited? (textbook, pp. 511–512, 529–530; video segment 2)

4. Why did Lincoln eventually authorize the use of black troops in Union forces? How were these troops initially organized and treated? What were the black troops fighting for? (textbook, pp. 511–512, 529–530; video segment 2)

5. Generally, how did black troops perform in the war? Why was the Fifty-fourth Massachusetts regiment famous? How important would black troops be in the outcome of the war? How did participation in the war affect the lives of African Americans? (textbook, pp. 530, 532–533; video segment 2)

6. What actions did the Confederate government take in its attempts to sustain the war effort? What limited the effectiveness of the government's actions? (textbook, pp. 530–531, 534; video segment 4)

7. What sort of hardships did the war cause in the South? Were these deprivations shared equally? What effect did this have on southern unity? How did the war affect women in the South? (textbook, pp. 534–535; video segment 4)

8. How did the wartime experiences in Augusta County, Virginia, reflect the general nature of the southern home front? (video segment 4)

9. How did slavery in the South begin to disintegrate during the war? How was the master-slave relationship altered? How did slaves react to the war? (textbook, pp. 535–536; video segment 4)

10. Once the war began, why and how did the U.S. Congress enact legislation that affected industrial, agricultural, educational, and financial institutions? What were the short- and long-term effects of this legislation? (textbook, pp. 536–537; video segment 3)

11. What sort of hardships did the war cause in the North? In what ways did northern women of all classes and geographic areas contribute to the war effort? (textbook, pp. 537–538; video segment 3)

12. In what ways did life in Franklin County, Pennsylvania, during the war reflect the northern home front? How was it different? (video segment 3)

13. How did the war affect northern politics? How did the two-party system operate during the war? How and why did Lincoln exert unusual presidential authority? How were dissenters treated? (textbook, pp. 538–539)

14. How was conscription handled in the North? Why did draft riots break out? (textbook, pp. 538–539)

15. How does the emergence of "digital history" affect the study of history in general and the Civil War in particular? (video segment 5)

16. In summary, how did the war affect the economy, society, and politics of both the North and the South? How did the developments on the home fronts affect the eventual outcome of the war? (textbook, pp. 524–539; video segments 2, 3, 4, 6)

HISTORICAL EXPERTS INTERVIEWED

Gary Gallagher, John L. Nau III Professor of History, University of Virginia, Charlottesville, VA
James Oliver Horton, Benjamin Banneker Professor of American Civilization and History, The George Washington University, Washington, DC
James McPherson, Professor of History, Princeton University, Princeton, NJ
William Thomas, Director of Virginia Center for Digital History, University of Virginia, Charlottesville, VA

PRACTICE TEST

The following items will help you evaluate your understanding of this lesson. Use the Answer Key at the end of the lesson to check your answers or to locate material related to each question.

Multiple choice: Choose the BEST answer.

1. When the Civil War broke out, President Lincoln chose not to make the conflict a struggle over slavery because he _____.
    A. believed slavery to be a relatively insignificant issue
    B. doubted his right to tamper with the "domestic institutions" of any state, even those in rebellion
    C. was not completely confident that destroying slavery was the best thing for African Americans
    D. thought that eradicating slavery would unleash millions of angry freedmen on the white South

2. In the video, Professor James Oliver Horton points out that the Emancipation Proclamation _____.
    A. freed all slaves in the United States
    B. reflected President Lincoln's racist views
    C. focused the war on the South's attempt to preserve slavery
    D. appeased the non-slaveholding Southerners

3. To most African Americans, the Civil War was _____.
    A. a political struggle for power between whites in the North and the South
    B. a military struggle that they avoided being a part of
    C. an attempt to save the Union
    D. a struggle to overthrow slavery and gain racial equality

4. The Confederacy's efforts to centralize its government and production facilities encountered resistance in _____.
   A. the general unwillingness of white Southerners to support the war effort after 1863
   B. the South's traditional values of states' rights and individualism
   C. the conviction on the part of slaveholders that the Davis government meant to confiscate some of their slaves
   D. frequent riots by soldiers, who were paid inadequately or not at all

5. Strikes by workers in northern industries calculated to improve wages during the Civil War _____.
   A. often proved remarkably successful
   B. drastically undermined the patriotism of most workers
   C. were more effective for women than for men
   D. rarely succeeded

6. "Digital history" opens up new opportunities for _____.
   A. students to become historians
   B. universities to offer fewer classes
   C. businesses to alter records
   D. libraries to restrict access to sources

Short Answer: Your answers should be one or two paragraphs long and specifically address the points indicated.

7. How was the Civil War a "rich man's war and a poor man's fight" on both sides? Do you think this is typical of most wars? Why or why not?

8. How did Augusta County, Virginia, and Franklin County, Pennsylvania, illustrate the issues of the home fronts during the Civil War?

Essay Questions: Your answers should be several paragraphs long and express a clear understanding of the points indicated.

9. Slavery was the fundamental issue leading to the outbreak of the Civil War and remained a key issue during the war. Explain the background, purpose, and results of the Emancipation Proclamation. How was slavery disintegrating during the war? How did the use of black troops alter the course of the war? What did all of these wartime developments indicate about the future of slavery in the United States?

10. Compare and contrast the home fronts of the North and South during the Civil War. In your answer, be sure to address how the war affected the economy, politics, and society of both sections. How did the developments on the home fronts affect the eventual outcome of the war?

ANSWER KEY

Answer	Learning Objectives	Focus Points	References
1. B	LO 1	FP 1	pp. 511–512, 524–528; video segment 2
2. C	LO 1	FP 2	pp. 528–529; video segment 2
3. D	LO 2	FP 4	pp. 511–512, 529–530; video segment 2
4. B	LO 3	FP 6	pp. 530–531, 534; video segment 4
5. D	LO 3	FP 11	pp. 537–538; video segment 3
6. A	LO 4	FP 15	video segment 5

7. ....LO 3...........FP 7, 11, 14 ....pp. 534–535, 537–539; video segments 3, 4

- Consider who was in a position to benefit from the Civil War.
- Describe how conscription was handled in the war. Who could be exempt?
- From what you know, how does the Civil War compare to other wars in this regard?

8. ....LO 3..............FP 8, 12 .... video segments 3, 4

- How was the economy affected by the war in these areas?
- To what extent was physical damage due to battles (or the threat of fighting) a factor?
- Consider how slavery was disintegrating in Augusta County and the experience of Franklin County with refugees.
- How were families most affected?

9. ....LO 1–3, 5.....FP 1–5, 8, 9, 16............... pp. 511–512, 524–539; video segments 2–4, 6

- Consider the pressures Lincoln faced prior to the Proclamation.
- Clarify the purpose of the document. What exactly did it do?
- How did the Proclamation transform the nature of war?
- How did slaves take their own initiatives toward emancipation in areas in rebellion?
- How important were black troops? How did they get involved in the fighting?
- What expectations were raised? Could slavery survive if the Union won?

10. ....LO 3, 5...............FP 16 .... pp. 524–539; video segments 2–4, 6

- Consider the economic challenges and opportunities of both sides.
- How could the North maintain a two-party system? How much power could and did Lincoln exercise? How did the South's emphasis on states' rights affect their war effort?
- How did class issues surface? How was the race issue addressed?
- Consider how and why the North was able to marshal its resources and maintain the war.
- How could the South sustain the support of the civilian population?

ENRICHMENT IDEAS

These activities are not required unless your instructor assigns them. They are offered as suggestions to help you learn more about the material presented in this lesson.

1. Imagine yourself to be an advisor to either President Lincoln or President Davis. In a well-developed position paper, convince the president of the need to use black troops. Be sure to anticipate arguments against your position.

2. Imagine yourself to be a woman trying to manage a farm in either the North or the South during the Civil War while your husband is away in the military. Write a series of three letters to him in which you describe your thoughts and feelings.

3. Read the novel *Cold Mountain* by Charles Frazier. Then write a review of the book, emphasizing what you derived from the story. Would you recommend this book to others? Why or why not?

4. Research the history of the draft in America. Who has to register? Who is usually exempted from the draft? Who ends up being drafted and does the bulk of the fighting in wars? What do the answers to the preceding questions mean? Finally, take a stand on whether women should have to register for the draft.

5. The video for this lesson mentions "The Valley of the Shadow" website. Research this project to find out how this project was accomplished. Submit a paper in which you report your findings. How can "digital history" change our study of the past? What are the challenges inherent in this type of historical database?

SUGGESTED READINGS/RESOURCES

See the "Bibliography" on pages 548–549 of the textbook if you wish to examine other books and resources related to the material presented in this lesson.

Lesson 24

Union Preserved, Freedom Secured

OVERVIEW

By 1863, President Abraham Lincoln had transformed the Civil War into a war to preserve the union *and* to free the slaves. If those goals were to be accomplished, the South would have to be defeated on the battlefields. Two key turning points in the war came in July 1863: one at Vicksburg, Mississippi, and the other at Gettysburg, Pennsylvania. Once General Ulysses S. Grant secured Union control of the Mississippi River and General Robert E. Lee retreated to the south, the stage was set for northern victory. But the cost was horrifying. Lincoln's eloquent Gettysburg Address gave meaning to the appalling sacrifices of war and called upon the nation to pursue a new birth of freedom.

During the final stages of war, General Grant employed a comprehensive military strategy to crush the Confederacy. Benefiting from the Union's military successes, Lincoln was reelected in November 1864. That political victory assured that President Lincoln's war aims would be pursued. In his second inaugural address, he appealed for a just and lasting peace. Five weeks later, on April 9, 1865, General Grant accepted General Lee's surrender at Appomattox. And then, at the moment of triumph, Lincoln himself became a victim of war.

LESSON ASSIGNMENTS

Text: Roark, et al., *The American Promise*, Chapter 15, "The Crucible of War," pp. 539–551

Video: "Union Preserved, Freedom Secured" from the series *Shaping America*

Document:
          "The Gettysburg Address" found at the end of this lesson

LEARNING OBJECTIVES

This lesson examines why the Union won the Civil War and what that victory meant to the nation. Upon completing this lesson, you should be able to:

1. Explain the significance of the battles of Vicksburg and Gettysburg.

2. Analyze the meaning of Lincoln's Gettysburg Address.

3. Explain the significance of the military operations of the Civil War during its final eighteen months.

4. Assess why the North won and the South lost the war.

5. Assess the place of Abraham Lincoln in U.S. history.

6. Analyze the role of the Civil War in the shaping of America.

LESSON FOCUS POINTS

The following questions are designed to help you get the most benefit from the resources selected for this lesson. For reference purposes, the titles of the video segments are: (1) Introduction, (2) "The Beginning of the End," (3) "The Gettysburg Address," (4) "Total War," (5) "The End," and (6) Summary Analysis: "The Legacy."

1. Examine Map 15.3 in the textbook. Where did the bulk of fighting take place? How was the "divide and conquer" strategy of the Union implemented in the South? (textbook, p. 541)

2. What happened at the battle of Vicksburg? Why was this victory so important to the Union? (textbook, pp. 539–541; video segment 2)

3. What happened at the battle of Gettysburg? Why did General Lee engage the Union forces there? Why did Lee fail? What was the significance of the Union victory there? (textbook, pp. 539–541; video segment 2)

4. Why is President Abraham Lincoln's Gettysburg Address significant? What ideas did he express? How did he give meaning to the war? (document; video segment 3)

5. Why did Lincoln eventually appoint U. S. Grant to be commander of all Union armies? What strategy did Grant and his subordinates, Philip Sheridan and William T. Sherman, use to try to beat the Southerners into submission? (textbook, pp. 540–541; video segment 4)

6. What happened during Grant's military engagements with Lee in Virginia in 1864–1865? Why did Sherman march to the sea? What was important about that? (textbook, pp. 540–541, 544; video segment 3)

7. Why did so many soldiers die in the Civil War? How did the death toll compare to other wars involving the United States? (textbook, pp. 542–543)

8. How did the developments on the battlefields affect the elections of 1864? How did the Republicans broaden their appeal? What was significant about the results? (textbook, pp. 544–546; video segment 4)

9. Why did the Confederacy collapse in the late winter and early spring of 1865? (textbook, pp. 546–547.; video segments 4, 5)

10. In summary, why did the North win and the South lose the Civil War? (textbook, pp. 511–551; video segment 6)

11. Why can the Civil War be considered to be the "Second American Revolution"? (textbook, pp. 547–548; video segment 6)

HISTORICAL EXPERTS INTERVIEWED

Gary Gallagher, John L. Nau III Professor of History, University of Virginia, Charlottesville, VA
Howard Jones, University Research Professor and Chairman, University of Alabama, Tuscaloosa, AL
James McPherson, Professor of History, Princeton University, Princeton, NJ

PRACTICE TEST

The following items will help you evaluate your understanding of this lesson. Use the Answer Key at the end of the lesson to check your answers or to locate material related to each question.

Multiple choice: Choose the BEST answer.

1. Vicksburg, Mississippi, was an important military objective for the Union because seizing it would allow the Union to _____.
   A. stop the export of cotton
   B. divide the Confederacy
   C. force General Lee to surrender
   D. implement the Emancipation Proclamation in that area

2. General Robert E. Lee invaded Pennsylvania in June of 1863 for all of the following reasons EXCEPT to _____.
   A. take the war out of Virginia
   B. gather food and fodder
   C. engage Grant's army in a final showdown
   D. shatter northern civilian morale

3. In the Gettysburg Address, President Abraham Lincoln _____.
   A. framed the Civil War as a test of American principles
   B. called for the immediate emancipation of all slaves
   C. recognized the values of the Confederacy
   D. promoted General Meade to commander of all Union forces

4. The strategy employed by the Union forces in 1864–1865 was one of _____.
   A. coordinated offensives
   B. passive resistance
   C. massive retaliation
   D. aggressive defense

5. The purpose of General William T. Sherman's march from Atlanta to the sea was to _____.
   A. trap the Confederate army at Savannah
   B. escape a Confederate attack
   C. demoralize the civilian population
   D. link up with Grant's forces

6. The death toll from the Civil War was _____.
   A. almost equal to the death total from all wars in which the United States has engaged
   B. significantly smaller than the death toll of U.S. personnel in World War II
   C. relatively light compared to U.S. casualties in Vietnam
   D. grossly overstated by journalists covering the war

7. All of the following contributed to Lincoln's reelection in 1864 except _____.
   A. massive voter registration of northern blacks
   B. Union military victory on the eve of the election.
   C. the Democratic candidate's stance on the war issue
   D. Andrew Johnson's selection as Lincoln's running mate

8. In March of 1865, as the Confederacy was close to defeat, Jefferson Davis proposed the final desperate strategy of _____.
   A. paying German mercenaries to fight against the North
   B. using women in combat
   C. assassinating Lincoln
   D. having slaves become soldiers

Short Answer: Your answers should be one or two paragraphs long and specifically address the points indicated.

9. Describe and explain the significance of the battles of Vicksburg and Gettysburg. How did the results of each battle shape the course of the Civil War?

10. How did Abraham Lincoln give meaning to the Civil War in the Gettysburg Address? What were the main ideas that he expressed? Why does that speech live on in American memory?

11. Describe and explain the major features of the Union's military strategy after Gettysburg. How did Generals Sherman, Sheridan, and Grant implement that strategy?

Essay Questions: Your answers should be several paragraphs long and express a clear understanding of the points indicated.

12. Describe and explain why the North won and the South lost the Civil War. In your answer, be sure to consider both the civilian and military aspects of the war.

13. Why is Abraham Lincoln considered to be the nation's greatest president? In your answer, be sure to analyze the essence of the Lincoln legacy and consider how he lives on in American memory.

14. How did the Civil War fundamentally transform America? In your answer, consider why some refer to the war as the "Second American Revolution" and how the Civil War lives on in American memory.

ANSWER KEY

	Answer	Learning Objectives	Focus Points	References
1.	B	LO 1	FP 2	pp. 539–541; video segment 2
2.	C	LO 1	FP 3	pp. 539–541; video segment 2
3.	A	LO 2	FP 4	document; video segment 3
4.	A	LO 3	FP 5	pp. 540–541; video segment 4
5.	C	LO 3	FP 6	pp. 540–541, 544; video segment 4
6.	A	LO 3	FP 7	pp. 542–543
7.	A	LO 4	FP 8	pp. 544–546; video segment 4
8.	D	LO 4	FP 9	pp. 546–547; video segments 4, 5

9. ....LO 1.............FP 1, 2, 3 ....pp. 539–541; video segment 2
   - How were Grant and the Union forces able to attack Vicksburg, place it under siege, and eventually force it to surrender?
   - How did the victory at Vicksburg give the Union a strategic advantage?
   - What advantages did the North have in the battle of Gettysburg?
   - Why was the Union victory at Gettysburg a tremendous morale boost for the North?
   - How did the Union victories at Vicksburg and Gettysburg alter the course of the Civil War?

10. ....LO 2.................FP 4 .... document; video segment 3
   - How did the Gettysburg Address explain the significance of the battle at Gettysburg from the northern perspective?
   - How did Lincoln bring forward the ideals of the Declaration of Independence?
   - How did Lincoln add the element of a "new birth of freedom," and what did that mean?
   - How was "freedom" given a more inclusive definition?
   - What is your opinion on why the Gettysburg Address lives on in American memory?

- How did the Union plan to conquer the South?
- What did General Sherman do to destroy the South's ability and willingness to fight?
- What role did General Sheridan play in Union victory?
- Why was General Grant able to push through to victory?

- How and why was the Union able to capitalize on its advantages?
- How and why was the Confederacy not able to defend its claimed territory?
- How important was President Lincoln to the Union cause?
- What is your assessment of the most significant factors in the outcome?

- What factors determine presidential greatness?
- How important was Lincoln's role during the Civil War?
- What were Lincoln's strongest personal qualities?
- How was Lincoln able to transform the nature of the Civil War?
- What is your assessment of Lincoln's legacy, and how do he and that legacy live on?

- How did the war alter the economic and political landscape of America?
- How did the war affect African Americans?
- What aspects of the war do you consider to be revolutionary?
- Why does the Civil War have an enduring place in our national memory?

ENRICHMENT IDEAS

These activities are not required unless your instructor assigns them. They are offered as suggestions to help you learn more about the material presented in this lesson.

1. In a well-reasoned essay, compare and contrast the military leadership of Generals Robert E. Lee and Ulysses S. Grant. Who do you think was the superior commander? Why?

2. If you live in an area that experienced significant military action during the Civil War, visit the relevant historic site(s). Then summarize that you learned from the visit. How does the Civil War live on in your area?

3. Read the book *The Killer Angels*, and then write a critical analysis of it.

4. Watch the movie "Gettysburg," and then write a critical analysis of it.

5. You are an advisor to President Jefferson Davis. In a well-reasoned position paper, try to convince him either to use or not to use black troops.

6. Research the effects of the Civil War on American culture (literature, poetry, music, monuments, etc.). Then submit a thoughtful essay describing what you discovered.

SUGGESTED READINGS/RESOURCES

See the "Bibliography" on pages 548–549 of the textbook if you wish to examine other books and resources related to the material presented in this lesson.

DOCUMENTS

President Abraham Lincoln's address at Gettysburg is considered to be among America's most important documents.

As you read this document, focus on answering the following questions:

1. How did he give meaning to the Civil War?
2. What were the main ideas that he expressed?
3. Why does the speech live on in American memory?

"The Gettysburg Address" November 19, 1863

Four score and seven years ago our fathers brought forth on this continent, a new nation, conceived in Liberty, and dedicated to the proposition that all men are created equal.

Now we are engaged in a great civil war, testing whether that nation, or any nation so conceived and so dedicated, can long endure. We are met on a great battle-field of that war. We have come to dedicate a portion of that field, as a final resting place for those who here gave their lives that that nation might live. It is altogether fitting and proper that we should do this.

But, in a larger sense, we can not dedicate—we can not consecrate—we can not hallow—this ground. The brave men, living and dead, who struggled here, have consecrated it, far above our poor power to add or detract. The world will little note, nor long remember what we say here, but it can never forget what they did here. It is for us the living, rather, to be dedicated here to the unfinished work which they who fought here have thus far so nobly advanced. It is rather for us to be here dedicated to the great task remaining before us—that from these honored dead we take increased devotion to that cause for which they gave the last full measure of devotion—that we here highly resolve that these dead shall not have died in vain—that this nation, under God, shall have a new birth of freedom—and that government of the people, by the people, for the people, shall not perish from the earth.

Lesson 25

Reconstructing the Nation

OVERVIEW

When the Civil War ended with northern victory, the Union was preserved and freedom for slaves was secured. However, important political, social, and economic issues remained on the agenda, and the America people now faced the daunting task of reconstructing the nation. To what extent would the shape of the reconstructed nation resemble the old?

Before his death, Abraham Lincoln had called upon his fellow Americans to approach the unfinished work before them "with malice toward none; with charity for all." During the twelve years after the war, the idealism projected by Lincoln could not be sustained by his successors, and the realities of power politics and resistance to change impeded progress.

One of the key questions facing the nation concerned the status of the states that had seceded or attempted to secede from the United States during the Civil War. Many of those who had denied the legality of secession now wanted to impose conditions for *readmitting* those states. Others who had defended the right and practice of secession now acted as if nothing had happened in the previous four years. Leaders of Congress disagreed sharply with President Andrew Johnson on who should control the process of reconstruction. Of course, the ex-Confederate states did rejoin the Union, but the "ideals" of the Old South lingered for generations.

An essential issue of reconstruction involved the status of the ex-slaves. As the video for this lesson illustrates, establishing a new birth of freedom for African Americans was contested at almost every step. While some significant gains were made, the hope of aligning the nation with its revolutionary ideals of freedom *and* equality was only half accomplished in the short term. More than a century later, the ideals are still there, and the challenge continues.

LESSON ASSIGMENTS

Text: Roark, et al., *The American Promise*, Chapter 16, "Reconstruction," pp. 552–589

Video: "Reconstructing the Nation" from the series *Shaping America*

Documents:
     "The Meaning of Freedom" found on pp. 558–559 of the textbook

LEARNING OBJECTIVES

This lesson examines how and why the choices made and the actions taken during the era of Reconstruction helped shape America. Upon completing this lesson, you should be able to:

1. Explain the major political, social, and economic issues of the Reconstruction era.

2. Describe the evolution of presidential and congressional plans for reconstruction.

3. Describe the conditions of ex-slaves after the Civil War and the attempts to help them adjust to a new status.

4. Analyze how southern whites resisted and eventually overthrew reconstruction.

5. Explain why northern whites abandoned reconstruction.

6. Assess the short- and long-term effects of reconstruction.

LESSON FOCUS POINTS

The following questions are designed to help you get the most benefit from the sources selected for this lesson. For reference purposes, the titles for the video segments are: (1) Introduction, (2) Short-take: "The 13th Amendment," (3) "Early Reconstruction," (4) Short-take: "The 14th Amendment," (5) "Radical Reconstruction," (6) Short-take: "The 15th Amendment," (7) "The End of Reconstruction," and (8) Summary Analysis: "The Battle of History."

1. What were the major issues and opportunities facing the nation at the beginning of the Reconstruction era? (textbook, pp. 552–555; video segment 1)

2. Why did both the President and Congress want to control the process of reconstruction? Why did controlling the process matter? (textbook, pp. 555–556)

3. What characterized Abraham Lincoln's initial plan for reconstruction? Why did some oppose it? How did Congress actively dispute Lincoln's plan? (textbook, pp. 555–556)

4. What does the Thirteenth Amendment say and mean? (video segment 2)

5. What kinds of labor systems evolved in the Union-occupied areas of the South during the war? Why did these systems satisfy neither southern whites nor blacks? (textbook, pp. 556–557)

6. Why did blacks think that the federal government might distribute land to freedmen after the war? Why wasn't this done? Why did the sharecropping system evolve? (textbook, pp. 556–557, 578–580; video segment 3)

7. What was the Freedmen's Bureau? What did it do? (textbook, p. 557; video segment 3)

8. What did "freedom" mean to the ex-slaves? How would you answer the questions posed in the textbook in the section entitled "Documenting the American Promise"? (textbook, pp. 557–560; video segment 3)

9. How did Andrew Johnson's personal and political background shape his views? What were his strengths and weaknesses as a politician? Why and how did he alter Lincoln's reconstruction plan? (textbook, pp. 561–562)

10. Who dominated southern politics immediately after the war? What acts of defiance were made in the South? Why were black codes passed? What did these state laws attempt to do? How did President Johnson and Congress react to these developments in the South? (textbook, pp. 562–565; video segment 3)

11. Why was the Fourteenth Amendment proposed? What are its most important provisions? What were the short-term effects of this amendment? (textbook, pp. 565, 568; video segment 4)

12. Why did Radical Republicans enact the Military Reconstruction Act (1867) and subsequent acts of "radical reconstruction"? (textbook, pp. 568–570; video segment 5)

13. Why was President Andrew Johnson impeached? Why did the Senate fail to convict him? What lessons were learned from this experience? (textbook, pp. 570–571)

14. Why was the Fifteenth Amendment proposed? What did it do? Why did women feel betrayed by the Fifteenth Amendment (and some of the wording in the Fourteenth)? (textbook, pp. 571–572; video segment 6)

15. What three groups formed the majority of the Republican Party in the South? What did each group want from this coalition? How did black politicians perform? Why was this an "extraordinary moment in American politics"? (textbook, pp. 572–573; video segment 5)

16. Who resisted the Republicans in the South? When was the Ku Klux Klan formed? What did it really want to accomplish? How did it go about its business? What did Congress do to try to curb the Klan? (textbook, pp. 573–575; video segment 5)

17. What changes did new reconstruction state constitutions introduce into southern life? What initiatives did the state legislatures make in the areas of public education, civil rights, and economic development? What limited further changes? (textbook, pp. 573, 576–578; video segment 5)

18. Why was Ulysses S. Grant elected president in 1868 and 1872? Why did corruption become so common during his administration? Did he have any accomplishments as president? What happened to the economy during his tenure? (textbook, pp. 581–582)

19. Why was the Civil Rights Act of 1875 passed? Despite this act, how and why did northern resolve to sustain reconstruction begin to wither in the 1870s? What decisions by the Supreme Court limited reconstruction? (textbook, pp. 582–583; video segment 7)

20. Who were the "Redeemers"? What was their agenda? How did they go about driving whites from the Republican Party and eliminating black voting power? How successful were they by 1876? (textbook, pp. 583–585; video segment 7)

21. Examine Map 16.3 in the textbook. Answer the questions posed below the map. (textbook, p. 584)

22. Who were the candidates in the 1876 presidential election? What was so peculiar about the initial results? What was the Compromise of 1877? How and why did it end Reconstruction? (textbook, pp. 585–587)

23. In summary, what were the short-term political, economic, and social effects of Reconstruction? In what ways was the Civil War only a "half-accomplished" revolution by the end of the Reconstruction era? What were the long-term effects of the choices made and the actions taken at that time? How was the American memory of Reconstruction affected by historians? (textbook, entire chapter; all video segments)

HISTORICAL EXPERTS INTERVIEWED

Richard Blackett, Moores Professor of History and African American Studies, University of Houston, Houston, TX
W. Fitzhugh Brundage, Professor of History, University of Florida, Gainesville, FL
Michael Perman, Professor of History, University of Illinois at Chicago, Chicago, IL
James Roark, Samuel Candler Dobbs Professor of American History, Emory University, Atlanta, GA
Bertram Wyatt-Brown, Richard J. Milbauer Professor of History, University of Florida, Gainesville, FL

PRACTICE TEST

The following items will help you evaluate your understanding of this lesson. Use the Answer Key at the end of the lesson to check your answers or to locate material related to each question.

Multiple choice: Choose the BEST answer.

1. In the video, Professor Richard Blackett observes that for black Americans the Reconstruction era began as a period of _____.
   A. despair
   B. hope
   C. fear
   D. prosperity

2. In the attempt to establish a reconstruction policy after the Civil War, _____.
   A. Lincoln's primary goal was to extend full political rights to ex-slaves
   B. Lincoln rejected the "10 per cent plan"
   C. Congress and the president disagreed about which had authority to devise a plan of reconstruction
   D. Congress wanted to ensure the return to power of the former southern ruling class

3. After the Civil War, African Americans believed that ownership of land _____.
   A. meant social equality with white landowners
   B. would give them income equity with white workers
   C. was a moral right and was linked to black freedom
   D. would mean economic and social equality

4. The black codes were essentially an attempt to _____.
   A. subordinate blacks to whites and regulate the labor supply
   B. extend rights, although limited, to the freedmen
   C. extend to blacks the same rights as whites enjoyed
   D. provide economic equality but restrict social and political equality

5. "Redeemers" were _____.
   A. reformers who hoped to establish public education in the South
   B. economic reformers who believed Confederate dollars should be redeemed in U.S. dollars to revitalize the southern economy
   C. evangelical reformers who hoped to heal the breach between northern and southern churches of the same denomination
   D. southern Democrats who wished to restore white southern control to the South

6. The role of the Supreme Court in reconstruction could be summarized as _____.
   A. an important agent in the Radical Republican agenda for civil rights
   B. a decisive agent for the expansion of civil rights and federal power
   C. a reactionary agent which undermined reconstruction
   D. a progressive, but objective, arbitrator over civil rights issues

7. The Compromise of 1877 essentially _____.
   A. spelled the end of Reconstruction and the Republican commitment to the civil rights of African Americans
   B. destroyed the efforts of the Redeemers and helped rebuild the southern economy
   C. shifted the racist political strategies from the Democratic Party to the Republican Party
   D. had little impact on southern blacks

Short Answer: Your answers should be one or two paragraphs long and specifically address the points indicated.

8. What did "freedom" mean to African Americans in 1865? How did ex-slaves begin to exercise freedom?

9. Why was freedom "contested territory" in the South during reconstruction? How was it contested?

10. What are the key provisions of the Thirteenth, Fourteenth, and Fifteenth Amendments? To what extent did these amendments bring about a "Constitutional revolution"?

11. How and why did sharecropping emerge during reconstruction? What were the short- and long-term consequences of this arrangement?

12. Why did the Ku Klux Klan emerge in the late 1860s? How did their terrorist activities affect the course of reconstruction?

13. Explain the following statement: "By 1870, Northerners had begun a retreat from the ideals of reconstruction."

14. Explain this statement: "The North won the war, but the South won the peace."

Essay Question: Your answers should be several paragraphs long and express a clear understanding of the points indicated.

15. In 1865, former Union General Carl Schurz referred to the Civil War as a "revolution but half accomplished." During the subsequent twelve years, the American people grappled with serious economic, social, and political issues. Describe and explain how these major issues were resolved. In what ways was the revolution still only half accomplished by 1877? What did that mean for the future of America?

ANSWER KEY

Answer	Learning Objectives	Focus Points	References
1. B	LO 1, 3	FP 1	pp. 552–555; video segment 1
2. C	LO 2	FP 2	pp. 555–556
3. C	LO 3	FP 6	pp. 556–557; video segment 3
4. A	LO 4	FP 10	pp. 562–565; video segment 3
5. D	LO 4	FP 20	pp. 583–585; video segment 7
6. C	LO 5	FP 19	pp. 582–583; video segment 7
7. A	LO 6	FP 22	pp. 585–587
8.	LO 3	FP 8	pp. 557–560; video segment 3

- Consider elements of personal freedom that had not been possible before, e.g., regarding mobility, family, expression, religion, education, etc.
- How did slaves pursue economic freedom?

9.	..............LO 4 ....FP 10, 16, 20..........pp. 562–565, 573–575, 583–585; video segments 3, 5
   - Consider why black codes were passed and what they tried to do.
   - What happened regarding land and labor?
   - What motivated the Ku Klux Klan and other terrorist groups? How effective were they?

10.	...........LO 2, 6.......FP 4, 11, 14, 15................pp. 565, 568, 571–573; video segments 2, 4–6
   - How did these amendments affect slavery, citizenship and equal rights, and voting?
   - What fundamental changes did this mean for the American people?

11.	..........LO 1, 3, 6..............FP 6...................................pp. 556–557, 578–580; video segment 3
   - Consider the needs of landowners and laborers.
   - How did this system address those needs?
   - Were there benefits of the system?
   - What was the major fault with this system?

12.	..............LO 4.................FP 16..pp. 573–575; video segment 5
   - Who joined the Klan? What were their motives?
   - What effect did the Klan have on black participation in politics?
   - How did Klan activity affect Northerners and reconstruction policies?

13.	..............LO 5.................FP 19..pp. 582–583; video segment 7
   - Why would a shift in attitude set in?
   - How did the Grant administration indicate a different direction in northern policies and emphasis?
   - What role did racial prejudice play?

14.	..............LO 6.................FP 23...pp. 582–587; video segments 7, 8
   - How had the South successfully resisted northern efforts to reshape their society?
   - Who was in power in the South by 1877? What did that mean for African Americans?
   - Who told the story of Reconstruction for generations?

15.	.... all ....all..pp. 552–589; video segments 1–8
   - What were the major economic issues involving land and labor?
   - How was freedom for blacks going to be protected? How would equality be expanded?
   - How would black participation in the political process proceed?
   - How did resolution of these issues take place? What was the status of the ex-Confederate states by 1877? What was the status of the ex-slaves?
   - Do you think a golden opportunity was missed by the American people during Reconstruction? What issues were postponed for later generations?

ENRICHMENT IDEAS

These activities are not required unless your instructor assigns them. They are offered as suggestions to help you learn more about the material presented in this lesson.

1. At the beginning of the twenty-first century, there has been renewed discussion about making reparations to African Americans for the deprivations brought about by slavery. In a well developed essay, take a stand on this issue. Be sure to acknowledge the arguments presented by those who would disagree with your position.

2. Imagine how Reconstruction could have worked out differently. Put yourself in a position of authority in the North in 1865. In a thoughtful essay, present your plan to redistribute land to ex-slaves and to provide them with resources to exercise their equal rights as citizens of the United States.

3. Research the establishment and work of the Freedmen's Bureau. Then submit a report on the success of this social program. Was this the first government effort at a large-scale welfare program? How was it similar/different from social programs of today?

4. In 2001, the president's pardoning power was in the news. In a well developed essay, explain the basis of the pardoning power and then compare the use of that power by President Bill Clinton and President Andrew Johnson.

5. Both President Andrew Johnson and President Bill Clinton were impeached. Write a report in which you compare and contrast the two proceedings.

6. The results of the presidential elections of both 1876 and 2000 were hotly disputed. Write a report in which you compare the elections and the resolutions of the disputes. What lessons were learned? Should the current system of elections be changed?

SUGGESTED READINGS/RESOURCES

See the "Bibliography" on page 587 of the text if you wish to examine other books and resources related to the material presented in this lesson.

Lesson 26

Looking Backward, Looking Forward

OVERVIEW

In 1876, the United States marked the occasion of its centennial by taking time to look back and to look forward. While we do not have an event of that magnitude to commemorate the last lesson in our course, it is altogether fitting that we pause here and reflect upon what we have learned and what lay ahead. In particular, we want to focus attention on the themes tracked throughout our study of the shaping of America.

We began our journey by examining the geography and the indigenous peoples who lived in America long before the area was named by Europeans. Over time, different people settled and different cultures emerged in America. As we revisit the areas of New York, St. Louis, San Francisco, Portland, Santa Fe, and Charleston, ponder the changes that have taken place and why they have occurred.

From colonial times to the time of the centennial, freedom has been contested territory in America. The boundaries of freedom were expanded for millions of people, while others, most notably American Indians, had less freedom by the 1870s. Women and African Americans had gained some legal guarantees of freedom, but they were not yet allowed to practice it on par with white men. The story of freedom then, like now, remains unfinished and changeable.

The story of American identity is closely linked to ideas of freedom and equality. Moreover, American identity has involved race and ethnicity throughout our history. As you will see, in this lesson we use the story of the relationship between Thomas Jefferson and Sally Hemings to provoke thought on what it means to be an American. How have we constructed American identity in the past? How will we reconstruct it in the future?

Our final reflection in this lesson grows out of a sampling of comments from some of the truly outstanding historians who have enriched this course. Listen carefully. History has always mattered. It is based on choices. Every generation can shape America and what it means to be an American. Create your own history!

LESSON ASSIGNMENTS

Video: "Looking Backward, Looking Forward" from the series *Shaping America.*

LEARNING OBJECTIVES

This lesson is about what America and its people had become by 1876–77 and what that teaches us. Upon completing this lesson, you should be able to:

1. Describe the state of the nation at the time of its centennial.

2. Explain how the story of freedom in America evolved and why it is unfinished.

3. Assess what American identity means and how and why that meaning changes over time.

4. Explain how the idea of equality became a core principle of the United States and what that has meant to the American people.

5. Describe how each individual and each generation creates history.

LESSON FOCUS POINTS

The following questions are designed to help you get the most benefit from the source selected for this lesson. For reference purposes, the titles for the video segments are: (1) Introduction: "The Centennial Exhibition," (2) "The United States in 1876," (3) "The Story of Freedom," (4) "Who We Really Are," and (5) Program Close: "Creating History."

1. What was being celebrated at the Centennial Exhibition? (video segment 1)

2. How would you characterize the cities of New York, St. Louis, San Francisco, Portland, Santa Fe, and Charleston at the time of the centennial? (video segment 2)

3. How had the story of freedom changed by 1876? How and why was freedom limited, particularly as related to minority groups? Why was the story of freedom unfinished then? Why is it unfinished now? (video segment 3)

4. What does the story of Thomas Jefferson's relationship with Sally Hemings teach us about American history? What does it illustrate about American identity? (video segment 4)

5. How and why has race been a social construction in America? How might it be reconstructed? (video segment 4)

6. What does the study of the past teach us? How can you create history? Why does it matter? (video segment 5)

HISTORICAL EXPERTS INTERVIEWED

Robert Archibald, President, Missouri Historical Society, St. Louis, MO

Gerald Danzer, Professor of History, University of Illinois at Chicago, Chicago, IL

R. David Edmunds, Watson Professor of American History, University of Texas at Dallas, Richardson, TX

Eric Foner, Professor of History, Columbia University, New York City, NY

Charles Fracchia, President, San Francisco Historical Society, San Francisco, CA

Annette Gordon-Reed, Professor of Law, New York Law School, New York City, NY

David Gutierrez, Associate Professor, University of California at San Diego, La Jolla, CA

James Oliver Horton, Benjamin Banneker Professor of American Civilization and History, The George Washington University, Washington, DC

Linda Kerber, May Brodbeck Professor in Liberal Arts, University of Iowa, Iowa City, IA

James Merrell, Professor of History, Vassar College, Poughkeepsie, NY

Chet Orloff, Director, Oregon Historical Society, Portland, OR

Jonathan Poston, Director of Museums and Preservation Initiatives, Historic Charleston Foundation, Charleston, SC

Kathryn Sklar, Distinguished Professor of History, State University of New York, Binghamton, NY

Mike Wallace, Co-author of *Gotham*, John Jay College, New York City, NY

Richard White, Margaret Byrne Professor of American History, Stanford University, Stanford, CA

Gordon Wood, Alva O. Way University Professor and Professor of History, Brown University, Providence, RI

PRACTICE TEST

The following items will help you evaluate your understanding of this lesson. Use the Answer Key at the end of the lesson to check your answers or to locate material related to each question.

Multiple choice: Choose the BEST answer.

1. All of the following were innovations featured at the Centennial Exhibition in 1876 EXCEPT
    _____.
    A. radio
    B. telephone
    C. dishwashing machine
    D. 1,500-horsepower engine

2. In 1876, Mexican Americans in the Santa Fe region were _____.
    A. suffering an erosion of status
    B. dominating local politics
    C. benefiting from trade with the East
    D. receiving compensation for lands taken after the war

---

3. In 1876, all of the following characterized San Francisco EXCEPT _____.
    A. busy seaport
    B. sophisticated culture
    C. heavy damage from an earthquake
    D. high percentage of foreign-born residents

Short Answer: Your answers should be one or two paragraphs long and specifically address the points indicated.

4. Why was Chicago displacing St. Louis as the commercial center of the Midwest by 1876?

5. In what ways did American Indians enjoy less freedom in 1876 than in 1776?

6. Why were women still told in the 1870s that different treatment was really privilege?

7. How and why has race been a social construction in America?

Essay Questions: Your answers should be several paragraphs long and express a clear understanding of the points indicated.

8. We have examined the development of the cities of New York, Charleston, St. Louis, Santa Fe, San Francisco, and Portland. How and why had these cities changed between the time of their founding and 1876? How would you characterize each city in 1876?

9. How and why had the story of American freedom changed from the colonial period to 1876? How and why was freedom limited? Why is the story of freedom unfinished?

10. Who is an American? What does being an American mean? How and why did American identity develop and change from the colonial period to 1876?

11. The idea of equality has been a core principle of the United States since 1776. How and why was the United States pushed to uphold this idea between 1776 and 1876? What was the status of equality in America in 1876?

ANSWER KEY

	Answer	Learning Objectives	Focus Points	References
1.	A	LO 1	FP 1	video segment 1
2.	A	LO 1	FP 2	video segment 2
3.	C	LO 1	FP 2	video segment 2

4. ....LO 1...................FP 2...video segment 2
   - What effect were railroads having on commerce?
   - Why had St. Louis been slow to support railroad construction?

5. ....LO 2...................FP 3...video segment 3
   - In what geographic area did Indians have freedom in 1776?
   - How and why had they lost territory during the century?
   - What was their status in 1876?

6. ....LO 2...................FP 3...video segment 3
   - What rights were denied women in 1876?
   - Why did men fear granting women equal rights?
   - How did the "privilege" argument try to dispel women's demands?

7. ....LO 3...................FP 5...video segment 4
   - To whose advantage did racial definitions go?
   - Are there any biological reasons or natural law reasons to draw racial distinctions?

8. ....LO 1...................FP 2.................................. video segment 2; Lessons 2, 3, 5, 11, 19
   - Consider the role of geography in relation to each city.
   - How did population growth affect the cities? Who tended to settle there?
   - What sort of economic growth had taken place?
   - What is the status of each city in 1876?

9. ....All LOs .... All FPs................................. video segments 1–5; Lessons 6, 12, 18
   - Who was free in colonial America? How was freedom expressed?
   - How did the revolutionary period universalize and democratize freedom?
   - What role did manifest destiny have on freedom?
   - What was the free-labor ideal?
   - How did freedom change for minorities?
   - How do you think the boundaries of freedom will change in the future?

10. ....All LOs .... All FPs................................. video segments 1–5; Lessons 6, 12, 18
    - To what extent did American identity apply to all people living in America?
    - Did a distinctive American identity emerge in colonial America?
    - How did the Declaration of Independence and the Constitution affect American identity?
    - How did the Civil War result in a definition of citizenship?
    - Who was excluded from the full rights of citizenship in 1876?

11. ....All LOs .... All FPs................................. video segments 1–5; Lessons 6, 12, 18
    - What did equality mean in 1776?
    - How did society give meaning to equality?
    - Who was excluded from equal rights and opportunities? How did they try to be included?
    - Who was still excluded from equality in 1876? Why?

ENRICHMENT IDEAS

These activities are not required unless your instructor assigns them. They are offered as suggestions to help you learn more about the material presented in this lesson.

1. Read the historical novel *1876* by Gore Vidal. Then submit a report on it. How does the novel depict the times?

2. Research the Centennial Exhibition held in Philadelphia in 1876. In a well-developed essay, describe the main attractions and the main features of the Exhibition.

3. Research the cost and the time it would take to make a round trip across America taking the route described in the video for this lesson. Then submit a report on your findings.

4. In a thoughtful essay, describe how you will create history in your life.

SUGESSTED READINGS

In addition to the books listed in the bibliographies referenced in previous lessons, the following selections elaborate on the themes discussed in this course and are highly recommended to you:

> Joyce Appleby, *Inheriting the Revolution*
> Jon Butler, *Becoming America*
> Eric Foner, *The Story of American Freedom*
> Linda Kerber, *No Constitutional Right to Be Ladies*